WILLIAM D. RUBINSTEIN

William D. Rubinstein is an adjunct professor at Monash University in Melbourne, Australia. He was previously Professor of History at the University of Wales-Aberystwyth. He has written *Men of Property: The Very Wealthy in Britain since the Industrial Revolution*; *Britain's Century: Political and Social History 1815–1995*; and many other works. He is a Fellow of the Australian Academy of the Humanities, of the Australian Academy of the Social Sciences, and of the Royal Historical Society.

WILLIAM D. RUBINSTEIN

The World Hegemon

The British Isles 1832–1914

VINTAGE

1 3 5 7 9 10 8 6 4 2

Vintage

20 Vauxhall Bridge Road,

London SW1V 2SA

Vintage Classics is part of the Penguin Random House group of companies
whose addresses can be found at global.penguinrandomhouse.com.

Penguin
Random House
UK

First published in Vintage in 2015

www.vintage-books.co.uk

A CIP catalogue record for this book is
available from the British Library

ISBN 9781784700454

Printed and bound by Clays Ltd, St Ives Plc

MIX
Paper from
responsible sources
FSC® C018179

Penguin Random House is committed to a sustainable
future for our business, our readers and our planet.
This book is made from Forest Stewardship Council®
certified paper

Contents

List of Illustrations

1. The Great Exhibition of 1851 © The Trustees of the British Museum

2. The Forth Bridge © Royal Scottish Geographical Society

3. Eaton Hall © Getty Images

4. Archibald Campbell Tait © Fulham Palace Trust

5. Lloyd Family Butchers, Aberystwyth, 1911

6. Harriet Mellon © National Portrait Gallery, London

7. Hustings at Bury St Edmunds © Past & Present Society

8. Chartist Meeting on Kennington Common, Royal Collection Trust / © Her Majesty Queen Elizabeth II 2015

9. Suffragette Magazine march © Getty Images

10. St Pancras Station, reproduced by permission of English Heritage

11. English cricket team © Getty Images

12. Map of the British Empire © Mary Evans Picture Library

Chapter One

Material Cultures

In many respects, the nineteenth century belonged to Britain, just as – in many respects – the twentieth century belonged to the United States. For most of the period between 1800 and 1914, Britain was at the zenith of its power and influence, and, certainly prior to the last decades of the century, was universally seen as one of the world's superpowers, perhaps the greatest superpower. It is a cliché that every period is a time of transition and change, but certainly this was the case in the nineteenth century, when Britain experienced an industrial revolution, was transformed from a largely rural to a largely urban society, and formally became the head of a mighty empire. Yet, to a surprising extent, much about Britain did not change dramatically. In contrast to virtually all the other European nations its formal governmental structure was almost precisely the same in 1914 as it was a century earlier. Britain escaped revolution, invasion, internal turmoil and dictatorship, despite the changes it experienced. This chapter considers the major dimensions of British change and stability during the nineteenth century.

The demographic background and its evolution

Of all the changes which came over Britain during the nineteenth century, possibly none was as dramatic, or easier to quantify, than the enormous growth in population and the increase in size of, in particular, Britain's cities. Britain recorded its first national census in 1801. Every ten years thereafter censuses have been held and from them we have an accurate account of British population and change. (The first Irish census was held in 1821. No census was taken in 1941, during the Second World War.) While no official figures exist prior to 1801, it is generally estimated that the population of England and Wales totalled about 3 million in 1600, and rose to about 5.5 million in 1700 and to about 6.5 million in 1750, with Scotland's population about 1.3 million in 1755 and Ireland having a population of about 2.7 million in 1700, 3.2 million in 1750 and 5 million in 1801 – in other words, the total population of what would become known as the United Kingdom probably totalled about 10.8 million in 1750. The extraordinary rate of growth of Britain's population during the nineteenth century can be seen from these statistics:

Population of the United Kingdom and its components, 1801–1911 (000s)

	1801	1831	1851	1881	1901	1911
England	8,352	13,090	16,922	25,974	30,813	34,109
Wales	541	807	1,006	1,361	1,715	2,027
Scotland	1,608	2,364	2,889	3,736	4,272	4,751
Ireland	5,216	7,767	6,552	5,175	4,459	4,381
United Kingdom	15,717	24,028	27,369	34,885	41,259	45,268
Percent of total in England	53	54	62	74	75	75

During the half-century from 1750 to 1801, the population of Britain and Ireland probably increased by about 44 per cent. Over the course of the next century, however, it rose by 166 per cent, a rate of increase certainly without any previous parallel in history. The population of England more than tripled during the nineteenth century. Britain's population explosion, moreover, occurred alongside massive and unprecedented emigration overseas, chiefly to North America and other areas of the white empire such as Australia. Without this emigration, Britain's overall population growth would have been even greater.

While England, Scotland and Wales grew significantly during the nineteenth century, it is striking that, in complete contrast, the population of Ireland actually declined considerably. Ireland's population reached a peak of about 8.5 million in the mid-1840s, before being struck by the great potato famine of 1845–51, probably the greatest demographic catastrophe in any European country between the Thirty Years War of the seventeenth century and the First World War. In 1845, a fungal potato blight destroyed the majority of the single crop on which much of rural western Ireland depended for its sustenance. Starvation and disease, and an arguably inept British government response, meant that about 1.1 million people died in the famine, while no fewer than 2.1 million Irishmen emigrated in the decade 1845–55 (more than one quarter of the total Irish population), creating great Irish Catholic diasporas in many cities in England and Scotland, and powerful communities in the United States, Australia and elsewhere. Although anti-English feeling was long ingrained, the Irish famine was one of the most important causes of the lasting sense of hostility and grievance felt by nationalist-minded Irish Catholics towards the British government.

Elsewhere in Britain, however, there was uninterrupted population growth. The total increase in England (369 per cent) was greater than that in Scotland (266 per cent) or Wales (317 per cent). The most basic question is what caused this enormous and unprecedented increase. While this cannot be answered with precision, many historians would probably suggest that there was a lowering in the age of marriage after the mid-eighteenth century, as opportunities increased in the wake of economic growth. This lowering in the age of marriage (illegitimacies represented only a small percentage of births) enabled more children to be born into each family. The reasons for this decline in the age of marriage are controversial, but might revolve around wider social and geographical changes in society such as a shift towards greater urbanisation. Particularly during the period 1800–70, large families were the rule, even among the middle classes. As well, it would also appear that the incidence of virulent diseases also declined compared with earlier centuries. Inoculation and, later, vaccination for smallpox (introduced by Edward Jenner in 1796) certainly resulted in a decrease in the incidence of this notorious killer, while the plague, the scourge of Europe's population down the ages, failed to appear in its old form after about 1727, possibly because the brown rat replaced the plague-ridden black rat. Nevertheless, one should not exaggerate how healthy Britain had become. In 1860, about 15 per cent of infants died before their first birthday, while death by such infectious diseases as tuberculosis, typhoid and scarlet fever were still normal events.

In the last decades of the nineteenth century, the birth rate began to decline, a phenomenon first observed among the English middle classes from about 1870. The birth rate remained marginally higher in Scotland than in England and

Wales, and remained higher in England and Wales than in Ireland, where the overall population continued to decline, and many young men and women emigrated overseas. This decline in the birth rate was accompanied by an even sharper decline in the death rate, especially among children, meaning that it became more likely that some children would survive into adulthood even among smaller families. This process, of smaller families becoming more general, is known as the 'demographic transition', and was accelerated among middle-class (especially professional) families by the steep costs of educating sons at fee-paying schools and universities. By the late nineteenth century, late marriages became the rule, augmented in the twentieth century by contraception. By the 1930s, the British birth rate was less than one half of what it had been in the mid-nineteenth century.

The other major factors in population change are emigration and immigration. The nineteenth century was the era, par excellence, of massive European migration overseas, especially to the United States and, in the British case, to areas of new settlement in the white empire such as Canada and Australia. Comprehensive statistics exist only from the mid-nineteenth century, and these are startling in their scale. In 1853, the first year when official statistics are available, 278,000 British people emigrated overseas, about 1 per cent of the population, of whom 191,000 went to the United States. About 5–10 per cent of the British population emigrated overseas in most decades of the nineteenth century, extraordinary percentages. While disproportionate numbers of these were impoverished Irishmen, emigrants came from all ranks on the social scale. Emigration overseas has often been seen as a 'safety valve' to relieve potential discontent at home, with tens of thousands of possible troublemakers, even would-be revolutionaries, moving out of Britain each year. Many did well in their new homes and, paradoxically, often eventually became conservatives and empire super-patriots. The worldwide network of empire loyalty which Britain had built up by the time of the First World War was largely founded on just such successful émigrés. Immigration into Britain from Europe and elsewhere always existed, but, during the nineteenth century, was hardly noticed except in the last two decades when about 150,000 eastern European Jews escaped poverty and oppression by migrating to Britain, chiefly to London's East End. Immigrant entrepreneurs, intellectuals and political refugees were, however, a notable part of the British scene; until 1905, Britain had no barriers of any kind to immigration, and anyone could come. By far the largest number of settlers in Great Britain, however, were impoverished Irish Catholics – who, of course, were British subjects, not foreigners.

Just as significant as the sheer growth in Britain's population was the enormous expansion in the size of Britain's cities, and the changes in the nature of British urban demography which occurred as a result of population growth and industrialisation. Down the ages, Britain contained a city which was vastly greater in size than any other, namely London, the capital. Many of these were, officially, the administrative centres of Britain's counties, while a few of the largest – Bristol, Liverpool, Manchester – were not local administrative centres but commercial or industrial centres. At the beginning of the nineteenth century, the gap in size between London and Britain's other main cities was extraordinary, while all of Britain's other cities were surprisingly small. In 1801, the Greater London metropolitan area had a population of 1,117,000. Remarkably, not a single other city in Britain had a population of more than about 83,000, the six next largest being Edinburgh (83,000), Liverpool

(82,000), Glasgow (77,000), Manchester (75,000), Birmingham (71,000) and Bristol (61,000). Only a handful of other cities had a population which exceeded 40,000. In Ireland, there were no good population statistics before 1821. In that year, the population of Dublin was about 336,000, while the population of Belfast was only about 35,000. By 1910, Dublin had about 395,000 inhabitants, while the population of industrial Belfast had risen dramatically, to about 380,000, up from only 200,000 in 1881.

The nineteenth century witnessed an extraordinary growth in the size of Britain's cities, so that in 1911, apart from London, there were forty cities with a population of 100,000 or more, including Glasgow (1,000,000), Birmingham (840,000), Liverpool (753,000) and Manchester (714,000). Britain now contained recognisable urban conurbations – distinctive groups of adjacent cities and their outlying areas – with South-East Lancashire (Greater Manchester) containing 2.3 million inhabitants, the West Midlands (Birmingham) 1.6 million, West Yorkshire (Leeds and Bradford) 1.6 million, and Merseyside (Liverpool) 1.2 million. These new urban areas dwarfed the old commercial and administrative towns of Britain, whose population wholly failed to keep pace with the new areas of urban growth. For instance, Chester's population was 15,000 in 1801 but only 39,000 in 1911; King's Lynn numbered 10,000 inhabitants in 1801 but only 20,000 in 1911; Exeter grew from 17,000 to 59,000 in this period. Unless a town could attract new sources of industry or commerce, it often decayed. Some old towns and cities such as Aberdeen, Derby, Norwich and Nottingham managed to find new industries, sometimes because a few local entrepreneurs fortuitously established businesses there, developing the granite industry in Aberdeen and lace manufacture in Nottingham. Nevertheless, without

new forms of commerce and industry, numbers declined relatively, even absolutely. Counties bypassed by economic and
population growth included Cornwall, which grew from
192,000 in 1801 to only 328,000 in 1911; Westmorland (41,000
in 1801; 64,000 in 1911); most of northern Scotland; and much
of rural Wales.

Within each of the old British counties, the growth of
enormous new cities meant that the old structures of governance and the old ruling elites were swamped, even obliterated,
by the new urban order. Lancashire's county town and capital,
for instance, was Preston, which developed its own new industries and grew from 12,000 in 1801 to 117,000 in 1911. But its
role as county administrative centre was largely irrelevant to
the governance of the county's two huge cities, Liverpool and
Manchester, and to the host of smaller, but still substantial,
towns which grew with industrialisation, such as Blackburn,
Bolton and Oldham. The traditional, premodern elite structure which had governed at the local level in Lancashire (as in
all other counties) – composed of aristocrats and the larger
landowners, well-established merchants and lawyers, and
some Anglican clergymen – was now largely swamped, in
terms of wealth, economic power and ideologically driven
political intent, by the new men of industrial and commercial
Lancashire, often 'self-made' and uncouth, often Nonconformist
in religion, often politically radical (at least initially), often
regarding the traditional ruling elite – again, at least initially –
as their enemies. Accommodating this new elite thrown up by
industrial growth with the old elites became one of the major
themes of nineteenth-century political life. The pattern found
in Lancashire occurred throughout the new industrial areas of
Britain. Birmingham in Warwickshire, for instance, became
renowned as the great city where semi-socialist civic

improvement and public works – led by the great radical (and, later, Tory) leader Joseph Chamberlain – went furthest.

Dwarfing every urban area in Britain – indeed, in the western world – was London, in every sense the capital of the nation and of the empire. Despite the fact that London was so large (indeed, perhaps because of it), it has been easy for contemporary commentators and later historians to overlook: Manchester, with its hundreds of billowing factory smokestacks, was somehow regarded as the norm and the standard from which other cities deviated. London's growth was indeed extraordinary: from 1.1 million in 1801, it grew to 2.7 million at the time of the Great Exhibition in 1851, and then to 4.8 million in 1881 and, remarkably, to 7.3 million in 1911, when it was almost certainly the largest city in the world. London's continuing expansion had been checked to a certain extent between 1831 and 1851 (when it grew in size from 1.9 million to 'only' 2.7 million), as newer industrial cities attracted the economically insecure and as London's own infrastructure floundered just before the development of suburban railways and trams, gaslight and running water, but then again spurted enormously, nearly tripling over the next sixty years. London was virtually unique among the world's great cities in combining the formal role of national capital and administrative centre with a host of other functions of fundamental importance – the world's financial centre, in the 'Square Mile' of the City of London, a great shipping port, Britain's press and publishing centre, the focus of arts, entertainment and the intelligentsia, the centre of retailing, and the focus of all of high society, the court, the aristocracy and the wealthy. It was also the largest single manufacturing centre in Britain, producing a range of industrial and consumer goods, although London was not a factory town like Manchester or Leeds.

1. The Great Exhibition of 1851. Held in the Crystal Palace, an enormous building erected for that purpose in Hyde Park, London, the Great Exhibition was the first 'world's fair'. Attracting millions of visitors from Britain and overseas, it was symbolic of Victorian progress and peaceful development.

Since the Middle Ages, London had acted as a magnet for the footloose, and tens of thousands came from other parts of Britain each year to seek their fortunes. While some succeeded, the majority remained in the working classes. For women, the hazards of migrating to London were especially great, with prostitution a ubiquitous and shameful feature of London life, probably more visible and unavoidable than anywhere else in Britain. London's wide combination of roles, and its vast size, place it in a different category from other great world cities. Although New York was America's largest city, its capital was Washington, while in the late nineteenth century, Chicago grew as something of a rival to New York. In many other countries – Russia, Canada, Australia – two rival

large cities emerged. There were countries where a single capital metropolis paralleled London's multifaceted role, such as
(most obviously) Paris in France, but none matched London's
size in their respective populations. In 1911, for instance,
London contained about 16 per cent of the entire population
of the United Kingdom, while Paris was the home to only
about 5 per cent of the French population. As a result, none of
the great new cities of the north of England emerged to challenge London's dominance, which, if anything, increased in
the course of the nineteenth century with London's role as
capital of the empire and world financial centre.

The population of the entire western world grew enormously during the nineteenth century, and it is difficult to
imagine any situation apart from rapid British population
growth. This occurred, perhaps ironically, at a time when
Britain never saw a revolution but emerged at the end of the
century with arguably greater political and social stability than
at its beginning. Could this have occurred without the 'safety
valve' provided by the empire and massive emigration overseas? Was population growth in part the result of the fortuitous
absence of old-style plagues and pestilence? Would it have
occurred in the absence of an industrial revolution? Quite possibly; the population of Europe's backward areas, especially
Russia, grew just as rapidly as Britain's, without the emergence of more than a skeletal urban working class in these
regions. It is just possible, too, to imagine population decline,
as in Ireland – if, for example, a sustained great plague visited
Britain, or a period of sustained depression led to massive emigration overseas. Arguably, the long period of population
growth throughout most of nineteenth-century Europe was
merely fortuitous, the result of autonomous factors, and not
the product of economic growth or industrialisation.

These population changes helped to ensure the dominance of England within the United Kingdom. Nevertheless, population alone isn't everything, and in and of itself cannot explain the relations between the four parts of the United Kingdom. Ireland's population declined in absolute terms, yet the Irish contingent of MPs at the Westminster Parliament sometimes held the political balance of power between the major parties.

Chapter Two

The Evolution of the British Economy

Parallel to the extraordinary changes in Britain's population and its distribution during the nineteenth century was the growth and reorientation of the British economy. Between 1801 and 1911 Britain's total gross national income grew from about £232 million to £1.643 billion, a sevenfold increase, at a time when rates of inflation were either very low or non-existent. Economic growth thus outstripped population growth, as remarkable and unprecedented as this was. Historians from about the 1880s often began to depict the era after *c.*1760 as that of an 'industrial revolution'. This was usually seen as centrally entailing the application of steam power and other forms of advanced motive power to manufacturing production, through the factory system, and to transport, via the railway and steam-powered shipping. While these things certainly occurred, one must not forget that the non-industrial component of the economy – finance, commerce, the professions, the service sector – grew at least as rapidly. Nor ought one to forget that agriculture and farming remained major components of the economy. The Industrial Revolution was also seen as fundamentally altering the class basis of British society, instituting the growth of a huge urban proletariat of workers in factories and mines, alongside a small class of wealthy industrialists. Again, while these changes certainly occurred, it is also the case that there was never a time when the classical industrial proletariat – workers in factories and mines – constituted more than about 40 per cent of the male workforce, while industrialists never constituted a majority of the wealthy or middle classes. Many recent historians question whether there was a 'take-off into sustained economic growth', to cite the famous phrase of Walt Rostow, the American economic historian who believed that industrial revolutions, wherever they occur, are marked by spurts of much higher levels of economic growth, as measured by that country's national product. Instead, they argue that Britain's growth rate did not increase noticeably during the mid to late eighteenth century, but was fairly steady throughout this period. Such an interpretation might help to explain the relative lack of political unrest in Britain, except in limited periods such as the aftermath of the Napoleonic Wars.

Historians have often debated why it was Britain, rather than a rival nation such as France or the Netherlands, where these economic changes apparently occurred first. Britain was well placed for early industrialisation. It was in many (but certainly not all) respects already a 'modern' society, with no feudalism, peasantry or serfdom as was found throughout most of Europe until the nineteenth century or later. Instead, Britain was already what Thomas Carlyle later termed a 'cash nexus'-based society, where reward was in the form of money wages and enterprise for profit was broadly based. In the eighteenth century, Britain probably already had the highest per capita income of any European state, and was free of very sharp boundaries separating the traditional aristocracy from the rest of society. Self-made men could become aristocrats. Private property was invariably protected by law, and could never be arbitrarily taken by the state. It has often been noted that England (but not Scotland or Wales) was the only part of Europe without any distinctive traditional peasant costume: bearing in mind social class differences, of course, everyone dressed alike. A high per capita income, a growing population, and broadly similar tastes throughout society were major factors in creating strong internal demand for the goods which the British economy produced, especially for the cotton and woollen mass-market goods emblematic of the first phase of industrialisation. These demand factors were augmented by increases in productivity and by Britain's fortunate position as a prime exporting nation, but, many historians have argued, were important elements in generating economic growth.

Britain also controlled, or was dominant in, a large fraction of the external trade of the world. Britain already had a large empire, centred in India, Canada and the West Indies. It also exported to Europe, and ironically was significantly assisted after the rise of Napoleon when Britain successfully blockaded the French-dominated areas of the Continent, removing potential European rivals to Britain's export trade. After the American colonies gained their independence, economic ties between Britain and the United States resumed strongly. When most of Latin America gained independence from Spain in the early nineteenth century, the continent in many respects became an unofficial British economic colony. Above all, British world trading hegemony was crucially guaranteed by the dominance of the Royal Navy.

These potent factors were necessary, but not sufficient, preconditions for industrialisation. Arguably more important was Britain's propensity to engender both successful business entrepreneurs, especially in the newer manufacturing industries, as well as the new inventions that made industrialisation possible, which produced the supply which matched home and foreign demand. Britain had always produced successful merchants and entrepreneurs; what was relatively new was their success in large-scale manufacturing industry as well as in trade and finance. Many of Britain's successful early industrialists were Protestant Nonconformists, whose 'Protestant ethic' of hard work and situation outside the Anglican-dominated elite structure probably acted as sparks to success. However, it might be noted that the two richest industrialists of the early nineteenth century, Richard Arkwright and Sir Robert Peel – the father of the prime minister – were Anglicans and that there were certainly a very significant number of Anglican entrepreneurs. It is likely, in fact, that Anglican businessmen were just as successful as Nonconformist businessmen. Possibly, too, Anglican success regularly came in different areas of the economy, for instance in overseas trade and brewing, from the areas of success enjoyed by Nonconformists. It is quite possible that there were disproportionately more successful Nonconformist industrialists and manufacturers than Anglicans, especially in the new urban areas of the north of England. The first wave of successful industrialists, especially in large-scale cotton and woollen manufacturing, achieved their success before steam power was used in factory production, their factories powered by water in remote rural areas.

When steam power became more widespread, from the 1820s on, a second wave of large-scale industrial production began, far greater than anything seen before. Most of this production was done in factories in cities, where steam power could be used without the necessity of ample running water, and the classical factory towns of the Industrial Revolution, especially Manchester, grew enormously as a result. Factory production centred above all around the manufacture of cotton goods. Imports of raw cotton into England grew from 93 million pounds in 1815 to 554 million pounds in 1844, the decades when factory capitalism grew most strongly. Steam power also generated a vast increase in coal production, the basic source of energy for all steam power and almost all domestic heating, while the manufacture of iron and engineering equipment likewise increased astronomically. This was the classical Industrial Revolution, an image known to us all as hallmarked by belching smokestacks, small children employed as factory hands, and hard-nosed factory owners alongside a proletarian army. By 1841 about 1.5 million people were employed in manufacturing in the United Kingdom, along with another 220,000 in mining, out of a total employed labour force of about 6.8 million, about 25 per cent of the total. Their numbers continued to grow until after mid-century, reaching about 40 per cent of the workforce by 1861, but then remained fairly stagnant, as the service sector of the economy increased sharply.

The very symbol of the new age was the railway, as emblematic of nineteenth century Britain as the cathedrals and monasteries had become of the Middle Ages. Primitive railways, consisting of carts running on wooden tramways, had been in operation in mining areas since the sixteenth century; these were, of course, pulled by horses or human labourers. Although steam engines had existed since the 1760s, it took until about 1804 for anyone to combine the two, and until the mid-1820s for the railway revolution to begin, with the famous Stockton–Darlington railway. Britain's railway revolution and its railway 'mania' took another decade or more to erupt: in 1837 there were only 540 miles of railways in operation in the United Kingdom, and fewer than 5 million passengers carried. The slow development of Britain's railways suggests that, as some economic historians have argued, rapid and sudden transformations of the economy did not always occur in this period. The late 1830s and 40s, however, witnessed the railway mania in full flood: by 1850 there were 6,084 miles of railways built, and 67 million passengers. The rest of the nineteenth century saw the remainder of Britain's railway system fleshed out, reaching virtually every place of significance in the country, so that by 1911 there were over 20,000 miles of railways in operation, with 1.3 billion passengers carried. England always had more railway mileage, in terms of its size, than Scotland, Wales or Ireland. Nevertheless, by the early twentieth century much of the Scottish Highlands, Welsh hill country and Irish rural areas were connected to urban centres by rail.

As a system of transport, railways were vastly faster, more reliable, and more efficient than anything known before, but they still had many deficiencies: accidents, often fatal, were frequent, and railways were highly labour-intensive, employing 373,000 people by 1911. By definition railways could not leave the track, and both persons and goods still had to be met and transported from the station to their final destination, which left ample room for widespread horse-drawn carriage until the automobile age. Steam power was a mighty pollutant, and London's many mainline railway stations were deliberately situated at the edges of the central city, rather than at the hub. Perhaps uniquely in Europe, all Britain's railways were built, operated and owned by private capitalists and companies, rather than by the state, and the railway companies grew to become among the largest of nineteenth-century businesses. Some railway builders and managers became legendary, with Isambard Kingdom Brunel (1806–59), also a celebrated shipbuilder, emerging as the public face of British industrial capitalism. The great edifices of Victorian engineering such as the famous railway stations, the viaducts, and a structure like the Forth Bridge, were at the heart of industrialisation. The Forth Bridge, linking Midlothian with Fife, opened in 1890 after taking over ten years to complete, impresses even today by its incredible size.

2. The Forth Bridge. One of the greatest of all Victorian construction projects, the mighty Forth Bridge linking Edinburgh with the north of Scotland opened in 1890. Its truly staggering size, as seen in this photograph taken when under construction, must have seemed like science fiction to observers at the time.

As noted, there has long been a debate as to whether
Britain's industrialisation was rapid and sudden or steadier and
more drawn out. Many recent historians have seen a much
slower and less dramatic process of economic growth than did
historians of fifty years ago. Rates of economic growth were
surprisingly low, perhaps because the British economy was relatively advanced before industrialisation. It is very important to
remember that while industry and manufacturing were the
most dramatic aspects of Britain's growing economy in the
nineteenth century, they were not the only or, indeed, arguably
the most important sectors. Britain's service sector – commerce, finance, trade, and the professions – was of central
importance. Economic growth in the service sector is intrinsic-
ally more difficult to measure or quantify than in manufacturing
or industry, a fact which calls into dispute the accuracy of
Britain's statistics of economic growth. Britain had long been a
world centre of trade, commerce and finance; during the nineteenth century its centrality in these spheres increased and
consolidated. In particular, the role of the City of London as
the centre of the world's international finance reached its apo-
gee. The City – as the historical Square Mile centring around
Threadneedle Street, which contains London's financial district, analogous to Wall Street in New York, is known – financed
much of the world's economic growth and development
through merchant banks owned by renowned families such as
the Rothschilds and Barings. It also contained the Stock
Exchange, Lloyds of London insurance, the headquarters of
the great clearing banks and insurance companies, and many
company headquarters. The City established a reputation for
probity, and for the ability to finance large-scale government
loans, which made it the world's financial capital until this
mantle passed to New York after the First World War.

Much in the world's international economic life was governed by the gold standard, by which the value of any currency was fixed against gold bullion, and redeemable in gold. Each country's central bank set its exchange rate, which had to be preserved by the use of its gold reserve. The gold standard appeared to work harmoniously until the First World War destroyed the world's existing currency system. London was a great centre of commerce as well as finance, containing innumerable retail shops, wholesalers, warehouses, import–export houses, and the great docks of the Thames. Other major British cities, such as Liverpool and Bristol, were primarily oriented around commerce and trade rather than manufacturing. While employment in manufacturing reached 40 per cent of the total workforce in 1861, and then hardly grew, the service sector increased during the late nineteenth century, increasing from about 21 per cent of the workforce in 1861 to about 30 per cent in 1901. Edinburgh and Dublin flourished as governmental centres and as homes of the local professional elite, as did London in part on a vastly greater scale. The service sector also included an ever larger segment of professionals and semi-professionals. While the older professions – traditionally law, medicine, the Anglican clergy, and perhaps military officers, always regarded as occupations for gentlemen – increased substantially during the nineteenth century, they were joined by newer professions such as accountancy and engineering, as well as the so-called 'sub-professions' – schoolteachers in the state sector, nurses, librarians – with an increasing female presence. Nursing, in particular, emerged as arguably the woman's sub-profession par excellence, a nurturing, life-saving occupation whose icon was Florence Nightingale, but one in which its largely female workforce was expected to work like slaves, in

highly unpleasant ways, for a pittance, almost always ultimately directed by male doctors.

While industry, commerce and the professions comprised
the bulk of the nineteenth-century workforce, one should
remember that agriculture was still extremely important to the
British economy. In 1811, about 35 per cent of families in Britain
were engaged in agriculture. There was a continuous decline in
agriculture as a component of the employed workforce throughout the century, to 27 per cent in 1861, 19 per cent in 1881, and
11 per cent in 1911, but these still comprised substantial numbers of persons. In 1851 nearly 1.8 million males were employed
in agriculture and farming, more than any other occupational
category. Britain's overall national income still included a large,
albeit declining, agricultural and farming sector, which
accounted for 33 per cent of Britain's national income in 1801,
20 per cent in 1851, and 6 per cent even in the early twentieth
century. Many parts of Britain still remained visibly rural and
pre-industrial down to the First World War, with farmers and
agricultural labourers, to say nothing of the country-house life
of the aristocracy and gentry, being familiar props of English
novels, poems and other literary depictions throughout the
nineteenth century. Indeed, given the relatively efficient and
progressive nature of much of British agriculture (outside of
southern Ireland and other Celtic areas), Britain's landowners
and farmers grew ever wealthier at least until the late Victorian
agricultural depression, which began around 1880 when the
large-scale importation of foreign foodstuffs undermined
Britain's farming sector. The Highlands of Scotland, the Welsh-
speaking areas of Wales, and most of Ireland retained a larger
rural sector than did most of England, although rural areas predominated in parts of England such as Cornwall and East Anglia
until the twentieth century.

British agriculture had been based, throughout modern history, on the so-called 'triple division of land tenure'. A landowner, often a wealthy aristocrat, owned the land, which was worked by a tenant farmer who paid a rental income to the landowners, and who in turn employed agricultural labourers. (There were also smaller owner-occupiers of land, especially in the north of England, Scotland and Wales.) This type of landownership made efficiencies of scale and investment in the land and new equipment and methods of production possible, and gave many of those landowners a vested interest in increasing the profitability of the land. British agriculture was, as a rule, more profitable and advanced than anywhere else in Europe, where small peasant holdings were the norm. Only when British agriculture was itself challenged by the gigantic farms and their output of the United States, Canada and Australia, in the latter part of the nineteenth century, did it face serious competition.

During the eighteenth and nineteenth centuries, enclosure continued. Landowners secured Acts of Parliament to 'enclose' fields previously owned in common, taking them over as private property in exchange for fencing them and providing agricultural improvements. The alleged loss of rights by the rural poor, whose access to these fields often provided a significant component of their incomes, became a matter of great controversy, then and since. Proponents of enclosing argued that they greatly increased agricultural productivity and also increased demand for labour. It should also be noted that different parts of Britain had relatively different farming patterns, with some areas specialising in cattle and sheep farming, others in growing crops. In general, areas of cattle and sheep production were harder hit by foreign competition after 1880 than were others. Ireland, with its reliance on the single crop of potatoes, paid a heavy penalty for its lack of diversification.

By the early twentieth century, there was a pervasive sense that all was not well with Britain's economy. In particular, there was a sense that Britain was being overtaken by Germany and the United States as the world's economic superpowers. Germany appeared to be far ahead of Britain in harnessing what is often now termed the 'second Industrial Revolution' based on electricity, chemicals and novel technologies, while America's assembly lines of mass production dwarfed anything elsewhere. Unemployment in Britain probably grew, while rates of British economic growth appeared to stagnate. Net national income per head, at 1900 prices, had increased from £18 in 1855 to £38 in 1890, but then hardly grew at all, totalling £44 in 1913. Identifying and ameliorating Britain's apparent decline became an obsession at the time, as it was to become again from the 1950s until the 1990s. That Britain was in a state of relative economic decline by 1914 was widely believed at the time, and has been much debated by economic historians since. It is reasonable to argue that there were areas of the economy in which Britain was being overtaken by its major rivals. As noted, these were in the so-called 'second Industrial Revolution' activities, or in mass-production output such as automobiles. There were, however, areas of the economy in which no decline had occurred by 1914. These included the old staple industries – cotton, coal, shipbuilding – and the service sector, which was growing strongly. The reason why Britain failed to maintain its old lead across the board has been vigorously debated. Many argue that it would have been inherently almost impossible to maintain its old lead once great rivals such as America and Germany emerged. Other have pointed to the 'cult of the amateur' in Britain, with the sons and grandsons of the dynamic founders of a firm being educated at a public school and university and joining the landed gentry. Some have also singled out the alleged sharp division between the City of London and British industry, with British banks declining to invest in new industries, or to the propensity to invest overseas rather than in Britain itself. Some economic historians, however, have questioned the notion of a real British decline by 1914, viewing the growth of the service sector as itself evidence of a dynamic and modernising economy. What is undeniable is that the economic changes brought about by the First World War deleteriously affected, after 1918, Britain's staple industries leading to high unemployment in these areas during 1919–39, concentrated especially in those regions of Britain, such as South Wales, the North-East, and Clydeside, where they had been strongest.

One major point about the economy which is not easy to grasp today is that there was simply no notion of many of the economic concepts and perspectives which we now take for granted as the basis of debate about economic matters. In particular, there was no notion of such concepts as gross national product, economic growth, aggregate demand, or even of an accurate determination of unemployment, or of its rise or fall. All of these ideas relied on the twentieth century for both their enunciation and definition, and of their accurate measurement. Just as importantly, there was no assumption of any kind that the government could control these factors, or alleviate them in times of distress, by the deliberate use of such measures as deficit spending in times of high unemployment or of automatic counter-cyclical expenditures such as increased unemployment benefits or government expenditures designed to create work during a recession. All such economic concepts and measures had to await the interwar period of the 1920s and 30s for their development, where they were especially associated with the great British economist John Maynard Keynes (1883–1946), and for the post-1945 period, when they were first implemented throughout the world. For one thing, the British national budget was simply too small to have the profound effect on economic demand and unemployment which it has had in modern times. In 1871, for instance, the total British national budget was £67 million, about 7 per cent of Britain's national income of £936 million. Today, even Conservative governments rarely if ever deliver budgets which account for less than 35–40 per cent of the British national income. Today, often these large budgets are paid for by deficit spending, in order to promote economic growth and job creation. Such a strategy would have been almost inconceivable in the nineteenth century: except in a national emergency such as a major war, budgets had to balance, either by increasing taxation or by cutting expenditure. There were no economic structures in place to promote economic growth as such. Governments relied on 'natural' means of economic adjustment, such as the gold standard (where the value of the pound, compared with other currencies, could move up or down); interest rates, set by the Bank of England; the yield on 'consols' (government-issued stocks which produced a fluctuating rate of interest, generally between 2.5 and 3.5 per cent in our period); and free trade or tariff agreements on certain goods with other countries. During times of very high unemployment, as occurred every ten years or so, there were no state unemployment benefits or anything of the kind, apart from the occasional ad hoc emergency measures. The unemployed had to rely on their savings, private charity, the workhouse (see below), or migration elsewhere in the UK or abroad. There were no locally enacted minimum wage rates, and it was also assumed that, desperate for work, labourers would agree to work for lower wages, cutting the total costs of the industrialist, which would enable him to lower his prices and recover his market share, eventually restoring equilibrium. After a fashion, this did work, and there were almost always new sources of investment, such as in railways or steamships, to assist the economy. But the human costs of this pre-Keynesian approach to economic management were extraordinary and tragic.

Chapter Three
Modes of Identity:
Social Class

Social class is not easy precisely to define, and, as a concept, is made more difficult by the fact that while one might situate an individual within an ascribed social class, he or she might perceive their own class in quite a different way. By time-honoured usage, it is common to divide British society into three main social classes, the upper, middle and working classes, with many subdivisions within each. While, broadly, it may be reasonable to draw this division, it is surprisingly difficult to define or set limits to these three main classes in anything more than a general way. As well, British society as a whole evolved during the nineteenth century, in ways which affected its class structure.

During the nineteenth century (and before and after), Britain contained a titled aristocracy composed of peers, baronets (hereditary knights) and knights. Most (but not all) peers sat in the House of Lords, the Upper House of Britain's

Parliament. Down the ages, Britain's aristocracy differed markedly from its Continental equivalents. It was very small, comprising fewer than about 550 men at the end of the nineteenth century; only the eldest son of a peer inherited the title, younger sons and daughters being commoners; the eldest son normally inherited all the family's land and most of their wealth. In 1833, 366 peers were entitled to sit in the House of Lords, 551 in 1900, and 616 in 1910. Several hundred Scottish and Irish peers did not have an automatic right to sit in the Lords, and nor did female peers in their own right or peers who were minors. Overall, the British peerage numbered about 600 in 1833 and 750 in 1900. Above all, Britain's aristocracy was not exempted from any tax and enjoyed no legal privileges (apart from trial by their 'peers' in the House of Lords, if accused of a crime). Baronetcies (about 1,000 in number in 1900) were also inherited by the eldest son, while knighthoods (also numbering about 1,000) ceased with their holder's death. Many aristocrats were very rich, owning vast amounts of land. The very greatest aristocrats, such as the dukes of Westminster, Bedford, Devonshire and Northumberland, and the earls of Derby, were among the richest men in Europe. On average, about ten new peerages were created every year. After about 1870 (but not before) many new creations were great industrialists or businessmen who, generally, had bought landed estates, thus integrating a component of the new wealth with the old.

At the very apex of not merely the upper classes but of the British nation was the monarch, the head of state, who as well as being the head of the churches of England and Scotland was also the (nominal) head of the armed forces, head of the British Empire and, from 1876, Empress or Emperor of India – among many other titles and roles. The monarch opened Parliament,

3. The Stately Home. This is Eaton Hall in Cheshire, the home of the Duke of Westminster. In its vast palatial size it was typical of the country houses of the very richest aristocrats and landowners, as well as those purchased by some nouveau-riche businessmen. The Duke of Westminster (whose surname was Grosvenor) was probably Britain's wealthiest man. His affluence derived from owning the ground rents of much of Mayfair and Belgravia, two of the richest parts of London. He also owned landed estates, especially in Cheshire. Yet the first Duke of Westminster was a Whig and then a Liberal, that is, on the moderate left of the British political spectrum.

signed all laws and Acts of Parliament, officially made all government appointments, awarded all titles and honours, and met at least weekly with the prime minister, as well as automatically reading all government documents. Despite this imposing list, the monarch was, of course, not absolute, and had plainly lost power to Parliament even since the eighteenth century. The four monarchs of the period covered in this book – William IV (1830–7), Victoria (1837–1901), Edward VII (1901–10) and George V (1910–36) – continued to play an important role in the choosing of prime ministers and the formation of governments, but only to a limited extent. Queen

Victoria was known to detest William E. Gladstone (1809–98), the great Liberal leader, but was compelled to appoint him, the choice of the Liberal Party, four times. Her repeated attempt to appoint his moderate rival Lord Hartington to the premiership always came to nothing. Nevertheless, even in 1894 she chose the moderate Liberal Lord Rosebery as prime minister rather than the more radical Sir William V. Harcourt.

The sovereign could thus not ultimately ignore the will of the people as expressed at general elections, and was compelled to sign into law the legislation of the three (1832, 1867, 1884) Reform Acts, the increase in death duties on the rich in 1894, and the proto-welfare state legislation associated with Lloyd George in the Edwardian period, although it seems unlikely that these sovereigns were enthusiastic supporters of any of these measures. The continuing role of the sovereign depended upon his or her popularity. This was never in question, with the exception of the two decades or so after the death of Prince Albert in 1861, when Queen Victoria virtually withdrew from public life, leading to the growth of at least a tentative republican movement among radical Liberals. As the queen returned to public life, nothing came of this, and the monarch enjoyed a continuing, perpetual wave of public popularity which has lasted to this day, with the possible exception of the 1990s and the controversy over Princess Diana and Prince Charles.

The monarch also benefited from the fact that, until 1917–18, nearly all important countries were headed by emperors or kings, the only notable exceptions being France (briefly in 1848–52 and then permanently after 1870–1) and the United States (whose president was, nonetheless, a kind of elected monarch). Until the end of the First World War, Russia, Germany, Austria-Hungary and Turkey were empires, with

Japan retaining an emperor to this day and Italy a king (at least nominally, while Mussolini ruled as dictator) until 1946. There could thus be no realistic alternative to a British monarchy in the world which existed prior to 1914.

Nonetheless, the 'church and king' type of ultra Tory patriotism which existed prior to 1832, and which has been documented so well by Professor J. C. D. Clark, appears simply to have vanished, at least from the mainstream of British politics, by the Age of Reform. The monarchy remained shrouded in distant mystery, and was closely aligned with the established church, but much support of the sovereign reflected the fact that he or she embodied in living form the history of Britain, including all of its progressive changes. The monarch was also at the head of high society, of the London season, and of the presentation of debutantes and the like. The expansion of knighthoods and baronetcies (but not of peerages until the late nineteenth century) to include men (and, occasionally, women) from new forms of enterprise, from among Nonconformists, and from the empire plainly helped the institution to remain popular. That a woman was Britain's monarch for over sixty-three years, something unique in Europe, may well have made veneration for the institution more popular rather than less. Support for monarchy was also extraordinarily manifest throughout the empire. In Australia, founded only in 1788, two colonies (later states) – Victoria and Queensland – were named for the sovereign, while Adelaide, the capital of South Australia, was named for the consort of William IV. A royal visit, whether to the white empire or to India, was a never-to-be-forgotten event, one which produced outpourings of empire loyalty. It might also be noted that although the royal family was obviously wealthy, receiving around £600,000 from the Civil List in 1913, they were not super-rich in a private capacity. According to Bateman's *Great Landowners* of 1883, which recorded the acreages and annual landed incomes of all large landowners, the queen owned, in a private capacity, 27,441 acres worth £5,561 p.a., while the Prince of Wales owned 14,889 acres worth £9,727 p.a., far less than the wealth of most landed aristocrats. (These figures exclude, for instance, most of the income of the Duchy of Cornwall, nominally owned by the Prince of Wales.) In contrast, Kaiser Wilhelm II was widely believed to have been, in a private capacity, the richest man in Germany, while the wealth of the Russian tsar must have been almost incalculable. That perhaps dozens of titled aristocrats were far wealthier than the royal family arguably made them continue as something like first among equals, as was possibly the case in the eighteenth century, rather than stand out as the Everest of privilege, as after the First World War, when the wealth of most old aristocrats declined sharply.

What is perhaps most striking about the upper classes during the period concerned here, at least until the Edwardian period, was how successfully the traditional landed aristocracy and their close relatives clung to real power and to the levers of governance, despite both the rise of new forms of industrial and commercial wealth, and of increasingly democratic reforms to political process. Lord John Russell's first Cabinet, for instance – formed in 1846, fourteen years after the 1832 Reform Act, and Whig–Liberal in its party politics – contained two marquesses, four earls, two viscounts, two barons, and three knights or baronets; Russell was the youngest son of a duke. Only two members of the Cabinet were simply 'Mister' – Henry Labouchere, who had married into the astronomically wealthy Baring family, and, most anomalously, Thomas Babington Macaulay, the great historian, who was Paymaster

General. Even Lord Salisbury's Tory Cabinet of 1895 included a duke, two marquesses, two earls, a viscount, three barons and two baronets. Most of the other members of this Cabinet were untitled great landowners or the close relatives of great landowners, such as Arthur Balfour, Salisbury's nephew. Only three could be described as middle class, most notably Joseph Chamberlain, probably the most dominant figure in British politics, who was by background a Unitarian screw manufacturer from Birmingham, although his father had been wealthy and he had attended a public school. Sir Henry Campbell-Bannerman's Cabinet, formed in December 1905, was the first in which non-aristocrats were in a distinct majority, and even included one Labour working man, John Burns. Yet it still contained six members who sat in the House of Lords, with most of the others being successful middle-class professionals and businessmen, such as Herbert Asquith (who succeeded Campbell-Bannerman as prime minister), a leading barrister married to the daughter of the richest businessman in Scotland, Sir Charles Tennant.

That the traditional landed aristocracy, which could often trace its lineage back for centuries, continued to dominate British politics in an increasingly democratic age, was widely noted at the time. A well-known work published in 1865, *The Great Governing Families of England* by John Longton Sanford and Meredith Townsend, contained historical accounts of twenty-three of the most important political families in England. Only one of these was in any sense a 'new' family or engaged in trade: the Baring banking dynasty which had married into the whig aristocracy. After surveying the Stanleys, the Cavendishes, the Leveson-Gowers, the Cecils, et al., it began its account of the Barings by proclaiming 'A new family at last! In the roll of houses ... there is but this one belonging strictly to the merchant princes.' Nor was this book merely describing past glories. Its account of the Cecils, for instance, noted that 'the family credit is now chiefly sustained in public life by . . . Lord Robert Cecil MP, who displays much of the family astuteness.' This Robert Cecil was to become the third Marquess of Salisbury, prime minister for most of the period between 1885 and 1902, who was succeeded as prime minister by his nephew Arthur Balfour. Writing of the Grosvenors, the authors noted that 'the family wealth develops with every succeeding year', a remark made before the head of the family, the Marquess of Westminster, was given a dukedom in 1874, while in the Edwardian period, the second duke was certainly the richest landowner in Britain, probably worth about £14 million. (A century later, the present Duke of Westminster was generally found to be the richest British-born person in Britain, according to the annual *Sunday Times* Rich Lists.)

There were a number of important factors as to why the old aristocracy continued to dominate British politics: their wealth, boosted by their minerals, urban real estate and agricultural produce; primogeniture, which kept the bulk of their estates intact across the generations; their education at elite public schools and Oxbridge, which instilled in them the expectation that they were born to rule; the continuing sense of *noblesse oblige* across most of British society. On the other side of the ledger, however, is the question of why the middle classes, on the face of it now central after the 1832 Reform Act, failed to dominate British politics until the twentieth century. Here, too, many answers can be given. Businessmen and professionals generally entered political life late, after they had become affluent (Members of Parliament, apart from government ministers, were not paid a salary of any kind until 1908), whereas the sons and other relatives of the old aristocracy often entered politics when they came of age. They thus had a twenty- or thirty-year head start on the middle-class politicians, who were often far too old to start at the bottom and work their way up. (This was also often the case in the twentieth century with backbench Labour MPs, who were regularly retired trade union officials.) Middle-class men, it was often seen, lacked gravitas, or the kind of classical education and high-mindedness required of a senior minister of the Crown; even their accents betrayed them. Many were Protestant Nonconformists rather than Anglicans – no longer an insurmountable obstacle to a political career, but still a handicap. Many were closely associated with a particular city or town, or with a specific industry, and entered politics to champion these, rather than the national interest. This changed in a very significant way only from the 1880s, when the majority of traditional landowners who had been connected with the Liberal Party left it for the Tories, especially in the wake of the Liberal Unionist split over Irish Home Rule in 1886. From then (if not before), most Liberals MPs were businessmen or professionals, with many fewer genuine aristocrats or their relatives. Especially from the 1906 general election, a contingent of forty or more Labour MPs were now also associated with the Liberals, nearly all of whom at this stage were former working men or trade union officials, wholly unassociated with the old ruling classes. By the Edwardian period, the great majority of the traditional aristocracy were to be found in the Unionist (i.e. Conservative) Party, but even here they were also challenged for the leadership of the party by the many Tory businessmen and professionals who flocked to the Tories as the Liberals moved steadily to the left. This change was symbolised in 1911 when Andrew Bonar Law (1858–1923) became leader of the Unionist Party; a dour Nonconformist

Canadian-born iron broker from Glasgow who had no connection by ancestry, education, marriage or lifestyle with the
old aristocracy (but who proved to be an astute and very successful party leader and minister). By this time, too, the old
aristocracy was increasingly challenged by higher rates of taxation and death duties, and by the importation of frozen meat
and other agricultural produce from overseas, often threaten-
ing the economic bases of their wealth. After the First World
War, and although their decline can easily be much exaggerated, there was a pervasive sense that the old aristocracy had
been almost entirely displaced as the leaders of British society
and, indeed, were fortunate not to have shared the fate of
many of their colleagues in Europe.

The upper classes also certainly included very rich businessmen, who also increased rapidly in number during the
nineteenth century. Gauging how rapidly is, of course, difficult, but the number of estates left for probate of £100,000 or
more (about £12 million or $18 million in today's money) rose
from about twenty-five per year early in the nineteenth century to about 250 per year by 1900, a tenfold increase, although
the value of money was virtually unchanged. The very wealthiest businessmen of the century, such as the banker Lord
Overstone (d.1883), the warehouseman James Morrison
(d.1857), or the railway builder Thomas Brassey (d.1870) –
were nearly as rich as any landed aristocrat. Many (but not all)
bought landed estates, although the West End of London and
other upper-class areas swelled with their numbers. More –
perhaps 60 per cent – appear to have earned their fortunes in
London and other commercial centres than in the industrial
north of England. It is difficult to provide more than an estimate, but if one defines the 'wealthy' as those earning £5,000
or more per year (that is, an annual income of 5 per cent of a

fortune of £100,000 or more), then certainly only a fraction of 1 per cent of the adult male population could be considered 'wealthy'. Even if all their relatives be included as 'wealthy', certainly no more than 1 per cent of the population could be so classified. The wealthy lived primarily in the West End of London, in Mayfair, Belgravia and Kensington, in similar exclusive districts in other large cities such as Victoria Park in Manchester, and in large country houses throughout the nation.

Below the aristocracy are the middle class (or classes). Defining it has always been notoriously difficult, the nineteenth century providing no exception. Should the category 'middle class' be delineated by occupations (businessmen and professionals), incomes (with, say, anyone with an income between about £150 and £5,000 being included), lifestyles (living in large houses with several servants but not mansions), or in some other way? Because its definition is so imprecise, estimating the middle-class percentage of the population is difficult, but probably about 15–20 per cent of the population could be said to be middle class in some sense. To most Victorians, the 'middle class' consisted of businessmen and professionals below the very rich. The middle classes probably comprised a larger share of the population in London and the smaller towns of the south of England than in the newer industrial areas. The size of the middle classes employed in public administration and the professions rose rapidly during the nineteenth century, increasing by nearly 350 per cent between 1841 (there is no earlier data) and 1911, compared with about 154 per cent among the employed male population. Most middle-class men were businessmen or superior shopkeepers, with a minority in the professions. Most university-educated men emerged from the professional middle classes and themselves became professionals. It has always been particularly difficult to define the lower middle classes of small shopkeepers, minor officials, schoolteachers, or where on the income scale they were to be distinguished from the solid middle classes. Even more difficult is how to categorise farmers and rural owner-occupiers. Including all these categories on their widest definition probably raised the overall middle class share to around 30 per cent of the adult male population. There is also the separate question of middle-class attitudes or lifestyles. The stereotype is of liberal, anti-aristocratic radicals leading to the Age of Reform and then of increasing conservatism as the left moved to 'socialism'. This may have been true of many, although some ardent pre-1832 Tories were businessmen, and some early socialists, like the Fabian Society, were middle class. The middle classes were supposed to have craved respectability, which was also true for many, in contrast to the alleged depravity of the aristocracy and the working classes. Above all, perhaps, the middle classes desired security, and often preferred positions in the Civil Service, the Colonial Service, or as recognised professional men, with tenure or near-tenure. An accurate placement of women in the middle classes is even more difficult; as a rule – but not always – this depended upon the status and income of their male breadwinners.

The nineteenth century also saw the rise of the fee-paying public schools (i.e. elite private schools) as institutions where the upper and middle classes could, in a sense, merge, although one must be careful not to exaggerate this. Most aristocrats and the super-rich sent their sons to the poshest of the public schools, Eton and Harrow, although these also contained many sons of barristers, Anglican vicars, and middle-ranking businessmen. Most of the new or reformed public schools which were formed during the nineteenth century – Cheltenham, Marlborough, Wellington or Mill Hill, to name but a few – were basically schools for the sons of upper-middle-class parents, not the sons of the aristocracy. Oxford and Cambridge universities also provided venues where the sons of genuine blue-bloods, the sons of the nouveau riche, and the sons of very fortunate or very talented nobodies could meet and interact, to a certain extent as equals, and form lifelong networks of friendship and employment. The nineteenth century also saw the emergence of professional societies, such as the Law Society (founded 1825), the representative body for solicitors; the Institution of Civil Engineers (founded 1818); and the Royal Institute of British Architects (founded 1834). These were founded to give respectability to each profession, to discipline 'rogue' operators, to lobby Parliament, and also to establish procedures and limits to the entry to each profession of young men (only a handful of established professionals, if that, were young women). Membership in these associations conferred respectability and status, and demonstrated that professions would not tolerate dubious members. In many ways, by the interwar period in Britain, education at a public school and Oxbridge had replaced landownership or even titled status as the chief determinant of high social status. To say that someone was an 'Old Etonian' or an 'old Balliol man' (a leading college at Oxford) was enough to identify and define his social status: whether his father was a duke, a millionaire, or merely an ordinary solicitor or business proprietor became less and less relevant. To most observers, it seems that the great class barrier, often almost insurmountable, increasingly lay between the upper and middle classes on the one hand and the working class on the other. This barrier was probably greater than in the eighteenth century, with higher start-up costs for successful entrepreneurs and more obvious markers of upper-middle-class status, such as education at a public school, although accurate research on this matter is very difficult.

Most people belonged to the working classes, those employed for wages in factories or mines, or in a variety of menial occupations such as carrying and hauling, on railways, or as domestic servants. There was also a very large class of agricultural labourers, probably the most poorly paid sector of the workforce. It is common to divide the working class into three segments: the higher-skilled working class – about 14 per cent of the employed population in the 1860s; the lower-skilled working class – about 26 per cent of the population; and the unskilled working class and agricultural labourers – about 25 per cent of the population (although this percentage was much higher in Ireland). The higher-skilled working class comprised mainly artisans who required some training, senior male factory operatives, locomotive engine drivers, even the best paid among coal miners. Many of these groups were protected to a certain extent by trade union organisations; in Britain these originated among the skilled artisanal male working classes, and often had an important role as insurance providers and even as lodge-style fraternal orders. Incomes among the skilled working classes could reach £100 per year or even more among such groups as locomotive engine drivers and skilled printers, although £75 per annum was probably the average. Many in the skilled working class could aspire to a standard of living not far below the lower part of the middle class with little beside their occupations to distinguish them. The lower-skilled working class comprised most factory operatives and miners, senior shop assistants, and what has become known as the 'uniformed working class'

– soldiers and sailors, policemen, postmen, firemen and railway station personnel, among others – who were often
surprisingly poorly paid. The normal rate of pay for an ordinary London policeman was about £1 per week, for which he
was expected to risk his life virtually every day. The unskilled
working class comprised the miscellaneous 'residuum', ranging from carters to stablehands to casual dock workers,
stevedores and merchant sailors, down to the semi-criminal
demi-monde carving out a catchpenny income as best
they could.

As with the middle classes, the leitmotif of most of the
nineteenth-century British working class was its insecurity:
there was, of course, no welfare state, and no government net
in the twentieth-century sense to protect anyone (from any
class background) from unemployment, old age, sickness or
accident. The famous New Poor Law of 1834 mandated that
there would be no 'outdoor relief' provided by the government – that is, any kind of government welfare or insurance
payments to the poor or needy. Instead, virtually the only
form of state-provided welfare was to be the workhouse, of
which hundreds dotted the country. Anyone could enter a
workhouse, where he or she would receive a parsimonious
meal and a bed of sorts. It was a requirement that one remained
overnight, and the sexes were separated. By the notorious
'principle of less eligibility', conditions in workhouses had, by
law, to be worse than anything likely to be encountered outside. The aims of the workhouse were to compel the poor to
save for bad times and old age, and to keep the cost to taxpay-
ers as low as possible. Little in the way of state-provided
welfare net of any kind existed in Britain, even skeletally, until
1908, while the modern welfare state is largely a product of
the 1940s. The assumption of the relief of poverty in Victorian

Britain was that any excessive generosity to the poor would simply deter honest work, lead to drunkenness and dissolution, and remove the disincentive to family limitation.

In the main, however, unemployment was not caused by deliberate malingering, but by wider economic conditions, which differed from industry to industry and from place to place. Unemployment in factory areas of the north was highly cyclical, and largely dependent on economic patterns of boom and bust: in boom times, when all the factories in Manchester, Bolton, Bradford or Paisley had full order books, everyone worked and, indeed, labour was scarce; during a periodical recession, many, perhaps most, were unemployed. On the other hand, among the poor in London, in other port and commercial cities and in agricultural areas, there was chronic unemployment caused by the fact that the ever-swelling population was almost always greater than the jobs available. In neither case were the presuppositions of the New Poor Law, that there would be idleness without its severe deterrence, valid. Some parts of the working classes which enjoyed tenure, such as policemen and postmen, were to a certain extent protected from either cyclical unemployment or chronic underemployment, but they were very much the exception. The structure for the relief of poverty in nineteenth-century Britain, such as it was, also largely failed the sick, accident victims, and above all the elderly and most women.

One of the best-known twentieth-century historical debates about the British working classes is whether their standard of living rose or fell: the 'optimists' (as they are known) believe that it rose, at least in the long run; the 'pessimists' that it certainly did not rise during the first half of the nineteenth century, while the sheer awfulness of Britain's slum districts, especially in factory towns, or the hellishness of the life of a coal miner, simply cannot be quantified. It is likely that the 'pessimists' are correct for the situation in Britain before 1850. The main variables in this debate are the increase in population compared with the rate of economic growth and the pace at which the economic benefits of industrialisation reached the working classes. Given the unprecedentedly rapid rate of population growth in the first half of the nineteenth century, it seems reasonable to conclude that the relatively slow and steady pace of economic growth failed to provide perceptible economic benefits to many in the working class. After 1850, however, it equally seems very likely that per capita incomes and living standards rose for everyone, the product of what the historian Harold Perkin described as 'a viable class society' which emerged in mid and late Victorian Britain.

The objective facts of social class must be considered in conjunction with the subjective facts: to what class did people feel they belonged and how did this matter? A number of well-known episodes of nineteenth-century British politics were indeed fought out in class terms, for instance the movement for the Reform Bill of 1832 and for the repeal of the Corn Laws in the mid-1840s, which were widely perceived as benefiting the middle classes. Given the vast size of the nineteenth-century British working classes, and the chronic poverty which was a part of their lives, it might seem as if class bitterness, even class war, would be endemic to British society. Although the notion of the industrial working class in the sense we recognise is often dated to the years just after the Napoleonic Wars, specifically to the period around 1820 or so, it is striking that the concept of an active, oppositionist working class never really emerged in nineteenth-century Britain, at least until the 1890s and arguably not even then. That social class appears to have been so unimportant in nineteenth-century British politics is evidence, perhaps, that its significance was exaggerated by later observers and historians, especially Marxist historians who believed that class conflict 'should' have been present during Britain's industrialisation and urbanisation. But Britain (like the United States, which, it is often argued, is 'exceptional' in never having produced a class-based politics) might well have been different.

While major socialist parties and strong socialist movements took shape throughout the Continent after about 1870, these had no parallel in nineteenth-century Britain: the Labour Party was first formed only in 1900, and then clearly as a small tail to the Liberal Party. As suggested, one might adduce several reasons for this, including the multiplicity of other salient loyalties, especially religious loyalties, which united persons of different social classes; the long tradition of left-liberal reforms being led and enacted by the upper classes; the willingness of both the Conservative and Liberal parties to accommodate the trade unions and some working-class demands; the genuinely widespread traditions of working-class self help; and the 'safety valve' of large-scale emigration. While Britain thus contained the oldest and possibly the largest industrial working class in Europe, it was, paradoxically, also one of the least demonstrative and least radical. Trade unions remained relatively small until the late nineteenth century, with the Trades Union Congress (TUC), the representative body of the British trade union movement, not formed until 1868. While Karl Marx (1813–83) and Friedrich Engels (1820–95) lived most of their adult lives in Britain, ironically they had less impact there than in most other European countries. The British experience probably shows that the rise of a self-conscious, oppositionist, and politically significant trade union and working-class organisation was not inevitable in an advanced industrial society. (Similarly, the United States never developed a socialist movement of any importance.) The European pattern, of the growth of large and highly significant socialist movements such as in Germany and France, did not occur in the same form in nineteenth-century Britain.

By 1914 there is some evidence that this was changing, with the Labour Party increasingly important, especially at the local level, in England, Wales, and Scotland, and the government keen to bring the trade unions into the circle of governance through active negotiations with them to satisfy their demands. Labour militancy – which had erupted during the late nineteenth century in such acts as the great London Dock Strike of 1889 – definitely increased, especially around 1910–11 when a wave of crippling strikes hit Britain. Yet Britain remained different from Europe, and it is doubtful, had the First World War not occurred, whether the Labour Party would have emerged as the dominant left-of-centre party in British politics, or the unions have become as powerful as they did after 1914.

These class differences were not precisely the same throughout the United Kingdom. In Scotland, although deference to aristocratic clan or regional leaders still existed and probably exceeded anything in England, assertive working-class consciousness, especially in Glasgow and Clydeside, was also strong. In Wales the influence of the gentry and aristocracy was much weaker than in many parts of England, and in industrial South Wales was virtually non-existent. In Ireland the religious conflict arguably overshadowed everything, and the role and influence of the largely Anglican landed aristocracy declined markedly in the later nineteenth century in the south. In Ulster, Protestant loyalties were dominant in a largely urban, industrial society. In England itself, aristocratic and 'society' figures and influence remained strongest in London, the south, and rural England. They were far less strong in northern and industrial England, although in places like Liverpool the divide between Protestantism and Catholicism largely determined politics after mid-century. A charismatic political leader could make a major difference to loyalties throughout society from top to bottom. In Birmingham, Joseph Chamberlain carried most of the local population with him in his journey from the political left to the right, including most of the local working class.

Eventually central to working-class representation and activism were trade unions. Although trade unions ultimately became the most important form of working-class defence and activism, and the most important base upon which the twentieth-century Labour Party was built, their history in the nineteenth century was halting and anything but smooth. The Combination Acts of 1798–1800 severely restricted the organisation of trade unions. Led by Francis Place (1771–1854) and Joseph Home MP (1777–1855), these restrictions were modified by the Combination Act of 1825 ('combination' was the term used to define a group of workers who 'combined' for a purpose such as increasing wages). Attempts to organise nationally based trade unions, such as the Grand National Consolidated Trades' Union of 1834, invariably failed at this time. The successful, continuing organisation of trade unions began in the second half of the century. The so-called 'New Model Unionism' is generally dated with the foundation of the Amalgamated Society of Engineers in 1851, organised among relatively skilled workers. As noted, the TUC, eventually to become one of the most powerful bodies in Britain, was founded in 1868. Trade union organisation only spread to

relatively unskilled and semi-skilled workers in the late nineteenth century, the so-called 'New Unionism', which is
generally seen as beginning in 1889 with the organisation of
gas workers by Will Thorne (1857–1946), later a Labour MP
(he remained a Labour MP until 1945), and of London dock
workers by Ben Tillett (1860–1943), following the famous
London Dock Strike of 1889. The Edwardian era saw a considerable growth in trade union membership, from 870,000 in
1890 to 2.6 million in 1910 and to 4.1 million in 1914. Labour
militancy also grew, with radical movements such as syndical-
ism (which advocated that the economy be managed and run
by groups of trade unions) becoming significant. The years
1911–12 were particularly notable for the number of strikes,
especially among mine workers, which the Liberal government managed to pacify only with difficulty. The Labour Party
now had a significant presence in Parliament, with forty-two
MPs in the Commons at the outbreak of the First World War.
Labour was still very much the tail to the Liberal Party dog,
and whether, without the war, it would have become an
entirely separate and major party is very unclear.

Extreme examples of working-class militancy were, nonetheless, arguably rare. The Newport Rising of November
1839, in which thousands of armed Chartist sympathisers
tried to free arrested Chartist supporters in Newport,
Monmouthshire, is sometimes described as the last armed
rebellion in Britain: soldiers killed about twenty-two rioters;
their leaders were convicted of high treason and originally
sentenced to be hanged, drawn and quartered, a punishment
then commuted to transportation to Australia for life. Violent
working-class acts, such as the so-called 'Sheffield Outrages'
of October 1866, certainly diminished, at least until the period
just before the First World War. (The Sheffield Outrages were

a series of violent acts, including murders, directed by union militants in Sheffield against both employers and workers who refused to join a trade union. Sheffield, home of a major steel industry, was notorious for its terrible working conditions.) Most working-class organised activity was actually directed towards forming organisations of mutual benefit, such as the co-operative movement, which began in 1837 and became well known with the 'Rochdale Pioneers' of 1844, a group of working men who opened a shop selling goods to other workers at reduced prices. By the 1870s, the Co-operative Wholesale Society, which bought in bulk and sold goods cheaply, had become significant. Ironically, successful private retailers, such as the founders of Marks & Spencer and Woolworths, imitated this sales technique of 'piling 'em high and selling 'em cheap'. Friendly societies, in which working men (and those in the middle classes) paid in a small sum every week and received unemployment and sickness benefits and other payments when these were necessary, also flourished in the absence of a welfare state. While these developments were important, they could not assist the very poorest, or those chronically ill, widows, and other categories whom they simply could not cover. Universal entitlement to state assistance would have to await the twentieth century, especially the Labour Party's famous measures of 1945–51.

As noted, many historians representing different perspectives have dated the birth of a self-conscious working class from about 1815–20 (for instance, E. P. Thompson and Harold Perkin). In some respects, this may be accurate, and working-class spokesmen from about that time noted the attributes of a unified class perspective – for example, a 'martyrology' of victims of upper-class suppression (apart from the normal oppression of capitalism) such as the Peterloo Massacre of

August 1819, when eleven protestors were killed in Manchester, or the Tolpuddle Martyrs of 1834, six agricultural workers from Tolpuddle in Dorset who were transported to Australia for seven years for attempting to form an agricultural workers' union. Such events were certainly remembered for generations. But the extent to which there was a unified self-conscious 'working class' in nineteenth-century Britain is not at all straightforward. Rather, members of the working class were deeply divided along several lines, especially that of religion and sectarianism. It has been shown that Nonconformist workers were loyal to Nonconformist industrialists, Anglican workers to Anglican industrialists, in such matters as voting for the candidate of the relevant denomination, preferring to work at their co-religionist's factory, and the like. Many extreme Protestant workers, especially those involved in the Orange orders or other Protestant groupings, detested Irish Catholic workers; Irish Catholics were also seen as rivals for jobs and prone to crime and drink. Deep divisions also existed between highly skilled workers, whose incomes bordered on those of the lower middle classes and who had trade union representation, and the so-called residuum of the chronically unemployed, criminals, and itinerants in the worst slums such as those in London's East End. While a radical ideology clearly can be found among some working-class spokesmen during the nineteenth century, most British workers were certainly patriots and even 'conservatives' of a kind (as Disraeli argued), supporting the monarchy, the empire, and Britain's established institutions, and cheering every British military and naval victory as loudly as any Old Etonian. Even in the twentieth century, when the Labour Party replaced the Liberals as the normal left-of-centre mainstream party, its leader, Ramsay MacDonald, made a conscious decision that the party in office would keep and indeed defend all of Britain's traditional institutions, in order to reassure voters that Labour did not consist of Bolsheviks and could be just as trusted by moderate voters as the older parties. Extreme, revolutionary or semi-revolutionary views were perhaps more likely to be associated with middle-class radicals than with British workers.

Chapter Four

Modes of Identity: Religion

Religion was arguably the most important mode of individual self-identity in nineteenth-century Britain; quite possibly its importance grew compared with the previous century, although this can be disguised by the intellectual assault on the centrality of religion associated with Charles Darwin and by the consistent steps towards religious equality which took place during the nineteenth century. Certainly we look at Victorian Britain as a religious society, with evangelical Christianity at the heart of our image of it.

The continuing centrality of religion was supported by a host of intellectual, social and legal forces. Virtually everyone in nineteenth-century Britain believed in the truths of organised religion: death often came suddenly, regularly to infants and children. A family with eight children could routinely expect to lose two or three in infancy or childhood. Religion, with its central promise of eternal life, was an ever-present source of solace. In many ways, the decline of organised religion in Britain followed upon the limitation, except in rare tragedies, of death to the elderly. At least as importantly, from the Reformation through the nineteenth century religion in Britain was an aspect of national identity: the Church of England was the national church of the English people, the religious component of being English in the same way as were English citizenship and speaking the English language. So, too, the Church of Scotland was the national church of the Scottish people. In a real sense, those who failed to conform to the national churches of the English and Scottish peoples, Protestant and reformed, were seen as disloyal to their national identities, in particular Roman Catholics, whose religion went hand in hand with allegiance, explicit or implicit, to the papacy and to Britain's traditional enemies France and Spain. Arguably, it was primarily for this reason that religion, now seen as chiefly if not wholly a private matter, was so bitterly contested during the three or four centuries after the Reformation.

The religious history of nineteenth-century Britain, however, consists to a significant extent of the disassociation of specific religious affiliations from any concept of national loyalty or identity, Ireland being the obvious exception. This occurred both because non-established religions were given full citizenship rights, and because the notion of citizenship became increasingly redefined such that religion became irrelevant to the concept of loyal citizenship, a change strongly implied by the growth of a mass democratic polity in which all adults participated. In particular, nineteenth-century England saw the gradual incorporation of the large Protestant Nonconformist sects within the 'Pale of the Constitution', while the Church of Ireland, the minority Anglican Church in Ireland, was disestablished in 1869. Nevertheless, there were limits to the changes which occurred: the Church of England

and the Church of Scotland were still established churches in 1914, just as they had been in 1800. In many respects, indeed, the Anglican Church was stronger in 1900 than a century earlier. Only in the case of Ireland did this process of the removal of religion from the concept of national loyalty and identity fail to diminish religious dispute: there, the religious basis of communal loyalty became central and paramount, ironically as the religious disabilities of the Roman Catholic majority were gradually removed, leading to a situation of virtual religious civil war by 1914.

Organised religion, especially the Church of England, continued to enjoy a near-monopoly in the conducting of the rites of passage (baptisms, marriages, funerals). In 1844, for instance, 91 per cent of marriages in England and Wales took place in an Anglican church, while only 7 per cent took place in non-Anglican places of worship. Even in 1911, 61 per cent of marriages were conducted in an Anglican church, compared with 18 per cent in some other place of worship, and 21 per cent in civil ceremonies. The Anglican clergy probably constituted the largest single profession in England, outnumbering lawyers and doctors. In 1871 there were 21,000 Anglican clergymen; in 1911, over 25,000. In 1910, there were over 45,000 clergymen of all denominations in the United Kingdom. Until the 1870s, more than half of all graduates of Oxford and Cambridge universities became Anglican clergymen. The two Anglican archbishops and twenty-four bishops sat in the House of Lords, and the senior hierarchy of the Anglican Church still exerted enormous influence at the local level, normally being regarded as among the most influential and prestigious of local notables, whose views on a wide variety of subjects were sought and respected. The surprising growth of numbers among the Anglican clergy was paralleled among the main Nonconformist denominations, with, for instance, the number of Wesleyan Methodist ministers rising from 736 in 1831 to 1,675 in 1901. There were 4,270 Methodist ministers of all strands of Methodism in 1910, as well as 3,195 Baptist ministers, and 4,908 Catholic priests in Great Britain (excluding Ireland). In Ireland in 1911, there were 3,924 Roman Catholic priests, along with 1,575 Anglican clergymen, 667 Presbyterians, and 244 Methodists. As Catholics comprised 74 per cent of the Irish population, it will be seen that Protestant clergymen were far more numerous in proportion to the size of the Protestant minority (26 per cent) of the population, contradicting the frequently heard Protestant claims of a 'priest-ridden' mass of Catholic peasants. Religious worship offered one of the few public spaces in which women were not merely allowed to participate but encouraged to do so. Women almost certainly constituted the majority of worshippers at most church services, and were increasingly the backbone of the ancillary structure of volunteers and minor employees on whom all churches relied, as Sunday school teachers, voluntary assistants, local committee members, home visitors and the like. Many women took readily to these ancillary roles, despite the total monopoly which males continued to enjoy in the power structure of all churches except for a few, such as the Salvation Army (founded in 1878), on the fringes of Nonconformist religious life.

Intellectual life in nineteenth-century Britain continued to revolve around religious questions. Probably most books and pamphlets published in Victorian Britain were religious in nature, and were printed in vast numbers. In the 1860s, for instance, the Religious Tract Society printed 33 million books and pamphlets each year. A major religious controversy, such as the quasi-Catholic challenge presented by the Oxford

Movement to the Church of England, had the power to divide the entire literate nation. The most important intellectual debate of the nineteenth century, that sparked by the publication of Charles Darwin's *Origin of Species* in 1859, became central to Victorian intellectual life *because* it was seen primarily as an attack on orthodox Christian religion. In part because of Darwin and the apparent conflict between science and religion, the 'Victorian crisis of faith', as it has been termed, became a familiar aspect of the youth of many from the well-educated middle classes of late Victorian Britain: those raised on strict literalistic belief in the Bible read Darwin and the works of freethinkers and agnostics, and experienced internal crises of doubt which persisted throughout their lives.

At the beginning of the nineteenth century, and for several decades thereafter, the Church of England continued to hold a monopoly position as the church of the English political nation. Theoretically, only Anglicans – those prepared to testify their assent to the Thirty-Nine Articles of the Anglican creed – could hold any political office in England and Wales. The Test and Corporation Acts, which enforced this monopoly, had long ago become a dead letter in the case of most Protestant Dissenters, especially at the local government level, but the overwhelming majority of the Members of Parliament were Anglicans. The Anglican Church oversaw the coronation of the monarch, the coronation being in large measure a religious ceremonial attesting to the monarch's role as head of the Anglican Church. The Anglican Church also had a role in areas seemingly far removed from religious worship. For instance, until 1858 it enjoyed a legal monopoly on the probating of wills in England and Wales, through a system of Anglican Ecclesiastical Courts. England's only two universities at the beginning of the nineteenth century, Oxford and

Cambridge, were Anglican institutions. Until 1872, only Anglicans could matriculate at Oxford or graduate from Cambridge.

In the course of the nineteenth century, a major component of the privileged position of the Anglican Church was modified or removed entirely. Protestant Dissenters (in 1828), Roman Catholics (in 1829), Jews (in 1858) and avowed agnostics (in 1885) were allowed to take their seats in the House of Commons. After the sweeping local government reforms of 1835, probably a majority of elected local councillors and mayors in England's large cities were Protestant Dissenters. Although some forms of legal discrimination remained in place against Roman Catholics, by the late nineteenth century only a handful of public offices existed which were not open to men of any religion.

Despite its initially privileged position, all was not well within the Anglican Church. Although their range and scope may be exaggerated, well-known abuses such as pluralism (one cleric holding two or more parochial appointments) and a vast differential between the princely incomes of most bishops and the near-poverty of many ordinary clergymen certainly existed. Areas of rapid population growth, such as the northern industrial towns, lacked churches or vicars, with the cumbersome structure of the Church of England, and its need to receive parliamentary approval for any changes in its framework, making reform difficult. The arguably unfortunate condition of the Anglican Church in the eighteenth and early nineteenth centuries resulted in the rapid growth of Protestant Dissent in regions where Anglicanism was weak – remote rural areas such as Cornwall and East Anglia, the new urban centres of the north, London and Wales – which brought a more immediate, vivid and personal form of worship. In March 1851, at the time of the famous Religious Census, it was found that 10.4 million persons attended a religious service in England and Wales, of a total population of 17.9 million. Of these, while 4.9 million attended an Anglican service, 5.1 million attended a Dissenting service (and 365,000 a Roman Catholic service).

The Church of England was also racked by bitter internal disputes which were nationally known. During the eighteenth century, the evangelical movement, aimed at religious regeneration through sincere repentance and conversion, earnestness and austerity, became extremely influential. Its best-known leader, John Wesley (1703–91), was originally an Anglican clergyman, but found the structure and hierarchy of the Church of England too rigid and, from about the 1770s, organised his followers outside of Anglicanism (these followers later fragmented into many separate Wesleyan sects). Wesley always denied that he was forming a separate church, but sometime between about 1790 and 1810 Wesleyanism generally became recognised as a separate denomination apart from the Church of England. Many evangelicals remained within the church, prominent in such groups as the Clapham Sect, formed around 1790 under the leadership of Rev. John Venn. Influential in such reforms as the campaign for the abolition of slavery, evangelicals like Hannah More (1745–1833) were tireless writers of religious tracts. Evangelicalism is, in particular, often seen as one of the most important forces behind the abolition of slavery. Evangelicals and Quakers were among the progenitors of the Slave Trade Abolition Act of 1806, and were central to the abolition of slavery throughout the British Empire in 1833. Parliament abolished slavery with compensation to the slaveowners (almost all in the West Indies), a great humanitarian act to which religion was central.

In the United States, slavery remained institutionalised in the Southern states until it was ended by a civil war in which 600,000 soldiers died.

From the 1830s, another influential movement arose from the opposite end of Anglican theology, the Oxford Movement (also known as Tractarians or Puseyites, after one of its leaders, Edward Bouverie Pusey, 1800–82). The Oxford Movement claimed that, despite the Reformation, the Church of England remained a 'Catholic' church whose authority derived from its unbroken linkages with Jesus, the Apostles, and the original bishops of the Christian church. The main intellectual leader of the Oxford Movement, John Henry Newman (1801–91), is regarded as one of the greatest theologians of modern times. The Oxford Movement seemed to many to want to pull the Anglican church away from Protestantism and towards Roman Catholicism, an outcome feared by its critics. Newman's conversion to Catholicism in 1845 deeply shocked many, and was an event of national importance. Broadly speaking, the evangelical and Oxford movements were associated with what became known as 'Low Church' and 'High Church' Anglicanism (although 'High Church' Anglicanism predated it and in some respects was separate from it) which persisted throughout the century and, indeed, up to the present.

Despite the internal challenges it faced, in 1914 the Anglican Church appeared in a (perhaps surprisingly) satisfactory state. Although non-Anglican churches had been granted equal status, Anglicanism unquestionably remained the religion of the great majority among the English upper- and middle-class 'Establishment', and had found a new role as a major religious force throughout the white empire and through its successful missionary activity in the Third World, especially black Africa and Oceania. By the beginning of the twentieth century, the

4. Archibald Campbell Tait (1811–82) was Archbishop of Canterbury (the head of the Church of England) from 1868 until his death. The Church of England was still one of the most important institutions in Britain, and its head was a central figure in English public affairs. Yet the Church was racked by internal controversy, by a growing 'Crisis of Faith' over the theory of evolution and other matters, and by the popularity of non-Anglican religions like Methodism.

Anglican Church had recovered some of the ground it had lost to Nonconformity. It had reformed the worst abuses known a century before, and appeared to have discovered a new vigour and even a new popularity.

The nineteenth century in England in many ways belonged to the Nonconformist churches. It is common to divide Protestant Nonconformity into 'Old Dissent' – sects such as Congregationalism, the Baptist faith and Quakerism, founded in the seventeenth century – and 'New Dissent', chiefly Methodism, and a variety of newer, often strange churches founded in the nineteenth century such as Mormonism. Both 'Old' and 'New' Dissent grew during the nineteenth century, although it is very difficult to give anything more than a general estimate of numbers. The Religious Census of 1851 found that, in England and Wales, 1.2 million people had attended Independent or Congregationalist services on a particular Sunday, 930,000 Baptist services, and no fewer than 2,484,000 one or other Methodist service, with smaller but not insignificant numbers attending services led by the Unitarians (50,000), Quakers (23,000), Plymouth Brethren (18,000) and Moravians (11,000). These figures may well be exaggerated – they count morning, afternoon and evening services separately, and devout individuals might well have attended more than one service – and group together denominations with a range of distinctive, often rival subsects (for instance, nine varieties of Methodism were detailed in the census). Nevertheless, they give something of the sense of how large and important Nonconformity had become. Nonconformity, especially Methodism, arguably became the dominant religion in Britain's industrial areas. It usually – although not always – went hand in hand with political Liberalism, and with the package of ideals – free trade, opposition to aristocratic 'privileges', 'self-help', temperance – which were bound up with mid-Victorian Liberalism, just as Anglicanism was seen as connected with Toryism.

By the late nineteenth century, many viewed Nonconformity as past its peak, or at least as not likely to make further gains. Sunday school enrolments, a potent indicator of the health of a religion, after a long period of steady growth appear to have peaked around 1900, before beginning a notable and then a catastrophic decline after the First World War. About 55 per cent of school-age children attended Sunday school (of any denomination) in 1900. This percentage never rose in the period to 1914, although it is also true that it did not markedly decline until the early 1930s. (In 2000, about 4 per cent of school-age children attended a Sunday school of some Christian denomination.) Evangelical Nonconformity, what many commonly see as the essence of 'Victorianism', probably reached a peak in the 1840s before being overtaken by increasing signs of protosecularism. By granting legal religious equality to Nonconformity, Parliament removed much of the sense of grievance which lay behind Dissent, the shared sense of historical persecution which helped to bind Dissenters together. By 1900, there was little to 'dissent' from, although Nonconformist grievances could still explode in nationally significant ways, as they did at the time of the 1906 general election over education and other matters.

As Dissenters climbed the economic ladder and sent their sons to public schools and universities, many inevitably became Anglicans and moved to the right politically and socially. Probably the most well-known Nonconformist in politics in the later nineteenth century, Joseph Chamberlain (1836–1914), illustrates this common progress. A Unitarian and originally a fiery radical leader of the Liberal Party's left wing, Chamberlain broke with the Liberals and, within a decade, had become the best-known Tory imperialist, the main architect of the Boer War. Chamberlain's two sons, Sir Austen (1863–1937) and Neville (1869–1940), were both educated at Rugby; both were Anglicans and both became leaders of the Conservative Party. To be sure, the pre-1914 decline of Nonconformity should not be exaggerated. The greatest victory of the Liberal Party in 1906 owed much to Nonconformist discontent, especially over the Education Act of 1902, and the 1906–10 parliament was said to have been the first since Cromwell's time with a Nonconformist majority. But this proved to be Dissent's last political triumph.

Roman Catholicism in England also grew during the nineteenth century. English Catholicism was composed of pre-Reformation recusant families, numerous in Lancashire and Sussex and often well connected, to which were added significant numbers of converts and very large numbers of Irish and some European Catholic migrants. The Roman Catholic church re-established an official hierarchy in England in 1850, amidst great controversy. Considerable anti-Catholicism still remained in England, even in 1914, at both the elite and mass levels, fanned in places like Liverpool by the Orange Order and extreme Protestant activists and societies. In contrast, the small Jewish community in England, which grew from about 25,000 in 1800 to 200,000 a century later, is noteworthy for attracting little or no hostility. In contrast to much of the Continent, Jews did not 'control' the economy and were not strongly associated with radical or modernist movements; on the contrary, they were often admired by Protestant philo-Semites. As a result, Britain escaped the anti-Semitism of tsarist Russia or Dreyfusard France, with hostility to Jews emerging only in the wake of large-scale immigration to London's East End after 1881, and then only fitfully. It is often said that the career of the century's best-known Jewish politician, Benjamin Disraeli (1804–81), who became leader of the *right*-wing party, would have been impossible anywhere else. The religious histories of Scotland, Wales and Ireland are intimately bound up with their national identities and will be examined in those sections of the next chapter devoted to each country.

Chapter Five
Modes of Identity:
Nationality

The nineteenth century was a time of intense national loyalties in Britain, although it is important to see these in an international context. Unlike many other varieties of nationalism, British patriotism, or patriotism for the component parts of the United Kingdom, made few or no overt demands on its citizens. Indeed, it might be queried whether Britain possessed a significant ideology of nationalism, as distinguished from an older sense of patriotism. Britain never had to achieve independence. It felt no sense of national 'relative deprivation' – to use a well-known sociological term – and, throughout the period 1800–1914, was always a successful and satiated nation which never felt a need for national revenge or aggrandisement. Britain's minority nations, Scotland, Wales and Ireland, might well have failed to share in this sense of national satisfaction, and the mood in each must be considered in turn. In general, the success enjoyed by the United Kingdom was enough to dampen strong nationalistic movements aimed at achieving national independence in the minority nations, with the exception of Catholic Ireland. There were other ways, too, in which Britain was anomalous. Virtually alone among European states, Britain had no conscription and relied entirely upon a voluntary military and naval force. Until the First World War, passports were not legally required to leave Britain, and, as noted, Britain had no effective immigration barriers of any kind until 1905. Britain had no annual national holiday like the Fourth of July in the United States, with its tradition of tub-thumping patriotic speeches, the nearest equivalent, perhaps, being Guy Fawkes Day, which (as early as 1661) was transformed from a rather sinister anti-Catholic commemoration to a noisy celebration for youths.

British patriotism was notable for almost never being officially compelled. Nevertheless, it was real and deep, and could occasionally erupt unexpectedly. Lord Nelson's state funeral in London early in 1806 possibly saw the highest percentage of the city's population as spectators to a state occasion of any event in history. Coronations, royal weddings, and the two jubilees of Queen Victoria, in 1887 and 1897, also saw vast outpourings of apparently genuine public enthusiasm and support, while Mafeking Night, following the relief of the Boer-besieged British outpost in Bechuanaland in May 1900, became notorious for the totally unexpected saturnalia which accompanied London's spontaneous public celebrations. There were radical gatherings which were attended by tens of thousands, for instance the great Chartist meetings at Kennington Common in April 1848, but these were dwarfed in number and possibly enthusiasm by ceremonies of patriotic feeling. In 1914, whatever was the case in Ireland, Great Britain enthusiastically went to war as a united nation, political differences being put aside.

What, precisely, British patriotism celebrated was also never really made clear. If there was a central British narrative commonly depicted and probably consensually agreed upon, it was, overwhelmingly, an English narrative consisting of the familiar triumphalist verities of English history, essentially a Whig account of perpetual improvement, which was evidence of the favour of divine providence. In recent decades, historians have often depicted British history in terms of the coexistence, peaceful or otherwise, of the four 'nations' which comprised the United Kingdom (England, Scotland, Wales, Ireland), but it should not be forgotten that, in popular terms, the United Kingdom was predominantly English. It is therefore not surprising that the ruling historical narrative was primarily English. Paradoxically, however, it is difficult to identify a specifically English nationalism during the nineteenth century, in contrast to the situation in Scotland, Wales and, most emphatically, Ireland. England was widely seen as being hallmarked by a number of readily identifiable alleged national qualities – justice tempered by mercy, fair play, gentleness, the 'stiff upper lip', eccentricity and marked individuality – which distinguished the English from foreigners, and which was underpinned by the English historical description of continuous improvement and success. It is probably fair to say that most of these alleged English qualities became widely accepted as actual hallmarks of the English only in the nineteenth century, and generally in its second half. For instance, few in the late eighteenth century would have conceived the English as particularly gentle, or, perhaps, as especially 'eccentric'. Like all national stereotypes, they are, of course, half-truths – which means (as is sometimes now forgotten) that they are half true as well as half false.

There were alternative historical narratives of 'Englishness', but these perhaps did not dissent from the mainstream narrative as much as one might suppose. The best-known radical account emphasised the 'freeborn Englishman' who had been corrupted by (it was often said) the 'Norman yoke' (in other words, the traditional landed aristocracy) and grasping London politicians. As enunciated by such populist publicists as William Cobbett (1762–1835), it also attacked 'Old Corruption' (venal office-holders among the aristocracy), London and finance capital, and looked to champions of Protestant liberty such as John Milton and John Bunyan as heroes. This radical populist tradition was certainly still alive among radical Liberals of the Boer War period. How radical the 'freeborn Englishman' story actually was might be disputed: its populism could have a very nasty edge and was often anything but benign. It is doubtful, too, whether a more radical historical narrative about 'Englishness' existed. There were other widely held historical myths about English history, but these were often rather odd and are now virtually forgotten. For instance, there was belief in some quarters in the movement which became known as the British Israelites, who argued that the British were – literally – one of the Lost Tribes of Israel, who had migrated in ancient times from Palestine to the British Isles. Made popular in such works as Rev. John Wilson's *Our Israelitish Origins* (1840), this notion struck a chord in extreme Protestant circles, by setting out and emphasising a view of British 'Chosenness' similar to that found in Judaism (and similar, too, to other notions of Chosenness so popular in the United States, for instance, the religious doctrines of the Mormon Church, which claims that Jesus lived and preached in America in ancient times). The great vogue for Freemasonry and other secret fraternal orders in late Victorian Britain plainly drew on similar sensibilities and roots.

Nevertheless, alternative visions of 'Englishness' never challenged the common one. Indeed, the notion of an English national 'grand narrative' was seldom explicitly articulated in detail, because it was never seriously challenged. Those who might have been engaged in constructing an alternative vision of English history normally found other modes of presenting a challenge to the deficiencies of the Establishment. After 1835 (when local government was reformed) urban civic govern-ance, for instance, often came into the hands of Nonconformist business and civic leaders whose challenge to the Establishment took the form of developing cities which were to be models of progressive improvement and reform, and which were also to challenge laissez-faire by the active use of state powers and money for social improvement. The best-known example of this was probably in Birmingham where, from the 1860s, Joseph Chamberlain and his allies attempted to create a model city. The foundation of new civic universities in Manchester (1851), Newcastle (1852), Birmingham (1900), Liverpool (1903) and elsewhere were important hallmarks of this movement.

There are many ways in which Scotland, Wales and even Ireland became less *sui generis* and more fully integrated into a United Kingdom in the period 1832–1914. The Welsh, Scottish Gaelic and Irish Gaelic languages steadily declined in terms of the number of their speakers, and monolinguistic speakers of these languages were increasingly confined to remoter rural areas. The process occurred even in Wales, where the old Celtic vernacular survived the longest. In 1800, virtually every-one in Wales spoke Welsh as his or her vernacular. By 1900, two thirds of the population were bilingual in Welsh and English while, especially in the industrial south, the majority of the population was almost purely English-speaking. For instance, Aneurin Bevan (1897–1960), probably the greatest

Welsh Labour politician of the twentieth century, could not speak any Welsh, although he grew up in a coal mining town in the Rhondda. The tiny number of speakers of Cornish, Manx and Norn (a Norse dialect spoken in parts of the Shetlands and Orkneys) declined to zero, or nearly to zero, by the early twentieth century. In 1900, probably all significant political and even cultural discussion and debate took place in English, and attempts by nationalists and romantics to revive the pre-English vernacular almost always came to little or nothing. Even in southern Ireland, where a Gaelic League was founded in 1893 to revivify Ireland's ancient language, and where Gaelic was made an official national language when the Irish Free State achieved independence in 1922, today only 2 per cent of the Irish population speaks Gaelic on a regular basis. All of the others, including the entire Irish political leadership, spoke and speaks English, the language of their alleged oppressors and conquerors, and all attempts to reverse the dominance of English have failed. With minor exceptions, all significant writing and literature in the British Isles during the period 1832–1914 was in English, even among Irish writers with a nationalistic edge such as Yeats, Synge or Joyce. There were minor exceptions, especially among some Welsh authors, but in effect British literary culture was monolinguistically English. Moreover, spoken English came increasingly to recognise the upper- and upper-middle-class speech forms of respectable London, Oxford and Cambridge – the so-called 'Queen's (or King's) English' – as the norm of correct speech, and all other accents and dialects as below standard, mimicked on stage and in cartoons as humorous or ignorant. These depictions applied to regional accents in Scotland, Wales, Ireland and northern and rural England, and as well to working-class accents, above all, perhaps, to the 'cockney' accent of London's East End. The explicit or unconscious acceptance of the Queen's English as the norm from which all other accents departed was arguably an important force in creating and maintaining a status hierarchy centred in middle-class London. Acquisition of proper speech, too, became an important marker of social respectability.

The English language became the near-universal vernacular of the British Isles (except in central and northern Wales and parts of the Scottish Highlands) in part because of profound technological changes, and changes in transport and communications, which did not and could not occur before the nineteenth century. Although it is a schoolboy's cliché that Britain after c.1825 was in the 'railway age', one must remember that all of British history before the nineteenth century took place in times of premodern, and invariably slower, transport and communications, and that this had fundamental consequences for the unity of Britain. By 1880 or so at the latest, probably any town, even the remotest in Great Britain, could be reached from London in less than a day, and any town in Ireland, even the remotest, in two days, whereas a trip from London to the Scottish Highlands even in Dr Samuel Johnson's age took weeks. By the 1880s, a trip by rail from London to Edinburgh on a fast steam train took about eight or nine hours, a time which would have seemed unimaginably rapid in the eighteenth century, and was vastly more comfortable than on stagecoach or other means of pre-railway travel. Communications, thanks to the telegraph, were even more rapid. News in London reached any major provincial city almost instantaneously, and was reported in local newspapers on the same day. This astonishing increase in the speed and ease of transport worked both ways: tens of thousands of those living in provincial Britain, even among the working classes, travelled to London, with the famous Great Exhibition of 1851, the first World's Fair, having lured several million to London on the new railway network, often for the first time.

There were other major institutional changes and circumstances which also worked to unify the British Isles. The nineteenth century was the first century in 1,000 years in which no attempt was made to change the ruling dynasty by force of arms. Even in the eighteenth century, and despite its largely peaceful constitutional changes, two serious attempts were made, in 1715 and 1745, to restore the Stuart dynasty by armed invasion. The death of the last Jacobite pretender, Henry Benedict Stuart, Cardinal York, in 1807 (known to his Jacobite supporters as King Henry IX, and generally called 'Cardinal York' because he was the Duke of York in the Jacobite peerage), closed the dynastic question. At his death, Cardinal York left the Jacobite crown jewels to King George III. By the Napoleonic Wars, if not before, the very notion of an armed invasion to place a different king on the English throne was surely absurd to the great majority of people. In so far as the question of the British head of state was ever raised again, it occurred in the context of proposals by some extreme Liberals or socialists to replace the monarchy with a republic. As noted, these surfaced, in particular, in the decade or so after the death of Prince Albert in 1861, when Queen Victoria withdrew almost entirely from public life. But any republican sentiment then completely disappeared in the last three decades of the queen's life, when she re-emerged as a genuinely popular figure linking all parts of Britain and the empire. Her jubilee celebrations in 1887 and 1897 were occasions for sincere national rejoicing. As discussed, with the exception of France after 1870–71 and the United States, all of the world's major nations at this time were monarchies, and would continue to be until the European cataclysms at the end of the First World War. In the twentieth century, republican sentiment might have re-emerged during the First World War had Britain lost, and King George V was forced to change his surname from the German Saxe-Coburg-Gotha to Windsor. But popular anti-monarchical sentiment in the United Kingdom did not become a significant force in twentieth century Britain, even with the rise of the Labour Party. Queen Victoria and her successors maintained a Scottish residence at Balmoral from 1848, and made infrequent but highly popular trips to most important provincial towns in Britain – but even less frequently to Ireland, visiting it only four times during her reign of sixty-three years, in itself a likely cause of Irish dissatisfaction with the British government. The new king, George V, visited remote India in 1911, the year after he had come to the throne.

Most of the aristocrats and members of the landed gentry in the four countries certainly moved closer to a unified traditional upper class in the period 1832–1914 than earlier, although the process was already well under way before then. This occurred in a variety of ways and for several reasons. Most wealthy, senior aristocrats from (in particular) Scotland, Wales and (probably to a lesser extent) Ireland were educated increasingly at a leading English public school and at Oxbridge, just as were their English counterparts. For instance, Archibald Primrose, the 5th Earl of Rosebery (1847–1929), Liberal prime minister in 1894–95 who was known as the 'King of Midlothian' because of his extensive and valuable landed holdings near Edinburgh, was educated at Eton and Oxford, married a Rothschild heiress, and spent most of his adult life in London and the Home Counties. Similarly, his contemporary Henry Petty-Fitzmaurice, 5th Marquess of Lansdowne (1845–1927), foreign minister and one of the largest landowners in Ireland (who declined the title of Duke of Kerry), was also educated at Eton and Oxford, where he was heavily influenced by Benjamin Jowett, the famous master of Balliol College. Aristocrats, wealthy gentry and the rich and titled came together every year in London for the 'season', several months each autumn in which levees, soirées and 'coming out' dances for debutantes were held in the great London town houses, sometimes presided over by royalty. While the aristocracy had of course been centred in London for many centuries, the ease of travel and universal acceptance of the norms of high society made such gatherings more popular and central, down to the First World War, than before. Intermarriage between aristocrats and near-aristocrats of all four countries (and with the overseas wealthy, especially the so-called 'dollar princesses', mega-rich American heiresses) almost certainly became more common. For instance, in 1908 Winston Churchill, then a rising Liberal MP and the grandson of the Duke of Marlborough, married Clementine Ogilvie Hozier, the daughter of Sir Henry Hozier, a wealthy groundrent landlord in Glasgow. Traditional Welsh and Irish aristocrats and gentry were also increasingly drawn into this pattern, as were some Irish landowners. But, as in most things, Ireland was an exception because much of its landed elite were Roman Catholics, at the time a virtually insuperable bar to intermarriage with Protestants, although they often married into the English 'Catholic Cousinhood' of aristocratic recusant families or recent converts.

In some respects, this merging of the elites also occurred among the business and professional middle classes, although in different ways and less categorically. The growth of public schools, many of which were founded or re-established during the nineteenth century, and which became the most popular secondary education among the upper middle classes, greatly facilitated this. With a common and virtually ubiquitous programme of education among all of the many dozen public schools in existence by 1914, based in the Greek and Latin classics, games and 'muscular Christianity', they instilled a common outlook among most of their pupils, whatever their geographical origins. So too did Oxford and Cambridge universities, although these educated a smaller portion of the middle classes after the foundation of London University and the provincial 'redbricks' which grew up after mid-century. But perhaps the greatest source for unity among the upper and upper middle classes was their increasing fear of socialism and radical Liberalism, with their agenda of paying for social reform by taxing the well-off. In particular after the Liberal Unionist split of 1886, when many moderate Liberals left the party led by Gladstone, most (but not all) of the wealthy belonged, increasingly as a matter of course, to the Conservative Party (known at the time as the Unionists). Increasingly, the Tories united wealthy businessmen fearing trade union power, higher taxes or outright socialism, landowners fearing land nationalisation in the wake of confiscatory reforms to landholding in Ireland and proposals for a 'single tax' on land throughout Britain, and Irish Protestants fearing a Catholic-dominated Home Rule Parliament in Ireland, all of whom came together into a unified upper-class movement of resistance. Not all joined in this – Nonconformist businessmen and many middle-class intellectuals often remained loyal to Liberalism – but the marked trend to a class-based British politics after about 1880 was a common feature in most parts of the United Kingdom. The rise of the (in theory) explicitly class-based Labour Party in the twentieth century, and the regrouping of anti-socialist forces in the Conservative Party, in itself probably acted as a major deterrent to a nationality-based British politics, especially after the Irish question was seemingly settled in 1922, the same year that the Labour Party first became the official opposition.

On the other side, however, there were also important reasons why the 'four nations' comprising the British Isles should have moved further apart, and nationality politics became more important, in the period 1832–1914. The Romantic movement, with its emphasis on folk and national traditions and national historical narratives, was arguably of central cultural importance throughout virtually the whole of this period, as exemplified, for instance, by the popularity and renowned historical novels of Sir Walter Scott about medieval and early modern Scotland. The Romantic movement might well have given rise to a politics of national assertion, such as explicitly developed in Catholic Ireland. During this period, too, the direction of British national life was firmly rooted in the central government in Westminster and in the Civil Service in Whitehall. Ireland was largely governed from Dublin Castle, but with the chief secretary for Ireland, always a member of the Cabinet, and the Lord Lieutenant of Ireland, also an appointed member of the government and almost always a British aristocrat, constituting in effect the governors of Ireland. Scotland was even more centrally governed from London: the first secretary for Scotland was appointed only in August 1885. Previous to that date, Scotland had no specific representative in the British government of the day, although the Lord Advocate (a Scottish legal official) acted through the Home Office as the 'manager' of Scottish affairs in Parliament. Wales had no specific government minister responsible for its affairs until the first Minister for Welsh Affairs was appointed in 1951, and no separate Cabinet minister until 1964. Prior to the First World War, the only specifically Welsh administrative office of any kind was a Welsh Department of the Board of Education, established in 1907. It would be easy to understand if Scotland and Wales, as well as Catholic Ireland, had each developed a powerful feeling of what sociologists term 'relative deprivation', the sense that they are treated invidiously and gratuitously worse than others.

Yet, except in the case of Catholic Ireland, this did not occur in our period, at least not with the urgency and significance with which Scottish and Welsh nationalisms emerged in the latter part of the twentieth century. Explaining why a historical event or phenomenon has not occurred is always more difficult than explaining why it has (which is itself hard enough!) but one might point to a number of important reasons why no such powerful nationalisms arose. Within Scotland, Wales and Ireland there were serious internal divisions which prevented any unity on such goals as increased internal self-rule. A movement for Welsh Home Rule briefly appeared in the 1880s, for instance, paralleling the major movement for Home Rule in Ireland. While this movement had some following in Welsh-speaking Wales, it had none in English-speaking South Wales, where many inhabitants were actually recent immigrants from elsewhere in Britain (or abroad), and which was economically dependent upon its links with England. Welsh self-assertion at this time concentrated instead on achieving the disestablishment of the Anglican Church in Wales, a goal which was finally realised in 1920. Scotland was similarly divided into a more 'Gaelic' Highlands and an English-speaking Lowlands, with Edinburgh, its capital, being more conservative and more closely linked with other parts of Britain than Glasgow, its largest city. There were as well other reasons why Scotland baulked at anything like Home Rule, above all that it was doing well out of its existing arrangement. Only in Ireland, with its Catholic peasant masses, did a genuinely popular and ultimately successful Home Rule movement arise at this time, one which was bitterly opposed by the Protestants of Ulster and elsewhere.

Similarly, the later nineteenth century and the earlier twentieth century was the zenith of the empire and of imperial loyalty. It also seemed to most observers that the twentieth century would certainly be the century of world-empires rather than of small nations, which would inevitably be absorbed into larger units or face decline. For a small component of the United Kingdom actively to seek to go its own way – which many feared would be the ultimate aim of 'Home Rule' – appeared totally contrary to the spirit of the times, and seemed so to many Scotsmen, Welshmen and even Irishmen. So long as the British Empire remained an existing world super-power, pressures for independence or semi-independence from any part of the United Kingdom were almost certain to be muted. The exception, as always, was Catholic Ireland. But even here it should be remembered that the stated aim of the Home Rule Party in Ireland was not full independence from the United Kingdom but a local Parliament in Dublin with powers over purely local matters. Under all of the three Home Rule bills considered by Parliament (in 1886, 1893 and 1913), such powers as foreign policy, war and income taxation were entirely reserved to the Westminster Parliament, and Ireland was to remain a part of the United Kingdom. Only after the Dublin Easter Uprising of 1916 and the rise of Sinn Fein was actual independence for Ireland a mainstream goal, an aim abetted by the Wilsonian settlement of Europe in 1918–19 which favoured independence for small national groups.

As well, in the period 1832–1914 England itself and the United Kingdom seemed to many to represent progressive values, in contrast to the 'backwardness' associated with, in particular, Britain's Celtic areas. Welsh-speakers were often despised by other Welshmen as quaint peasants who spoke a barbaric language, with the English language seen as a ticket to modernity and the United Kingdom itself in the forefront of progress. Similar views were held by many Scotsmen (and others) about Highlanders and, above all, by virtually everyone else about the majority of the Irish Catholic peasantry, viewed as a priest-governed mass of sometimes humorous but generally feckless, illiterate, alcoholic semi-barbarians, who stood in stark contrast to the industrious Protestants of the north.

Finally, an important reason for the failure of strong nationalist movements to emerge is that each needed allies in other parts of the United Kingdom, and these did not appear, again with the exception of the Irish, both north and south. Instead, disproportionate numbers of Scotsmen and Welshmen became members or allies of the Liberal Party, joining with the larger group of English Liberals to elect Gladstone, Campbell-Bannerman and Asquith as prime ministers. Many of these English Liberals were themselves Protestant Nonconformists, and thus political and social 'outsiders' to the Anglican-centred Establishment. Most of the time after 1832, and certainly after the 1867 Reform Act, it was normal for many more Liberals than Tories to be elected in Wales and Scotland. In 1868, for instance, twenty-two Liberals and eight Tories were elected in Wales, fifty-two Liberals and eight Tories in Scotland, compared with 243 Liberals and 220 Tories in England. At the last general election before the First World War, in December 1910, Wales elected twenty-six Liberals, five Labourites (closely allied with the Liberals) and only three Tories. In Scotland the totals were, respectively, fifty-eight, three and nine. In the United Kingdom as a whole, the Liberals and Tories each acquired 272 MPs, with forty-two Labourites and eighty-four Irish Nationalists keeping Asquith and the Liberal Party in office. Throughout this period, as will be clear, England often elected a Tory majority, whatever the case in the 'Celtic fringe'. In 1895, for instance, the Tories and their Liberal Unionist allies gained 293 MPs in England, compared with 112 Liberals; Ireland, as always, was a separate case, with the Irish Nationalist Party normally winning virtually all of the seats in southern Ireland, the Ulster Unionists most of the seats in the north. The Irish Nationalists were almost always allied with the Liberals, although never incorporated into any Liberal government, while the Ulster Unionists were an active part of the Conservative and Unionist Party, as it was known after 1886. The Celtic areas thus depended politically at all times on the goodwill of England with its much larger population, while in general forming an important component of the Liberal Party, its Liberal MPs serving in Liberal Cabinets. This situation, of simultaneous dependence and active participation, almost certainly worked to diminish political nationalism in Scotland and Wales.

These two countervailing trends, towards separateness and towards unity, occurred against a backdrop of English predominance in the United Kingdom, always constituting a clear majority of its population.

Scotland

England, being dominant, had no need to specify what constituted 'Englishness' or an English national identity. The need to define their national identities was greater, however, in Scotland, Wales and Ireland. Yet each of the other parts of the United Kingdom was quite separate, with obviously distinctive histories and cultures. Scotland, with 1.7 million inhabitants in 1801 and 4.5 million a century later, and religiously relatively unified, might, as noted, have been expected to have evolved a serious and continuing tradition of overt opposition to English rule, perhaps as extreme as in Catholic Ireland. Scotland had, of course, been a separate country with its own Parliament until 1707. Unlike Wales, it had its own distinctive established religion, aristocracy and legal system. Unlike Ireland, its established religion was that of the majority while its traditional aristocracy was not necessarily hated by the majority. During the late eighteenth and early nineteenth centuries it had experienced what in recent years has become known as the 'Scottish Enlightenment', more renowned throughout Europe than its English equivalent, and it possessed four old and distinguished universities, compared with just two for the whole of England (and none at all in Wales) before the 1820s. The image of Scotland was arguably reinvented during the eighteenth and early nineteenth centuries to emphasise the age-old historical legitimacy of the Highlands as authentically Scottish, famously depicted in works of art and literature, above all in Sir Walter Scott's novels. Despite its internal differences, the materials were seemingly all there for a vigorous, perhaps subversive, assertion of Scottish autonomy, even of Scottish independence. Yet this did not occur. Why not?

The most important reason is that Scotland and the Scots did very well out of their membership of the United Kingdom. The Industrial Revolution made Glasgow into one of the very greatest manufacturing and industrial centres of the world, and sparked the economic development of its surrounding areas and of other Scottish cities such as Dundee, which became the world centre of jute manufacturing. Scotland itself was at the core of a worldwide web of overseas Scottish entrepreneurship. It is, indeed, almost no exaggeration to view the nineteenth century as the time when Scottish enterprise conquered the world. Scottish firms such as Jardine Matheson predominated in Hong Kong and the Far East. Australia was virtually a Scottish (and Scots–Irish) continent in terms of the extraordinary number of successful Scottish pastoralists and merchants, as were New Zealand and the English-speaking parts of Canada. Scottish merchants were a significant component among the leading British entrepreneurs in Britain's 'unofficial empire' in Latin America, as were many of the leading British merchants in Russia and eastern Europe. (A trend which had begun earlier: the father of Immanuel Kant, the great German philosopher, was a Scottish merchant named Cant who had settled in Germany.) Even in the United States, probably the most famous among rags-to-riches millionaire tycoons was Andrew Carnegie (1835–1919), who began as an operative in a Scottish factory.

Scottish entrepreneurship and its spread around the world went hand in hand with other Scottish-led activities overseas at this time, such as missionary work on behalf of the Protestant churches. Dr David Livingstone (1813–73), the celebrated explorer and missionary who was 'found' by Henry Stanley in 1871, was a poor Glasgow boy who educated himself at Scottish colleges before being sent to Africa by the

London Missionary Society; there were hundreds of Dr Livingstones around the world at the time and later. Scotsmen (and, perhaps in particular, the Scots–Irish from Ulster) also certainly formed a disproportionate share of the officers and men of the British army, the East India Company and its successors, and even the Royal Navy. Without the worldwide empire presided over and governed from London, it would have been very difficult for this worldwide saga of success to have occurred.

It is often said as well that although the Scots had no means of governing themselves, through their role in the British government they governed the empire. Such a view might be an exaggeration in the earlier part of the nineteenth century but not in the late Victorian or Edwardian periods. The only Scotsman who became prime minister in the early and mid-nineteenth century was Lord Aberdeen (1852–55), although every Cabinet necessarily had its share of Scots. Gladstone, four times prime minister between 1868 and 1894, and arguably the greatest British political leader of the century, was the son of a typical Scottish merchant who made a fortune in the West Indies and Liverpool and then joined the landed gentry. After Gladstone, however, came the deluge: Lord Rosebery, the 'King of Midlothian', and his successor as Liberal prime minister, Sir Henry Campbell-Bannerman (1836–1908), another successful émigré Scottish merchant, this time in Manchester. Toryism, too, became a Scottish lake, with Arthur Balfour – although a Cecil on his mother's side, he was by paternity the son of a great Scottish untitled landowner – succeeded as Tory leader by yet another émigré Scot of a very different type indeed, the Canadian-born Andrew Bonar Law, son of a Free Church of Scotland minister. Even the early Labour Party imitated the bourgeois parties in one respect at least, that its two most important early leaders, Keir Hardie and Ramsay MacDonald, were Scotsmen.

What constituted Scottish national identity was also contested among the Scots themselves. Religiously, Scotland was officially Presbyterian, with an established church, the Church of Scotland, based upon a hierarchical system, in which authority theoretically went from the bottom up rather than from the top down, with congregations electing ministers (presbyters) and representative elders in the alleged manner of the early Christian Church. These in turn elected various more senior bodies, culminating in the General Assembly of the Church of Scotland, headed by a moderator elected for a year or two, although the sovereign was the official head of the church. Presbyterian doctrine is Calvinistic, and is often seen as grim and unforgiving, while the Church of Scotland has always been concerned to create a 'godly community' of well-behaved and devout believers. Since the Reformation, the Church of Scotland has certainly functioned as the Scottish national church, much more fully an aspect of Scottish national identity than the Anglican Church in England, with the annual meetings of the General Assembly of the Church of Scotland often being seen as a kind of substitute, after 1707, for a Scottish Parliament. Yet religious dissent always existed in Scotland, almost always from sources which were even more extremely Protestant and Calvinistic than the official church. During the eighteenth century, an evangelical Secession Church, which from 1847 was known as the United Presbyterian Church, was formed, generally from among extreme Protestants, mainly in Glasgow and Edinburgh.

A much more serious and traumatic fissure in the Church of Scotland, however, arose in the 1830s and 40s, leading in 1843 to what became known as the Free Church of Scotland.

Ostensibly the disputes that led to the formulation of a breakaway church included the non-recognition by the official
church of ministers appointed to newer parishes in urban
areas, and the widespread use within the Church of Scotland
of lay patronage, where (as in the Church of England), a lay
patron, normally a wealthy landowner, had the power to
appoint ministers to churches of which he was the patron, a
custom regarded by many as contrary to Presbyterian usage.
The movement towards forming a new church was led by Rev.
Thomas Chalmers (1780–1847), a professor at Edinburgh
University, and a tireless champion of this cause. Led by
Chalmers, in May 1843 at the annual General Assembly of the
Church of Scotland in Edinburgh there occurred the famous
'Great Disruption', when about 40 per cent of both the clergy
and laity of the Church of Scotland broke away from the old
church, dramatically symbolised by a mass walkout from the
General Assembly's meeting.

The Free Church of Scotland, as the breakaway movement was known, was strongly Protestant and Calvinistic,
and drew its support from, in particular, nouveau riche
Scottish businessmen, often living embodiments of the
'Protestant ethic' and from remote areas in the north of
Scotland. Within a few years it had not only attracted a mass
following, equal to the established church, but a remarkable
network of new churches, schools and institutions. The inten-
sity and spirit of the new church continued until the 1870s,
when it was widely noted that rigorous Calvinism began to
decline among all three Presbyterian churches. In 1900 the
United Presbyterian and Free Church merged, with most of
its members combining with the established Church of
Scotland in 1929. It is significant that Scottish 'nonconformity' almost always arose among believers who kept the name

and structure of the old established church, insisting on a purer and more uncompromising form of Calvinism. Although English Nonconformist sects such as the Baptists did exist in Scotland, and there was a growing Roman Catholic presence (deeply resented by many Scottish Protestants), the nature of Dissent in Scotland differed from that in England, where many sects, from the Quakers to the Primitive Methodists, were totally outside the structure of the Anglican Church and made no attempt to retain any remnant of its worship or dogma. One reason for this, arguably, was the self-consciously Scottish nature of the large breakaway movements: Scottish religious identity was almost consensually formulated through Scottish Presbyterianism.

That this was so might well have enhanced moves towards Scottish autonomy or even independence, but in the event this did not occur. Apart from Scotland's continuing success within the United Kingdom, the still very influential Scottish aristocracy and other components of its elite were probably drawing closer to their English counterparts. The notorious Highland Clearances – especially under the 1st Duke of Sutherland, the great Scottish magnate, between 1807 and 1821 – were motivated in part by the desire to introduce the highly efficient English 'triple division of land tenure' and large-scale sheep breeding into the Highlands, in place of farming by the impoverished crofters, small owner-occupiers or tenants. Sutherland, the largest landowner in Scotland, was also the Marquess of Stafford and a great English landowner. Thousands of crofters were cleared from the Highlands, many emigrating to Canada, leaving a lasting residue of bitterness. By the late nineteenth century, most Scottish aristocrats had probably been educated at a great English public school and university, although many spent some time as well at a Scottish university. By the twentieth century, Scotland's aristocrats were Janus-faced: linked ever more strongly to their English peers, but also still enjoying considerable local power and prestige.

Scottish 'nationalism' during the nineteenth century was extremely limited in its demands, centring around the desire for the appointment of a Secretary of State for Scotland in the Cabinet. This demand, first voiced in the 1850s, was crowned with success in 1885, with the appointment of the Tory Duke of Richmond as the first Scottish secretary. Vociferous Irish Nationalist demands for a Home Rule Irish Parliament had their parallels in Scotland, and the idea of 'Home Rule All Round' had many supporters in Scotland and elsewhere. But Irish Nationalist demands and extremism triggered a Protestant Unionist backlash, which had important echoes throughout Protestant Scotland. Whereas in 1885 Scotland had elected fifty-eight Liberal and eight Conservative MPs to Parliament, a year later, following the breakup of the Gladstonian Liberal party over Home Rule, the number of Unionist (Conservative and Liberal Unionist) MPs rose to twenty-seven. In 1900, for one of the only times at a normal two-party general election, Scotland elected a majority of Unionist MPs. In the twentieth century, with the long-term bifurcation of British politics along class lines and the rise of Labour, the middle and upper classes largely unified under the Conservatives. Until the 1990s, both Labour and the Conservatives opposed increased Scottish autonomy. The Scottish Nationalist Party, formed in 1928, did not gain an MP until 1945 and did not become a major force until the 1970s. Their rise occurred half a century after Scotland began its long-term decline as a major industrial centre.

Wales

The situation in Wales presented some parallels with Scotland, but also many differences. Wales was not, since the Middle Ages, an independent state, but rather a kind of appendage of England. It had never had a Parliament of its own, or its own legal system, or a separate, distinctive aristocracy. Cardiff, which became acknowledged as the capital of Wales, was on the principality's south-east coast, and had a population of only about 2,000 in 1801, compared with Edinburgh's 83,000. Wales's largest city in 1801 was Swansea, also on the south coast; it had a population of only about 10,000 and was smaller than Colchester or Shrewsbury. Most Welsh people lived in isolated, often almost inaccessible rural areas, and spoke Welsh. A far higher percentage of the population of Wales – about one half in 1851 – spoke Welsh as their vernacular tongue than did the Irish or Scots who spoke Irish or Scottish Gaelic. Wales was considered remote, exotic, even uncivilised, by many Englishmen; Anglican parishes in Wales were considered the least desirable in the country and were generally among the lowest paid. There was little or nothing in Wales to compare with the Scottish Enlightenment, and Wales had no real university of its own until 1872.

In the eighteenth and early nineteenth centuries one very significant change came over the Welsh people: most ceased to be Anglican and became adherents of one or another variety of Protestant Nonconformity, such that by 1880 'Wales' and 'Nonconformist' were virtually interchangeable terms. By the early twentieth century, when Welsh Nonconformity was at its peak, only about 25 per cent of the people of Wales and Monmouthshire were Anglicans, compared with 23 per cent who were Congregationalists, 25 per cent who were Calvinistic

5. Lloyd Family Butchers, Aberystwyth. This picture, taken in 1911, is of a typical family-run retail shop, similar to thousands of others at the time. The lines of unrefrigerated carcasses in the outdoors will probably seem utterly unhealthy to many today.

Methodists, 18 per cent Baptists, 6 per cent Wesleyans, and 3 per cent adhering to other denominations, chiefly Roman Catholicism. Although the four main Nonconformist sects had broadly similar doctrines, they had somewhat different clientele and histories and were, in many ways, rivals. They also had in common the ironical fact that all were English imports, while the Anglican Church regularly claimed to be the authentically Welsh ancient church of the principality, the successor to the early Christian Celtic churches, and that its translation of the Bible into Welsh probably saved the language from extinction. (Calvinistic Methodism was officially founded at Bala in 1811 by Rev. Thomas Charles (1765–1814), a Welsh Anglican vicar, but drew its doctrinal origins from English and Scottish sources.) By the early nineteenth century, the Welsh religious situation thus differed in many ways from the Scottish in that three quarters of the Welsh people made no pretence to belonging to the established church of the country in any sense, but viewed it, rather unhistorically, as a 'foreign' imposition. Nineteenth-century Welsh Nonconformity also developed a religiosity that, to many, embodied the essence of 'Welshness', emphasising rousing hymns in the 'Land of Song', and greatly prizing the minister capable of delivering spirited and gripping sermons (*hwyl*). In the absence of an entrenched local gentry or professional class, Nonconformist ministers often comprised a major part of the local leadership elite. Most Nonconformist sects in Wales were also associated with radical politics, first Liberal and then Labour, and their ministers normally emerged from working-class backgrounds, in marked contrast to the Anglican clergy.

Nevertheless, for much of the nineteenth century, Welsh Nonconformity was arguably not a disguised form of political nationalism: at least it had no nationalistic political agenda. Welsh politics in the nineteenth century before about 1868 was dominated, perhaps surprisingly, by its anglicised gentry, often Tory or Whig–Liberal, who were regularly returned to Parliament with little opposition. Historians have argued that the backwardness of 'Welsh Wales', and its lack of either a leadership elite of its own or a single charismatic leader akin to Daniel O'Connell in Ireland, were major factors in this, as was the relatively limited extent of the franchise in Wales before 1867, given that the right to vote was based largely on property ownership. A major turning point in Welsh politics came at the 1868 general election, the first held after the 1867 Reform Act, when a clear majority of Liberals were elected for the first time since 1832, twenty-two compared with the Tories' eight. By the end of the nineteenth century, Toryism in Wales was reduced to a fringe remnant in border and very middle-class areas, even in years of Tory triumph. Moreover, the social character of most Welsh MPs changed considerably, going 'downmarket' in a way unusual in the nineteenth century. One man elected in 1868 was the Rev. Henry Richard, a Congregationalist minister, who became leader of the Welsh MPs.

The mid and especially the late nineteenth century also saw the very rapid industrialisation of South Wales, symbolised by its coal mines, the very emblem of laissez-faire industrial capitalism at its grimmest and nastiest. Other forms of heavy industry and commerce developed rapidly in and around Cardiff, which increased in size from only 18,000 in 1851 to 182,000 in 1911, and Swansea which grew in the same years from 31,000 to 144,000. Sharing in the bounty provided by the mantle of the British Empire at this time almost certainly acted to dampen serious separatist aspirations, as did the growth (for the first time) of a class of native Welsh industrial tycoons, who were eventually ennobled with titles such as Lords Merthyr, Swansea, and Glantawe. Culturally, too, this was a time of the favouring of English over Welsh, epitomised by the famous 'Blue Books' controversy of 1847, when the authors of a government commission on education in Wales criticised the continuing use of the Welsh language as a significant factor in hindering the 'moral and religious progress' of the 'poorer classes' and in keeping Wales generally backward. While their conclusions scandalised the Welsh-speaking community, it was consistent with a long-term decline in the use of Welsh, especially in the south. Welsh 'nationalism' generally focused on improvements in Welsh education, some land reform, and especially on a move towards the disestablishment of the minority Anglican Church in Wales. A very typical Welsh historical myth and narrative also developed at this time, focusing on the (alleged) ancient Druids, the medieval kings of independent Wales, and the figure of Owain

Glyndower (Glyndwr, c.1354–1416), the medieval warrior king. Welsh disestablishment was almost achieved in 1895, and was finally enacted in 1919 when there was a Welsh prime minister, although a Tory parliamentary majority.

During the late nineteenth century, because of rapid industrialisation, the Welsh population evolved from one largely rural and agricultural to one largely industrial and urban (or situated in mining villages). As in Scotland, the rapid and comprehensive growth, first of Welsh radical Liberalism, and then of Welsh Labour, probably acted to reduce the somewhat contradictory pressures towards Welsh nationalism or even independence. By 1914 Wales was still firmly a part of the United Kingdom, although always on the left of politics and usually somewhat wary of imperialism and of Anglican gentry England. Its national mood was summarised in the career of the most famous and important Welsh politician of the age, David Lloyd George (1863–1945). Although Lloyd George was an almost perfect representative of Wales's national political culture, his life and career also illustrated the often contradictory nature of Wales and its place at this time: he was born in Manchester; grew up in the rural north of Wales and had little to do with the industrial south; magically transformed himself in 1914–18 from a 'Little Englander' and the 'scourge of the dukes' to the great champion of the empire; and died an earl. As in Scotland, overt Welsh nationalism came late to Wales, with Plaid Cymru, the Welsh nationalist party, founded only in 1925 and electorally unsuccessful until it elected its first MP in 1966.

Ireland

Ireland came to dominate British politics to such an extent that British political history between about 1845 and 1922 might, with little exaggeration, be said to consist of Ireland plus footnotes. If anything, what was known as the 'Irish question' became more central to British political life after the 1870s than before, leading to the break-up of the Gladstonian Liberal Party in 1886, to a near-civil war situation in Britain in 1910–14, to the downfall of Lloyd George in 1922 and to the decades of Tory ascendancy which followed. Presumed dead, the Irish issue sprang back to life in the late 1960s in a form more terrible than before.

The Irish question is so complex and proved so insoluble because it entailed several related but differing and very serious issues which, although linked in the minds of most Irish people, were not necessarily causally connected. Resolving one – no mean task in itself – would not necessarily resolve any of the others. Religion and ethnicity, the nation's economy and its economic structure, modes of domestic governance and the nexus between the Westminster government and Ireland and its various communities were the principal elements in the Irish question. Ireland, of course, is a separate geographical entity: this was itself a major element in the Irish question. To some extent, therefore, Ireland could not be governed from London, and some form of local autonomy (at the very least) seemed inevitable. From 1297 until 1801 Ireland – the whole island – had its own Parliament with limited powers under the British Crown, with an administration headed by a Lord Lieutenant appointed by the British government. In 1800 the Irish Parliament, whose powers had been increased in 1782, consisted, like the Westminster

Parliament, of two houses, an Irish House of Lords comprising twenty Anglican bishops and (at the time) 228 Irish peers,
and an Irish House of Commons of 300 members. As in
Britain, voting at elections was heavily restricted to a tiny
number of electors, with Irish peers and other landowners de
facto controlling nearly all elections. From 1727 only
Protestants could vote, although the vote was restored to
Catholics who met the requisite property qualifications in
1793. No Roman Catholic, however, could sit in the Irish
Parliament, which was restricted to members of the Church
of Ireland.

In the late eighteenth century, as a result of the French
Revolution, a number of potentially serious revolutionary
bodies were formed, such as Wolfe Tone's Society of United
Irishmen, which developed links with revolutionary France,
and a revolt among Munster peasants actually occurred in
1798. As a result, William Pitt's government in 1801 took the
drastic step of securing the consent of both Parliaments to a
union. Pitt envisaged this as part of a strategy including
Catholic emancipation (which King George III refused to
allow and which was not enacted until 1829) and an enlarged
market for Irish goods. From 1801 until 1922, a hundred (105
from 1832) Irish MPs sat in the Westminster House of
Commons, with Ireland governed both indirectly from
London and directly by the Irish viceroy and his staff at Dublin
Castle, while twenty-eight Irish peers (out of a total of 228)
elected from their own number sat in the House of Lords.
Ireland thus had no national legislature, although each county
and borough provided a local government structure. Increased
agricultural prices during the Napoleonic Wars kept Ireland
relatively quiescent, but after Waterloo agitation again began
to secure 'Catholic emancipation' – the right of Irish Roman

Catholics to be elected to the Westminster Parliament and hold the full range of civic offices – and, if possible, for the restoration of the Dublin Parliament. This agitation was led by Daniel O'Connell (1775–1847), an Irish Catholic barrister who became known as the 'Liberator'. O'Connell's Catholic Association, formed in 1823, skilfully exploited the fear of rural unrest to gain, with remarkable speed, the granting of 'Catholic emancipation' by Parliament in 1829. O'Connell is seen by historians not merely as one of the great figures in modern Irish political history, but one of the first leaders of a rural proletariat to emerge in Europe, who used mass public meetings to great advantage. O'Connell's political triumph in 1829 might have been expected to go very far towards resolving the Irish question, and O'Connell, a moderate property owner, did not further exploit the political power he and his Irish Catholic bloc held at the Westminster Parliament.

Catholic emancipation did not resolve the Irish question, but was only one step on a troubled road which lasted for nearly another century. This was largely because of the underlying religious demography and power structure of the country. In 1821 about 80 per cent of Ireland's population of 7 million were Roman Catholics. (By 1900, this figure had declined slightly, to about 75 per cent.) About 10 per cent were adherents of the Church of Ireland, the Protestant Episcopal church on the island, and about 10 per cent were Presbyterians or other Protestant Nonconformists. Catholics existed in great numbers throughout the island, except in the north-east corner, the Province of Ulster. Church of Ireland membership was also widely spread, but was especially concentrated in and around Dublin, where it comprised most of the Anglo-Irish Establishment, its governmental, military and mercantile leadership. Many (but not all) significant landowners were churchmen, some of whom spent part of the year in other parts of Britain, where they often owned estates. Ulster was the home of the Scots–Irish Protestants, who had come over from Scotland in the seventeenth century and whose national ethos and historical narrative revolved around a triumphalist anti-Catholicism. Despite being the religion of only 10 per cent of the Irish population, the Church of Ireland was the established church, and was closely intertwined with Ireland's governing classes. It was headed by no fewer than four arch-bishops, compared with only two (Canterbury and York) for the whole of England. Protestant Nonconformists like the Ulster Presbyterians did not form a true part of the Anglo-Irish Establishment, although, as Protestants, they faced fewer obstacles and barriers than did the Catholics. Today, when we are used to the Northern Irish conflict being depicted in terms of Irish Catholics v. Ulster Scots–Irish Presbyterians, it is important to realise that a third religious element, members of the Church of Ireland, the Anglican Church, existed at the time and were, in fact the ruling elite.

Irish Catholics thus felt a deep sense of grievance which was augmented by economic reality. Catholic landowning Ireland consisted chiefly of small sub-lessees and very small farmers, eking out a living in a manner reminiscent of a Continental peasant society. Beneath even this, the mass of rural Irish Catholics were not farmers at all, but an impover-ished rural proletariat of agricultural labourers, comprising an estimated 59 per cent of the rural population in 1841. Industrial growth largely bypassed – and would continue to bypass – Catholic Ireland, in contrast to Ulster, which became a major industrial centre after about 1850, the population of Belfast growing from 103,000 in 1851 to 387,000 in 1911.

Nevertheless, Ireland remained reasonably quiescent and

rather off politics' centre stage from 1832 until the Great
Famine of 1845–51, caused by a terrible fungal blight affecting
potatoes, the staple diet of much of Ireland's rural proletariat,
one of the greatest demographic catastrophes in modern history. The population of the west of Ireland declined
precipitously, County Galway diminishing from 440,000 in
1841 to 322,000 a decade later, County Tipperary from 436,000
to 332,000 in the same period. These areas continued to decline
through emigration after the famine, with Galway, for
instance, dropping to 271,000 in 1861 and to only 182,000 in
1911. Relief of the famine by Britain's Whig government
under Lord John Russell was uninspired and half-hearted,
although it must be said that, with the transport and communications available at the time, it would have been difficult to
transport food from overseas to the stricken area in time to
save many, while other areas of the British Isles, not dependent
upon a one-crop economy, avoided famine. Observers reported
scenes of starvation and utter misery strongly resembling the
horrors which greeted the liberators of Belsen and Dachau a
century later and, indeed, it was not long before Irish nationalist writers such as John Michel charged the British government
with a deliberate act of genocide in its minimal response to
the famine.

The famine had a number of lasting effects of considerable
importance. It altered the class structure in much of rural
Ireland, eliminating a large portion of the agricultural labourer
class, increasing, through mergers and purchases, the size and
viability of farms, and also, in the long run, increasing the
power of the landlords. The famine created an enormously
increased number of expatriate Irishmen, especially in the
United States, with a bitter hatred of England. In 1858, expatriate Irishmen in America founded the Fenian Society, known

officially as the Irish Republican Brotherhood, which advocated and paid for armed insurrection in Ireland and terrorism in England (and Canada, a symbol of British imperialism), and which came close to assassinating Queen Victoria. Its methods of random bombings and murders foreshadowed the policies of the IRA and more recent terrorists. In Ireland itself, the famine became a part of the dominant historical narrative, fundamental evidence of English wickedness and racism. The famine also probably acted to enhance the power of the Catholic clergy, relatively more numerous post-famine, who now adopted a more vigorous and visible role as leaders of the Irish rural masses, whereas previously they had been largely dormant.

Nevertheless, the famine had several beneficial effects in the medium term, reducing the size of the impoverished class of agricultural labourers and making Irish agriculture more profitable along English lines. It was thus possible that, Fenianism notwithstanding, Ireland might have remained quiet and offstage. Probably the first dent in this period of quiescence came with the election of Gladstone's Liberal government in 1868 with a large majority. Gladstone – a strange combination of evangelical and High Church Anglican, whose religiosity strongly influenced his actions according to rules which only he and the deity understood – decided, essentially for no apparent reason, that his central mission was to 'pacify Ireland'. His religious outlook and perception of the centrality of the religious question for Irish politics led him to make the centrepiece of his Irish policies the disestablishment of the Anglican Church in Ireland. For Gladstone, such a move would go far to pacifying Ireland's Catholic majority, as well as its Presbyterian minority, who were also outside the established church. It would also solidify Nonconformist support in

Britain for his agenda, since the eventual disestablishment of the Church of England was high on the long-term programme of radical Nonconformity. Although Gladstone's Irish church policies were opposed, they were not opposed with the vigour with which a previous attempt, in 1833, at reform of the Church of Ireland was opposed (when the number of its archbishops was cut from four to two and eight Irish bishoprics were abolished). This previous measure of 1833, the Irish Church Temporalities Act, led directly to the Oxford Movement and was regarded by strong Anglicans as heretical sacrilege. In 1868, the main questions were how generous financial terms should be given to the Church of Ireland, and whether there should be 'concurrent endowment' for all Ireland's denominations instead, a move favoured by some Catholics. Disestablishment of the Church of Ireland became law in 1869, making Ireland one of the few places in Europe without an established church. Gladstone also passed an Irish Land Act in 1870 which made the eviction of tenants more difficult.

Gladstone and many others thought that a healthier, happier Ireland would emerge, but this was not to be. While Irish unrest dampened down for some time, within ten or twelve years it re-emerged in a new, more extreme form. The English agricultural depression, which began around 1879 largely as a result of foreign competition, and a depression which struck the United States at this time, reducing the still large number of would-be Irish emigrants, produced considerable unrest again in Ireland, which by about 1880 had centred around demands for Irish Home Rule, that is, the restoration of an Irish Parliament for the whole island with considerable powers. This renewed radicalisation coincided with the ascendancy of Ireland's greatest political leader between O'Connell and the 1916–22 civil war, Charles Stewart Parnell (1846–91).

Parnell, an upper-class Anglo-Irish Protestant, became leader of the Irish Parliamentary Party around 1878, and from then made the achievement of Irish Home Rule his goal. In 1885 Gladstone, once again prime minister, announced his conversion to Home Rule, and proceeded to introduce such a measure into Parliament in 1886. It would have created a unicameral Irish Parliament consisting of two 'orders', one representing the old Irish aristocracy and the upper classes, the other the mass of the people, with limited powers to legislate on Irish affairs. The Westminster Parliament was to retain many powers, including exclusive control over foreign policy and defence. Irish MPs were also to continue to sit in the Westminster Parliament. The Home Rule Bill was accompanied by another Land Purchase Act, designed to buy out many absentee landlords.

Gladstone's Home Rule Bill set off an enormous storm of hostility and opposition without any parallel since the repeal of the Corn Laws in the mid-1840s. Opposition came from several sources. The first and most important was the Presbyterian community in Ulster, the Orangemen, who feared inevitable rule by the Catholic majority. Their fierce anti-Catholicism was augmented by a belief in the progressive nature of Protestant society in northern Ireland, in contrast to the Catholic south. Orangemen pointed out the enormous progress made by Belfast as an industrial powerhouse under Protestant domination, strongly linked to Protestant Glasgow and the industries of the Clyde. Belfast's biggest business, Harland & Wolff, was the largest shipbuilder in the world, and many other major industries were located there (although the most famous ship ever built by Harland & Wolff did little to enhance its reputation: RMS *Titanic*). In contrast, Catholic southern Ireland, priest-riddled and backward, had hardly any industries at all. Dublin's largest business was Guinness Breweries, and even the Guinness family was Protestant. The notion of the inevitable superiority of Protestant to Catholic Europe was, in 1905, given apparent scholarly credence when the famous German sociologist Max Weber published his renowned work *The Protestant Ethic and the Spirit of Capitalism*, which introduced the notion of the 'Protestant work ethic'. Protestant fears were that an impoverished Irish Catholic majority, led by Catholic priests with an ideology from the Dark Ages, would inevitably destroy the achievement of the Protestant minority through deliberate taxation and perhaps overt persecution. The Ulster Protestants wanted either a continuation of the existing state of affairs, or at the very least the exclusion of Ulster from the Home Rule Bill's provisions. They, and their supporters, also argued that Gladstone's appeasement of those who hated Britain at the expense of those loyal to it was immoral, and would not work: Irish nationalists would inevitably be back ten years later with some proposal still more extreme.

The Ulster Protestant community was strongly backed by many English Tories, who saw in them a winning cause. 'Ulster will fight, Ulster will be right', was Lord Randolph Churchill's famous phrase. Over the next thirty years Protestant Ulster evolved into a community whose *raison d'être*, almost to a man and woman, revolved around fierce opposition to Catholic-dominated Home Rule, underpinned by a spirit of militant national resistance. While the other minority nations within Britain looked back to a romantic, legendary past, reviving the Druids and the medieval Irish kings, Ulster saw its history as beginning with the Protestant conquest of northern Ireland in the seventeenth century and celebrated the suppression of the Catholics. Alone among the historical narratives and myths of Britain's minority nations, Ulster celebrated victory rather than mourning defeat and conquest; it did not look to a lost golden age before foreign oppression began. Gladstone and the Home Rulers certainly underestimated the strength of Ulster's determination to resist a Catholic majority, arguing that their civil rights would be protected, while a Home Rule Parliament would bring the communities together by forcing them to take part in the mundane process of local government administration, necessarily entailing compromise.

Apart from the Ulster Protestants and the Tories, several other major sources of opposition to Home Rule quickly emerged. Most serious was that within the Liberal Party itself. Both the party's Whig, moderate right wing and, rather surprisingly, a major portion of its left wing led by Joseph Chamberlain, were also bitterly opposed to Home Rule, Chamberlain and others arguing that it would weaken the British Empire. Many strong Protestants in England and Scotland also turned against Home Rule. As a result, in June 1886, Gladstone's Home Rule Bill was defeated by 341 to 311, when ninety-four Liberals voted against it. Many of these joined in forming a new political party, the Liberal Unionists, which by the mid-1890s had effectively become part of the Conservative Party. A further attempt by the minority Liberal government of 1892–5 to enact Home Rule also failed. A Home Rule bill, excluding Ulster for six years, finally passed in 1914 but was put into cold storage by the First World War. After the war and the Dublin uprising of Easter 1916, it proved impossible to reach any agreement short of Irish independence and the total exclusion of Ulster. In the period, too, an Irish nationalist historical myth and narrative took shape, based around the ancient and medieval independent kingdoms

of Ireland took shape, aiming at total independence, if neces-
sary by force. Although confined to the fringes until the First
World War, its strength was enhanced by the failure to enact
Home Rule and by the lack of inspiring political leadership in
Catholic Ireland after Parnell's career was destroyed in a
divorce scandal in 1891, followed by his early death.

The successful enactment of Irish Home Rule is one of the
great 'might-have-beens' of British history. Conceivably, a successful Home Rule Parliament, concentrating solely on
down-to-earth local issues and respecting the rights of all,
might have satisfied and disarmed Ulster while damping down
extreme Catholic Irish nationalism. A united Ireland might
have supported the First World War, and a significant number
of southern Irish MPs would have remained in the Westminster
Parliament, probably enhancing the electoral success of the
British left in the twentieth century. On the other hand, the
nationalistic forces of both Catholic Ireland and Ulster were
probably too strong to make compromise possible, while
Gladstone's programme was – as Chamberlain said – profoundly antipathetic to the spirit of the times, with its
perception of great empires as a prerequisite for great power
status in the twentieth century.

Although somewhat removed from the central discussion
of this section, it is worth noting that the nineteenth century
saw the emergence and growth of many colonies settled by
British émigrés, in Canada, Australia, New Zealand and parts
of South Africa. While these might have developed strong separatist tendencies, especially as many settlers came from
Britain's dispossessed, in fact without exception they developed strong feelings of loyalty to Britain, seen nostalgically as
the 'mother country', with all loyally going to war on Britain's
side in the war of 1914–18 and, indeed, in the war of 1939–45.

Britain's white colonies developed as British outposts overseas, the majority rejoicing in British law, government and civilisation. Only where large communities of Irish Catholics resided in the white empire was this sense of loyalty contested.

Perhaps the most important lesson to be drawn from this discussion of local nationalisms within the United Kingdom is that, Catholic Ireland alone excepted, a sense of Britishness and British triumphalism became ubiquitous everywhere, with Scottish, Welsh, Ulster and even moderate southern Irish opinion loyal to Britain and the empire. Nothing succeeds like success, and the unquestioned success of Britain in every sphere until, at the earliest, the end of the nineteenth century, proved sufficiently strong to dampen down centrifugal opinion, helped by the 'safety valve' of migration to the white empire and elsewhere. The doctrine of evolution helped, too, with large empires and continental nation-states (such as the United States) seemingly, by the end of the century, preordained to domination in the twentieth century. So too did Protestantism (outside of southern Ireland, of course), seen as a progressive religion generally in accord with scientific progress and democracy, as opposed to the backwardness of Catholicism and non-Christian religions. The nineteenth century was a time of the integration of the disparate parts of the British Isles into something like one whole, southern Ireland always being the exception.

Chapter Six

Modes of Identity: Gender

Many would suggest gender is the most basic mode of identity and self-identification. While this has been a constant throughout all human history, in some periods gender has been more of a constant than in others. Many would argue that Victorian Britain marked the zenith of ascribed gender differences and gender roles in modern history. Men and women, according to this viewpoint, were confined almost comprehensively to 'separate spheres', male domination, with the rarest exception, being normal. Like most historical generalisations, such a view is partially true, although its limitations are also clear.

It might be useful to outline those areas of public and private life from which women in Britain were debarred by law, custom or institutional bias. Britain was a western, liberal state, and such institutions as arranged and child marriage, the virtual imprisonment of widows and, a fortiori, such enormities as female infanticide, female circumcision, polygamy, suttee, and the range of anti-female practices routinely found in the non-European world, were always illegal. These practices were regarded with universal horror when reported in Britain. Legally, in nineteenth-century Britain women were debarred from voting or holding public office (except at the local level, where women ratepayers were increasingly given the right to vote and hold office), serving on juries, or entering most professions such as the law, although medicine was open to women by the end of the nineteenth century. Most hereditary titles of nobility passed to the eldest male heir. Until 1882, the property of married women became, upon their marriage, the legal property of their husband, although trusts were regularly established by the rich to get around this. After 1857 (and indeed until the 1920s), the grounds for divorce were different for husband and wife, a husband having to prove only adultery by his wife to be granted a divorce, while a wife had to prove not merely adultery, but some other heinous activity such as cruelty, incest or bestiality, the assumption apparently being that many normal men would routinely commit adultery, and wives should simply grin and bear it unless the husband was truly a swine as well. Women were automatically debarred from virtually all private educational institutions, although by the end of the nineteenth century there were women's private schools, and women's colleges at Oxford and Cambridge, with women admitted to many other universities.

While this list of legal disabilities suffered by women in nineteenth-century Britain is significant, it is also probably exhaustive: legally, British women could do anything else, such as own, inherit and leave property, live where they wished, sue or give evidence in court, or emigrate. Some degree of de facto equality also existed in public spaces: men and women, for instance, sat together in churches, performances and meetings, and on public transport. Women could, and frequently did, write books and comment on public affairs.

They could organise societies and associations and often, but not always, join learned and serious bodies. A queen sat on the British throne from 1837 until 1901, and gave her name to the age.

Of course, spelling out the legal and de facto rights of women offers no realistic description of their actual status. In fact, women's roles were automatically constrained and diminished in ways which men's never were. Women were at almost all times constrained by the pervasive notion of 'separate spheres', that women belonged in the home, as mothers and home makers. Women's occupational patterns differed markedly from those of men: while virtually all able-bodied adult males were in the labour force, only a minority of women were. (This situation might well have differed from that in pre-industrial Britain, when 'domestic' industries were often carried out in the home, and more women worked while also engaged as homemakers.) In 1841, while 76 per cent of males over ten were listed in the census as having an occupation, only 25 per cent of females over ten were so described. In 1911, 84 per cent of males stated an occupation compared with 32 per cent of women. Although these figures can be disputed – many women listed as having no occupation were actually involved in the businesses of their husbands or fathers – in fact most adult women spent most, or in some cases, all of their adult lives without gainful employment and dependent upon a male breadwinner for their incomes. The female occupational structure was also very different from its male equivalent. By far the largest single occupation among employed women during the nineteenth century was domestic service, with nearly 1 million females employed in 1841 and over 2 million in 1911. Textiles and clothing were the next largest occupational categories, with over half a million female employees in 1841 and 1.7 million in 1911. Many components of the factory production of textiles and clothing were female preserves, and wages were relatively high.

As the nineteenth century progressed, a female service and professional sector grew, based especially in the 'sub-professions' of teaching and nursing. A female clerical sector began rapidly increasing in size in the late nineteenth century (although not before), especially with the widespread use of typewriters in the 1890s. At the very top, a tiny handful of women became successful in business life, or even rich in their own right, such as Harriet Mellon (c.1772–1837), an actress who became the wife of the great banker Thomas Coutts (d.1822), inheriting his fortune and becoming the chief director of Coutts & Co. and eventually Duchess of St Albans; or, at the end of the century, Helen Carte (née Black, 1852–1913), a talented Scotswoman who became the secretary and business manager of Richard D'Oyly Carte (d.1901), the chief producer of Gilbert and Sullivan operas, whom she later married. Before her marriage, however, she was paid a salary of £1,000 per annum plus 10 per cent of Carte's profits as his business manager, and was probably the highest-paid woman in England. Among other things, Helen Carte oversaw the rebuilding of the famous Savoy Hotel in London, and left over £100,000 at her death. While there were a number of other such examples of highly successful businesswomen, even in the 1890s they were, of course, exceptionally rare. Inevitably, the mid and late nineteenth century saw a range of female 'firsts', as a microscopic number of highly qualified women were able to break through into the professions: the first woman architect in 1898, the first woman administrative civil servant in 1874 (Mrs Nassau Senior, the sister of the novelist Thomas

6. Few women in the nineteenth century became wealthy entrepreneurs in their own right. One of the most remarkable exceptions was Harriet Mellon (1777–1837). The illegitimate daughter of an actress, she also became an actress on the London stage, and then married Thomas Coutts, the millionaire founder of Coutts Bank. After his death in 1822, she became the managing partner in the bank, possibly the first British woman to hold such a position. She then married the Duke of St Albans and became a duchess. At her death, she left most of her vast fortune to Coutts's granddaughter (from a previous marriage), Angela Burdett-Coutts (1814–1906), who became a famous philanthropist, helping the poor.

Hughes, who was appointed a Poor Law inspector), the first woman dentist in 1895, the first woman doctor, Elizabeth Garrett Anderson, in 1865, and so on. Despite these breakthroughs, only after the First World War could British women enter such professions as the law.

One of the main obstacles to women's employment was the almost complete absence of a career structure in any female occupation with the exception of professions such as teaching and nursing. Invariably, the high peaks of every profession were dominated by men, while unskilled or semi-skilled women could expect to rise no higher than the factory floor.

Below this was the street. As Henry Snell, an early Labour politician, put it in *Men, Movements, and Myself* (1936):

> What of the women who had no male relatives, the young women with children to support, and the lonely working girls? How were they to live? ... [E]verybody knew the dangers to which they were exposed. The statesmen knew of them, the economists and the Church knew, but there was no evidence that their complacent philosophy of life was seriously disturbed.

There is no accurate way of knowing the extent of prostitution in nineteenth-century Britain other than that it was a ubiquitous part of life, especially urban life. Prostitution in London's West End, especially in the Haymarket and surrounding streets, was so flagrant and unavoidable that it was commented upon by most foreign visitors. In 1888, when Jack the Ripper brutally murdered five prostitutes in London's East End, the Metropolitan Police were asked how many prostitutes were potentially at risk. It reported that 1,200 prostitutes and sixty-two brothels were known to the police in the single police district of Whitechapel. Estimates of the total number of prostitutes in mid-Victorian London ranged from 40,000 to 120,000, although in 1861 Henry Mayhew pointed out, in an oft-quoted remark, that the census had no occupational category for prostitutes, and officially the number of women working as prostitutes was zero.

Mayhew was here noting the Victorian 'double standard' at its more egregious: few ever discussed the subject of prostitution, except in the context of venereal disease, or asked why so many women were driven beyond the fringes of respectable society to earn a living. As a general rule, prostitution was accepted as an unfortunate fact of life with which it was point-less for the state to interfere. Above the level of the streetwalker, many women certainly lived as the mistresses of rich men. St John's Wood, north of the West End, with its many blocks of flats, is often said to have been developed in part for wealthy City men to keep a second household; it was also conveniently near Lord's cricket ground, combining pleasure with pleasure. The fact that divorce was both legally difficult and socially stig-matised arguably meant that second households of this type were de facto widely tolerated. Only occasionally did the press intrude into the private lives of leading politicians, unlike the situation in our time. There is some evidence that prostitution declined, at least in its visibility, in the Edwardian era, presum-ably as more opportunities in the sub-professions and service sector opened for young women.

Because the life of unprotected and single women was often so precarious, it was probably the case that a higher per-centage of women married in the nineteenth century than before or since. About 85 per cent of women in Victorian Britain eventually married and conventional marriage was regarded as the normal and only really acceptable fate for most women, followed of course by motherhood. While many working-class women did work after their marriage, for the most part married women had to satisfy themselves out-side the home with voluntary work for charities and church groups. There was, therefore, an almost total reliance on the husband as head of the household and breadwinner. A fortu-nate marriage could bring lifelong security and affluence, while marriage to a ne'er-do-well or an alcoholic, or to a man simply unlucky in business or professional life, represented ever-looming disaster, as did the possibility, always real, that the husband would die young.

Given the central importance of marriage and its ubiquity, the historian naturally wants to know more about its inner nature: how many marriages were happy? Of course, a comprehensive answer to this is beyond our knowledge, since no evidence exists, and a range of conclusions is possible. It seems clear that a great many marriages were extremely happy, with the husband and wife as true companions in life, the wife sharing the husband's intimate concerns. Historians have pointed out that many of the surviving letters of British Cabinet ministers to their wives show an extraordinary level of intimacy, and there were many men who preferred the company of women, for instance Benjamin Disraeli. On the other hand, the image of the heavy, often brutal or even sadistic Victorian husband and father was a powerful one, and the nature of the institution of marriage in Victorian Britain gave ample scope for domestic male oppression. It is likely that unhappy marriages increased as one went down the social scale, where a lack of income, outside interests and communication skills greatly enhanced the potential for marital warfare, as did alcohol and domestic claustrophobia. Probably many men were only too happy to leave their wives in charge of the home, and to get out as often as possible to the world of social clubs, political societies and, above all, fraternal orders such as the Freemasons, which at the time were all-male domains; for the working-class male, there was the pub, the social club and, increasingly, weekend sporting fixtures, especially football. If women enjoyed a life outside the home, something which required adequate time and resources, this was normally in church and charitable groups. The Primrose League, a Tory fund-raising organisation founded in 1883, was possibly the first mass political movement actively to include women, and the Conservatives, then and later, probably mobilised women to a greater extent than did the Liberals or the nascent Labour parties, whose political culture was (at the time) more male-dominated and male-exclusive.

Concrete political gains for British women in the nine-teenth century were few, with the Married Women's Property Act of 1882 arguably the most important. It gave married women the right to retain their incomes and property upon marriage. Such measures as the Divorce Act of 1857 and the Matrimonial Causes Act of 1878, which allowed a wife beaten by her husband to apply for a separation order, were among the few other measures which touched directly on women's rights. The key was granting women the franchise, but there was no movement here except in 1894, when women received the vote in local elections on the same terms as men, enfran-chising mainly well-off widows and unmarried women. Intellectually, the case for women's rights had been made by writers such as Mary Godwin and John Stuart Mill, but the suf-fragette movement was still in a relative infancy. Motions in Parliament to enfranchise women had attracted a measure of support, but never enough to see it enacted, and the main women's suffrage movement, the Women's Social and Political Union, was founded only in 1903. Indeed, a component of social Darwinist theory as it emerged in the late nineteenth century saw the 'separate spheres' of men and women as a product of natural selection, while many women, including very clever ones, actually remained opposed to women's suf-frage or their direct participation in public life. The seriousness of the political, military and economic issues facing the British Empire in the late Victorian era also weighed against extend-ing the vote to women, with their alleged lack of practical experience or realism, and their supposed naive idealism. The enfranchisement of women, when it finally came in 1918, would by no means have been a certainty without the First World War.

Men are the other half of the gender equation, a fact often overlooked in today's age of feminism. Maleness and the male role must, by definition, mesh as complementary with the role and status of women. The relative absence of career opportunities for women, and the crucial importance of marriage and the family, weighed heavily on the life and career choices of adult men, adding to the sense of individual responsibility which was so important as a determinant of worthiness in Victorian life. Not all men rose to this responsibility: there was, for instance, the little-explored world of the bachelor, exemplified in such institutions as Oxbridge colleges (whose fellows had to be unmarried until late in the century) and the posh London club, many of whose members were lifelong bachelors. There was also a homosexual underground, which allegedly and notoriously existed in the public schools, universities and Guards regiments, but was always illegal and regarded with near-universal repulsion except in artistic circles. The most famous nineteenth-century British homosexual, Oscar Wilde (1854–1900), was perhaps noteworthy for having been almost universally condemned and ostracised after his jailing in 1895. As in many other spheres of life, social class played a major role in tolerance for male homosexuality, with public school and university men allowed a much greater degree of latitude by the police than their social inferiors, unless they engaged in grossly scandalous activities in public. The evidence suggests that attitudes towards anything resembling homosexuality probably hardened during the nineteenth century. For instance, it seems that (heterosexual) male friends often walked arm in arm in public until the closing years of the century, when this appeared to have ended owing to its implications of improper intimacy. On the other hand, there was far less prejudice against lesbianism, which was never illegal, and women were (and are) always allowed to kiss and hold hands with other women in a way which few men would tolerate with other men. In the real world, however, there were certainly so many variations and permutations in individual behaviour and lifestyles that historians could probably find many exceptions to any stereotype of what nineteenth-century Britain, especially Victorian Britain, was supposedly like.

Chapter Seven

The Political Nation, 1800–1914

In terms of its legal and constitutional forms, Britain changed less markedly between 1800 and 1914 than virtually any European nation. One might contrast the situation in Britain with that in France, which in the course of the nineteenth century transformed itself from a republic to an empire headed by an emperor, to a monarchy with broad monarchical powers, a constitutional monarchy, a republic, another empire with an emperor, and finally to a republic again, having experienced three revolutions and numerous attempted *coups d'état* along the way. By way of comparison, Britain had almost precisely the same formal institutions of government in 1914 as in 1800. Indeed, it is difficult to think of any formal change in the institutions of national governance which occurred in nineteenth-century Britain after the Act of Union with Ireland in 1801. Moreover, there was also a fair degree of genuine continuity in many of the informal institutions of British government: in 1800 Britain's actual executive consisted of a Cabinet headed by a prime minister, just as in 1914, while, by 1820, everyone knew that there was a Tory right-of-centre party (although it was not called the Conservative Party until the 1830s) and a liberal or radical party, then generally known as the Whigs. In 1914 these two parties still existed, broadly and with many permutations, as the descendants of the two earlier parties, now known officially as the Unionists and the Liberals. There was also something of a continuum among the families which produced a disproportionate number of the ministers in successive governments, mainly drawn from Britain's traditional landed aristocracy, although occasionally from families outside the aristocracy. For instance, Frederick John Robinson (1782– 1859), who entered Parliament in 1806, served as president of the Board of Trade and Chancellor of the Exchequer in the 1820s, was created Viscount Goderich in 1827 and briefly served as Britain's prime minister in 1827–8. In 1833 he became Earl of Ripon. Many decades later his son, the 2nd Earl (and 1st Marquess) of Ripon (1827–1909), served as Colonial Secretary in the Liberal government of 1892–5 and even continued to hold Cabinet office as Lord Privy Seal in 1905–8 in Sir Henry Campbell-Bannerman's Liberal government. The foremost political leader of the late Victorian period, Robert Gascoyne-Cecil, 3rd Marquess of Salisbury (1830–1903), was a direct descendant of Lord Burghley, Queen Elizabeth I's great minister, and some other leading politicians of this era – such as Lord Rosebery, the 8th Duke of Devonshire, Lord Randolph Churchill, and Arthur J. Balfour – could also trace their lineage back for many centuries.

To be sure, however, such evidence of continuity, impressive as it is, conceals far more than it reveals. The British political nation changed drastically and in many respects

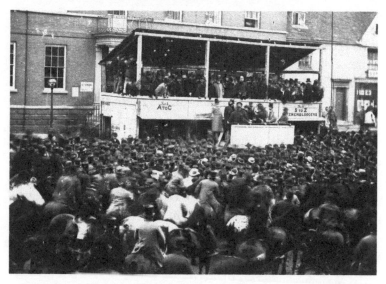

7. Hustings at Bury St Edmunds, 1865. Until 1872, voters in elections cast their votes in public by declaring aloud to an electoral officer the candidate for whom they wished to vote. Their name, and the name of the man for whom they voted, was then written down in 'Poll Books'. This was usually done on raised public platforms known as 'hustings'. From 1872 onwards, votes have been cast by secret ballot. Yet 'hustings', usually meaning the election campaign itself ('on the hustings') is still used.

fundamentally during the nineteenth century, probably far more than it had during the eighteenth century. During the nineteenth century Britain evolved from what for want of a better phrase might be termed a popular oligarchy, to a broadly based mass democracy in which most adult males had the vote and the nature of general elections and political leadership was, in many respects, recognisably similar to today.

While this process was continuous across the decades it has been common for historians to divide Britain's nineteenth-century political history into three different eras of approximately equal length, marked by different characteristics. The first, from the start of the century until the passage of the Great Reform Act of 1832, and which clearly forms a component of the 'long eighteenth century' (c.1660–1832), as it has come to be termed, was the last phase of what is sometimes called Britain's *ancien régime*, and was characterised by an aristocratic oligarchy but also, perhaps, by a consensual Tory rule which drew in much of the mercantile and professional middle classes. This period occurred during the reigns of King George III (1760–1820) and his son George IV (1820–30), who had previously held the legal powers of the sovereign as Prince Regent during his father's madness, in the years generally known as the Regency (1811–20). George IV was succeeded by his brother William IV (1830–7). The second period – lasting roughly from 1832 until the passage of the Second Reform Act of 1867 (or, perhaps, until Disraeli's famous Crystal Palace speech of 1872), often termed the Age of Reform – was marked by the ascendancy of laissez-faire, free trade, a series of key governmental reforms in the interests of modernised, liberal government, a fluctuating series of party alliances and governments, and a view of Britain's worldwide empire as secondary to the country's other international interests. The third period, roughly from 1867 (or 1872) until the outbreak of the First World War, is sometimes termed that of 'Imperialism and Social Reform', and was marked by the growth of a genuine mass political nation and modern parties, a mass press of growing importance, increasing awareness of poverty and inequality at home, with the enunciation of increasingly influential collectivist theories aimed at reducing poverty, and the centrality of the British Empire as crucially important to Britain's continuing great power status, even to its continuous existence.

This schema continues to be a fruitful way of viewing Britain's nineteenth-century political history, and will be used here to describe the broad political trends of the nineteenth

century. That profound changes occurred in Britain's governance during the century can also be illustrated by considering
many of the major political leaders in 1900. Such figures of
central importance as Joseph Chamberlain – arguably Britain's
most important political leader at the opening of the twentieth century – a Nonconformist manufacturer strongly
associated with an industrial city; Sir Henry Campbell-
Bannerman, a Scottish-born Manchester cotton manufacturer;
Herbert H. Asquith (1852–1928), a barrister who was the son
of a small Congregationalist woollen merchant in the West
Riding; or, still more, John Burns (1858–1943), in 1906 the first
working man to hold Cabinet office, could simply not have
risen to the top of British politics a century before or perhaps
fifty years before. These men and others of similar background, born with no connections to the traditional aristocracy
or governing circles, were able to rise only because of the profound political and social changes which had come over British
society during the nineteenth century. It can be argued that
what is known as the Edwardian period (technically 1901–10,
the years of the reign of King Edward VII, Queen Victoria's
son, but generally used for the years between 1901 and the
outbreak of the First World War in 1914) saw social class conflict enter British politics in a major way, with the 'New
Liberalism' that emerged at the end of the century aiming at
providing benefits to the working classes which were to be
paid for by taxing the well-off. At this time, however, both the
Liberal Party and the opposition Unionists increasingly looked
to collectivist measures of social improvement.

Although the schema used here is a fruitful one, there are
also other ways of viewing the 'long nineteenth century'.
Some historians see a broad continuity in British political culture from the eighteenth century until perhaps the mid-1880s.

The whole of the years before the 1880s saw a polity which revolved around a limited electorate, with Parliament always dominated by landed aristocrats in the Lords and their close relatives or associates in the Commons. From about the time of the Third Reform Act of 1884, in this view, the bases of British political life changed, with a genuine mass electorate and mass-based political parties replacing the former system. The old aristocracy, while it still existed and was certainly not negligible, became progressively less important than middle-class political leaders, and even a few working-class ones, who were able to organise mass constituencies around adversarial programmes, assisted by the mass popular press which arose for the first time in the 1890s and by mass political associations. British politics, according to this view, became dominated by rival collectivist visions, with the Liberal Party increasingly looking to progressive taxation and the Unionist (i.e. the Conservative) Party to a high tariff wall to raise revenue and exclude foreign imports, as the means of paying for a greatly enlarged state apparatus. This is also a fruitful way of viewing the 'long nineteenth century', and should be kept in mind.

While Parliament was dominated up until 1832 by the landed aristocracy and its close relatives, a significant number of self-made businessmen, wealthy professionals and East and West India 'nabobs' and merchants managed to get elected to the House of Commons. This was because the very small electorates in many borough seats were open to influence – or something like overt bribery – from any source, and wealthy businessmen regularly took advantage of this situation. Because of the continuing presence of businessmen in the pre-1832 House of Commons their number was not markedly higher after the 1832 Act, which supposedly gave political power to the middle classes. (There were about 179 businessmen in the House of Commons elected in 1830; 186 in 1831; and about 215 in 1832, in the first reformed Parliament.) That businessmen figure so prominently in the pre-reformed Parliament is evidence of what might be termed the consensual nature of the Tory government which dominated British political life between the 1780s and 1830. The *raison d'être* of pre-1832 Toryism was to augment Britain's national interests by increasing Britain's worldwide commercial greatness as well as by defending its traditional social structure and institutions, the landed interest, and a traditional 'church and king' vision of British patriotism.

Despite the unrest of the pre-1832 years, particularly the very troubled years between about 1815 and 1820, there was no British revolution and perhaps no really serious threat of one. That there 'should' have been a powerful revolutionary movement in industrialising Britain has long been a presupposition of radical and Marxist historians; indeed on even a superficial view it is somewhat surprising that no serious revolutionary effort occurred. One might suggest a number of reasons why no such movement came to Britain at this time, bearing in mind that few events in history which 'should' have occurred and did not were actually preordained. The aims of Britain's radicals at this time were primarily political in nature, chiefly aimed at the reform of Parliament and other institutions, rather than socioeconomic, lacking any concept of proto-socialist collectivism. Economic theory at the time revolved around removing state barriers and restrictions and establishing laissez-faire. A collectivist economic vision of society would not emerge until the time of Marx and Engels a generation later. Popular disturbances which were straightforwardly economic in nature – by food rioters or machine breakers – were often spontaneous and almost always

localised to a few communities. The French Revolution, with
the bloodbath of the Reign of Terror and dictatorial rule by
Bonaparte, deeply affected moderate opinion in Britain, alien-
ating many who might have been sympathetic to reform. The
British government was relentless and very effective in nipping
much serious popular protest in the bud, employing a network of spies, the apparatus of local and national government,
and severe punishments in a successful effort to suppress
insurrectionary movements.

No genuinely charismatic national radical leader emerged
who might have given such a movement a central focus. There
was also a religious dimension to the failure of the working
classes to rise up. Many historians, beginning with the great
early twentieth-century French historian of England Elie
Halévy, have credited the growing Methodist movement with
having prevented an English revolution during these years.
Wesleyanism was extremely hostile to radical political action
outside those channels which were legally permissible, and
gave consistent advice to its followers to obey legitimate
authority. So too did other forms of evangelicalism, including
the growing evangelical movement within the Church of
England, disseminated in countless tracts by influential writers such as Hannah More. With the possible exception of a
few fringe religious leaders, the whole body of organised religion in Britain, now of growing importance and popularity,
was set against radical, insurrectionary change, and especially
against anything which threatened to usher in the equivalent
of the French Revolution.

The Reform Act of 1832, the main product of the Whig
government of 1830–4 headed by Lord Grey, was, of course,
one of the most important pieces of legislation in British history. Briefly, it abolished nearly ninety 'rotten boroughs' – tiny

seats with virtually no inhabitants – and added 125 new seats in their place, generally in populous new areas of urban growth, but also in rural counties where (as was noted) the Whig landowners were strong and influential. Secondly, it rationalised the basis of the electorate, extending the vote, on the basis of the ownership or rental of houses or landed property, to much of the middle classes. In many respects, the Great Reform Act signalled a revolutionary change, although its limitations should be kept in mind. The electorate increased in size by an estimated 49 per cent, although 80 per cent of adult men (and all women) still lacked the vote. Large cities such as Bradford, Leeds and Sheffield received separate parliamentary representation for the first time (although its qualified inhabitants had previously voted in local county seats), but nothing had happened to the majority of parliamentary seats and, indeed, the influence of the great landowners remained the same or even grew. Most certainly, democracy was not introduced into Britain in 1832.

Perhaps the most important effects of the 1832 Reform Act were ancillary, creating the conditions and environment for a raft of other reform measures. For instance, in 1833–5 the Church of Ireland was reformed; the New Poor Law, which restricted welfare largely to the workhouse, was enacted; local government was rationalised; and a wider electoral system was introduced at the local level. Taxes on newspapers were greatly reduced and, in 1840 the first postage stamp was introduced. The spirit of the Age of Reform seemed to be predominantly liberal and utilitarian. Traditionally, it has been seen as benefiting the middle classes through a variety of measures aimed at reducing 'Old Corruption' (perquisites for aristocrats and their minions) and enhancing laissez-faire capitalism. On the other hand it is important to realise that the landed aristocracy and gentry certainly did not suffer as a result of the actual changes introduced during this time, and were probably just as politically important in the early 1860s as thirty years earlier. British liberalism in this period built on the foundations of Whig liberalism – religious freedom, freedom of the press, limits on the authority of the executive – to denote an attitude towards the role of government which wished to limit its authority to what was absolutely necessary, giving the maximum degree of liberty to the individual in most spheres, including the economic. A recognisable ideology of conservatism, based upon the veneration of traditional institutions and a mistrust of liberal and radical theorists and extremists, also grew up in the wake of Edmund Burke (1729–97) and later theorists.

1832–1867

The new political order left the Whig Party (increasingly known as the Liberal Party) in control of Parliament. At the 1832 general election, the first fought after the Reform Act, the Whig–Liberals gained 479 seats, the Tories only 179. Dominated by Whig aristocrats, the government enacted a string of reform measures noted above, such as the rationalisation of local government and the enactment of the New Poor Law. Yet Lord Grey and his successor as Whig prime minister, Lord Melbourne (in office 1835–41), soon came under a renewed strong challenge from the Tories, and in 1841 they were ousted by the Conservative Party (as it was now increasingly known, although they were – and are – also known as the Tories), now led by Sir Robert Peel (1788–1850), one of the great figures of nineteenth-century British politics. The son of a millionaire cotton manufacturer, but educated at Harrow and Oxford, he was a reforming Home Secretary in the 1820s, and had very briefly headed a minority Tory government in 1834–5. In 1834 Peel delivered what is known as the Tamworth Manifesto, in which he pledged future Conservative governments fully to accept the Reform Act and, indeed, to introduce 'careful' measures of reform aimed at 'the correction of proved abuses'. Peel thus began a long tradition wherein the Conservative Party almost always accepted reform measures introduced by radical governments; the post-1832 Tory Party would not aim at (as it were) turning the clock back, and – unlike Continental right-wing movements – would accept increasing democracy and careful measures of reform.

Peel's formula proved very popular with moderate Liberals, who remained wary of extremist tendencies in their party. On the other hand, this stance threatened to alienate many on the right wing of the Conservative Party, especially conservative landowners, who often believed that they had been weakened by reform, and who also feared the removal of tariff protection entailed in the mid-1840s by the repeal of the Corn Laws. While no one doubted Peel's competence, he was also seen as unusually supercilious and lacking in the common touch. Peel became prime minister in 1841 at a time of renewed economic difficulties: the decade is often known as the 'hungry forties'. While economic growth, especially the 'railway mania' of the decade, certainly existed, the rapid rise in Britain's population, especially in the urban slums, arguably engendered a considerable increase in poverty, while shortly afterwards Ireland experienced its catastrophic famine. In the late 1830s a new radical mass movement arose, known as Chartism because of its charter, advocating universal male suffrage and annual elections. Strikes and radical violence increased, and a repetition of the situation of mass unrest of the 1815–20 period seemed probable.

While forcefully repressing violent unrest, Peel believed that some very basic measure of reform, aimed at improving the living standards of the working classes, was necessary. In 1845 Peel became convinced, through a consideration of pro-laissez-faire economic arguments, that the best hope for rising living standards lay in the repeal of the Corn Laws. ('Corn' in England is the term given to what would elsewhere be known as wheat, the basic component of bread, at the time the main foodstuff of the working classes.) In order to protect British landowners and farmers, a tariff had long existed on the importation of corn from overseas. This kept the profits of the agricultural sector high, but also artificially increased the price of bread. Peel, a convinced Free Trader (as advocates of the removal of tariffs were known), was won over to the view that Repeal (as repeal of the Corn Laws was known) would have profoundly beneficial effects for working-class standards of living. According to its proponents, by reducing the cost of bread, it would also enable factory owners and manufacturers to cut wages (at least marginally), lower the cost of their products, and compete more successfully in international trade. Peel thus foresaw a commonality of interests between the middle classes, especially in manufacturing, and the urban working classes. The drive for Repeal was also aided by an efficient and powerful free-trade lobby, headed by Richard Cobden (1810–65) and John Bright (1811–89), two manufacturers whose names became synonymous with Victorian free-trade liberalism. Unfortunately for Peel, most Tory backbench MPs were landowners who were opposed to Repeal. Early in 1846, after a lengthy national debate, the Corn Laws were repealed. Peel managed to obtain the votes of 113 Conservative MPs, but 242 of his party voted against him. Peel fell from power in June 1846.

8. The great Chartist meeting at Kennington Common, in south London, held in 1848, the year of revolution throughout Europe. Chartism was a radical movement to establish democracy in Britain by enacting the 'People's Charter'. This remarkable photograph, taken by police while the meeting was being held, is regarded as the earliest photograph to be taken of an historical event as it actually occurred. It was unknown until it was discovered in 1977.

Within a few years, this split in the Conservative Party became permanent: Peel and the 'Peelites', those Tory parliamentarians who followed him, increasingly sided with the Whig–Liberal opposition, with most eventually joining them on a permanent basis. The fight over Repeal also helped bring to pre-eminence the two most famous politicians of the next generation. One of Peel's most talented deputies, who loyally followed him, was William Ewart Gladstone. Originally a right-wing Tory, enormously gifted, from a mercantile family background somewhat similar to Peel's and a product of Eton and Oxford, Gladstone moved steadily to the political left, becoming, by the late 1860s, the renowned leader of Victorian Liberalism. The Peelites included most of the younger men of

talent in the Conservative Party, creating a vacuum of leadership and ability. Into this void stepped the man who was
unquestionably the most implausible British political leader
of the nineteenth century, Benjamin Disraeli, eventually
Gladstone's great rival. Disraeli, a London Jew who became an
Anglican as a teenager, was a celebrated novelist, but unconnected by birth, marriage, education or lifestyle with the party
of landowners he eventually led. Disraeli had first attempted to
enter Parliament as a radical – like Gladstone he was initially on
the 'wrong' side of political life – but became one of the greatest intellectual and political figures of nineteenth-century
British conservatism. He was at this time a backbencher,
becoming one of the leaders of the Conservative Party in the
House of Commons a few years after Peel's resignation. The
residuum of the Tories in Parliament was officially headed,
from 1846 until 1868, by their leader in the House of Lords, the
14th Earl of Derby (1799–1868), who was known from 1846 to
1851 as Lord Stanley.

The next twenty-two years saw the Whigs, increasingly
with the assistance of the former Peelite Conservatives, dominate British political life under a series of aristocratic prime
ministers. Lord John Russell (1792–1878) was prime minister
in 1846–52 and again in 1865–6. Russell, the younger son of
the Duke of Bedford, introduced the Reform Act into the
House of Commons and was a consistent supporter of Whig
liberalism, the introduction and furtherance of liberal measures of reform by the Whig aristocracy and its supporters.
Britain's prime minister in 1852–5 was George Hamilton-
Gordon, 4th Earl of Aberdeen (1784–1869), a former Tory and
then leader of the Peelites in the House of Lords. His government, in which Gladstone served as Chancellor of the
Exchequer, signalled the movement of many Peelites into the

Whig–Liberal camp. Britain's longest-serving prime minister during this period was Henry John Temple, 3rd Viscount Palmerston (1784–1865): a colourful, outspoken, moderate Whig who had first held government office in 1807, he was known for his rousing (some would say bombastic) assertions of British patriotism. As Foreign Secretary in 1850, Palmerston had staunchly defended gunboat diplomacy against Greece when the house in Athens of a British citizen of Portuguese–Jewish background, 'Don Pacifico' (David Pacifico) had been pillaged by a mob, concluding 'As the Roman, in days of old . . . could say "*Civis Romanus sum* [I am a citizen of Rome]", so also a British subject, in whatever land he may be, shall feel confident that the watchful eye and strong arm of England will protect him against injustice and wrong.' Palmerston's stirring words became immensely popular with middle-class Britain, even those normally very lukewarm about the use of military force. As prime minister for nearly ten years, Palmerston did oversee the use of military force on several occasions. His government was responsible for the suppression of the Indian Mutiny in 1857–8, and for the Chinese War of 1857–8, but remained pointedly neutral during the American Civil War of 1861–5, despite considerable pressure to recognise the South's independence.

The one major war of this period was fought not by Palmerston but by his predecessor, Lord Aberdeen. In 1854, in an effort to keep the Ottoman Empire (Turkey) neutral and out of Russian hands, Britain and France declared war on Russia, sending a large contingent of men to southern Russia in what became known as the Crimean War, which lasted until 1856. This strange and destructive affair, which was 'won' by Britain and France in the sense that the peace treaty at the war's end guaranteed Turkish neutrality, is famous for a number of rather unenviable reasons. The incompetence and generally poor military leadership of the British troops led to the celebrated Charge of the Light Brigade at Balaclava in the Crimea in October 1854. Britain's heavy casualties brought lasting fame to the renowned nurse sent to Constantinople to attend to wounded British hospitalised there, Florence Nightingale (1820–1910), 'the lady with the lamp'. Journalism took a quantitative leap forward with the reporting by the *Times* correspondent in Crimea, William Howard Russell, whose brutally frank reports of appalling conditions, tele-graphed back to England in a few hours, created a sensation. The conflict also engendered probably the first anti-war move-ment in the modern sense, led by John Bright, the Free Trader and a Quaker. The war did, however, arguably check Russian expansionism into the Ottoman areas for several generations. The Aberdeen government's handling of the war proved so unpopular that he fell from office. He was replaced by Lord Palmerston, who had not held office under Aberdeen. This era also saw three minority Tory 'Protectionist' governments briefly holding office for three short periods, composed of the anti-free-trade core of the Conservative Party. The Protectionists (that is, those in favour of a tariff) first held office in 1852 under Lord Derby; this government is famous as the first in which Disraeli served as a minister, as Chancellor of the Exchequer, and, despite its name, for not re-enacting a tariff. The minority Tories were in power again in 1858–9, and finally in 1866–8. In February 1868, after Derby's retirement, Disraeli became prime minister for the first time. The third minority Tory government enacted the Second Reform Act in 1867.

Governance and public debate about governance during the period 1832–67 is seen by many historians as the zenith of national debate and careful discussion by informed members of the intelligentsia and politicians who acted in the national interest rather than in their party's interests. Famed writers such as Macaulay and Bulwer-Lytton actually held Cabinet posts; Disraeli, the leader of the Tories, was one of the greatest novelists of his age, while Gladstone, leader of the Liberals, wrote many books on topics ranging from Homer to theology; John Stuart Mill, the great philosopher, sat in Parliament in 1865–8. This period also probably marked the zenith of the intellectual journal of informed debate such as the *Fortnightly Review* and the *Westminster Review*. Most, if not all, of the great debates and movements of opinion of the time were carried on by well-informed, often brilliant, intellectual amateurs, rather than by university academics. Strikingly, the proponents of the theory of evolution – Charles Darwin, Alfred Russel Wallace, Thomas Huxley and Herbert Spencer – had little or nothing to do with the established universities during their careers (although Huxley held professorships for several years at two London medical schools). Many attributed these circumstances to the political conditions which existed between the 1832 and 1867 Reform Acts, when only a minority of propertied men held the vote, before the political process was corrupted by a mass press and well-organised party machines, and while the existence of the Peelites meant that no government was necessarily safe for a full parliamentary term.

The years from about 1850 until 1867 are also sometimes known as the 'age of equipoise', the height of Britain's mid-Victorian stability and prosperity. Britain avoided the revolutions which erupted throughout Europe in 1848, cleverly and decisively crushing any violent unrest from the Chartists or other radicals. The mood of stability was symbolised by London's Great Exhibition of 1851, the first 'world's fair', at which the fruits of British and foreign industry were displayed. In part a brainchild of Prince Albert, it has been seen as ushering in two decades of prosperity and rising living standards, and was emblematic of how industria-lisation, the growth of the railways, and other modern developments, had now improved working-class living stan-dards and introduced peace and prosperity.

In political terms, this mood of stability was to change in 1867. It was widely recognised in public commentary at this time that sooner or later a much larger percentage of adult males would have to be given the vote, and that the great cities were still under-represented at the expense of small towns and rural areas. The death of Palmerston in 1865 also seemed to presage the end of a long parliamentary truce. It was Disraeli and the Tories, in their third minority government, who brought in the Second Reform Act. Disraeli firmly believed that the lower middle classes of smaller shopkeepers and tradesmen, and the superior working classes, likely to be given the vote in any future reform, were probably more pro-Tory than their social superiors. The possibility of reform also attracted the fierce opposition of a group of conservative Whig politicians and intellectuals, headed by Robert Lowe, formerly the minister responsible for education, which became known as the 'Cave of Adullam', men who (in Carlyle's phrase) thought that enfranchising a component of the working classes would constitute 'shooting Niagara', going over the waterfalls in a barrel. Nevertheless, Disraeli and the Tories proceeded to enfranchise virtually all male householders and lodgers in boroughs, took fifty-two seats away from very small boroughs and gave new or increased representation to large and middle-sized towns. The size of the electorate was increased by 88 per cent, although about two thirds of adult males in England, Wales and Scotland, and five sixths in Ireland, were still not entitled to vote. If, however, Disraeli expected immediate political gains from his move, he was doomed to disappointment. In the general election held in 1868, just after the passage of the Second Reform Act, the Liberals scored strong gains in Scotland, Wales and Ireland (although not in England) and found themselves with a majority of 106. Gladstone now took office as prime minister for the first time.

1867–1900

There is agreement among many historians that the last third of the nineteenth century was the period when a recognisably modern political culture came into existence in Britain, with the 1880s often seen as a decisive turning point. This evolution came about in large measure as a result of both the Second and, perhaps more importantly, the Third Reform Act in 1884, which created a largely class-based electoral geography. By the early twentieth century a British electoral geography based mostly on social class was well established: middle-class seats were mainly Tory, working-class seats on the whole Liberal (or, in some areas, Labour). There were some variations in this pattern due to regional peculiarities or personal factors (for instance, the personal ascendancy of Joseph Chamberlain in Birmingham) but the overall picture is well documented. The fact that the electorate became so large necessitated the establishment of mass political machines and organisations, and enhanced the position of the leaders of the major parties as something more than first among equals. This apparent modernisation of politics was also augmented by such factors as the growth of a mass newspaper press, and of such institutions as the trade unions and of lobbying groups on behalf of special interests.

Gladstone's government of 1868–74 is usually seen as the greatest of the four ministries he headed. Although his Cabinet did not differ too markedly from previous Whig–Liberal governments, it was the first to have a significant representation from middle-class businessmen and professionals, including Protestant Nonconformists, which reflected the heightened importance of the middle classes among all Liberal MPs. Gladstone also had an agenda of reform, which included the disestablishment of the Church of Ireland, discussed earlier, along with Irish land reform, and the reform of the elementary education system of England and Wales. The Education Act of 1870 created Boards of Education and required all children to be educated to the age of thirteen. It outlawed religiously sectarian education in state schools. In a separate act, Oxford and Cambridge universities were opened to non-Anglicans. The army and the law courts were reformed and, by the Ballot Act of 1872, voting by secret ballot became the rule at all elections. Previously voting was in public, with the voter openly stating the candidate for whom he voted. This was held to be more honest and honourable than secret voting. To those who supported the secret ballot, however, it was felt that this procedure could be used by employers or landlords to penalise those who voted the 'wrong' way, although in practice the Ballot Act probably made little difference. After this spate of legislation, there was a widespread feeling among political commentators and politicians, which continued for perhaps another quarter-century, that reformist mid-Victorian Liberalism had run its course. The 'radical programme' of the 1880s, as it was termed, centred around such matters as the possible disestablishment of the Church of England and temperance reform, both strongly favoured by Nonconformists. These were more decisive than other reform measures and attracted much less support, even within the Liberal Party. Only with the growth of the so-called 'New Liberalism' at the end of the century, with its quasi-collectivist presaging of the welfare state, did the Liberal Party again develop a potentially nationally popular agenda.

The sense that Liberalism had run its course worked to the advantage of the Conservative Party. At the general election of 1874 Disraeli and his party won a large majority. The English middle classes, perhaps frightened by Gladstone's Irish policies, now gave a significant majority of their votes to the Tories, with the City of London (which elected four MPs) moving decisively into the Tory camp. Almost as many English borough seats went to the Tories as to the Liberals, justifying Disraeli's faith in the conservative instincts of much of the lower-middle-class and superior working-class voters enfranchised in 1867.

Disraeli's government lasted for six years and is known for a raft of social legislation which is often said to have introduced what in the twentieth century became known as 'One Nation Toryism' into the centre of Conservative Party policy, where it remained for a century. Disraeli wished to mark out a social policy agenda which was seemingly to the left of the Liberals, for whom laissez-faire liberalism remained in the ascendancy. Disraeli (and his Home Secretary R. A. Cross, who was responsible for much of this legislation) gave greater legal recognition to the trade unions, made slum clearance possible through an Artisans' Dwelling Act, and improved public health, river pollution and safety aboard British ships through enacting the famous 'Plimsoll line' on merchant vessels. The government did not, however, go beyond this, and did not, for instance, introduce any form of national insurance as Bismarck's right-wing government did in Germany. In foreign policy, Disraeli's government achieved a triumph at the Congress of Berlin, which again guaranteed Turkish independence and secured Cyprus for the British Empire. Previous to the congress, Britain came close to war with Russia over events in the decaying Turkish Empire in the Balkans, and a pro-war mood gripped much of England, symbolised by the famous music-hall song which began 'We don't want to fight / But by jingo if we do . . .'. 'Jingoism', outspoken xenophobia, entered the language of political abuse. That the mid-Victorian mood of Little Englandism had changed was also symbolised by the enactment of the Royal Titles Act of 1876, which gave Queen Victoria the title of Empress of India (but no additional or revised powers), thus declaring Britain to be at the head of an officially recognised empire. The British monarch was officially to remain Emperor (or Empress) of India until independence was granted to the subcontinent in 1947.

Disraeli signalled his fundamental changes in policy in a number of well-known speeches in London and Manchester in 1872 at which he expounded the need for 'social improvement' and the virtues of the British Empire, even foreshadowing the establishment of a 'representative council' for the whole empire in London. 'Imperialism and Social Reform' increasingly became the watchwords of both parties by the end of the century.

Yet Disraeli's popularity plummeted in the last two years of his great government. He was old and ill (from 1876 he sat in the House of Lords as Earl of Beaconsfield) and his government apparently ran out of steam in domestic legislation.

Worse, a severe depression, affecting both industry and agriculture, began in 1878–9, which undermined his government's popularity. Gladstone brought the spotlight upon himself through the so-called Midlothian Campaign, a series of popular speeches and mass meetings in and near Edinburgh in 1879–80, where Gladstone was campaigning for the forthcoming general election. Gladstone put international morality and religion at the centre of his campaign, denouncing the so-called 'Bulgarian Atrocities' carried out by the Turks against the Christians of the Balkans, and thus attacking Disraeli's defence of Turkey at the Congress of Berlin. The campaign, which was organised by Lord Rosebery, Gladstone's successor as prime minister in 1894, is often seen as the first modern election drive, at which the leader of a party seeks national attention for himself and his views. (It might be worth noting that, by tradition, peers cannot become directly engaged in an election campaign; this tradition debarred both Disraeli, now an earl, and his successor Lord Salisbury, from responding successfully.) The Midlothian Campaign succeeded brilliantly. As a result, Gladstone and the Liberals found themselves back in power at the 1880 general election, where they remained until 1885. Gladstone's second government, it has often been noted, had fewer achievements than his first, and was increasingly dominated by the Irish issue.

These years also saw the beginnings of a collectivist movement, fanned by the success of Henry George's famous book *Progress and Poverty* (1879), which advocated a single tax on land, and by the formation of the Fabian Society and the Social Democratic Federation (SDF), both in 1884. The Fabian Society, founded by intellectuals such as Sidney and Beatrice Webb and George Bernard Shaw, advocated the gradual growth of collectivist measures in the interests of an efficient and rational society. The SDF, founded by the writer H. M. Hyndman (1842–1921), organised working-class rallies and demonstrations involving tens of thousands of protestors. Although some mainstream Liberals such as Joseph Chamberlain were now advocating moderate redistribution, these movements as yet had little major impact on British politics, and nor did the death in London in 1883 of Karl Marx who wrote *Das Kapital* (published in three volumes, starting in 1867 and ending in 1895 after Marx's death) in the British Museum.

Despite these harbingers of collectivism, Gladstone's second government was still centrally concerned with completing the nineteenth-century British reform agenda. In 1884 it passed the Third Reform Act, which gave the vote to agricultural labourers and most other adult males missed by the two previous Reform Acts, and further redistributed seats in Parliament to urban areas on the basis of population. The 1884 Reform Act greatly increased the size of the electorate, which, it is estimated, grew in England and Wales from 2.6 million to 4.4 million, and gave much more real political influence to the poorer classes than before. That Britain now had something like a mass democracy was increasingly recognised by the two major parties. They began the organisation of mass parties in the modern sense, with annual party conferences, an infrastructure of party agents responsible to each party's central office, the enrolment and mass canvassing of voters, and the like. Although these had existed skeletally before, from the mid-1880s it became an absolute prerequisite for electoral victory to arouse enthusiasm among one's potential supporters across the nation. Each party developed a network of newspapers, both national and local, normally supportive of it, which, as newspaper circulation grew, made the great 'press lords' who owned these newspapers ever more influential. Both parties also used armies of volunteer workers – increasingly women, especially among the Tories – and rewarded wealthy donors with peerages and knighthoods. Both parties became recognisably identified with ideologically based agendas and drew their support from different types of constituencies, the Tories from the middle classes and (most but not all) rural areas, the Liberals from the working classes, many Nonconformists, and the Celtic areas. In many respects, the Third Reform Act marked a major departure from the assumptions of informed government by qualified voters underpinning the period after 1832, although it was generally seen at the time as following naturally and inevitably from the two previous Reform Acts. It did not attract as much heated controversy as did the 1832 and 1867 Reform Acts.

The mid-1880s were increasingly dominated by Gladstone's proposal for Irish Home Rule, described above. After the 1885 general election and before he was converted to Home Rule, Gladstone was defeated on a vote of no confidence after the Irish MPs voted with the Tories, and the Conservatives formed a minority government headed by their new leader Lord Salisbury, a skilful, very intelligent and cynical politician whose main forte was his mastery of foreign policy. Salisbury had succeeded to the leadership on Disraeli's death in 1881. In domestic policy he was almost equally adept, and gradually emerged as the dominant political leader of the last fifteen years of the century. A general election in late 1885 produced a Liberal win, although with the Tories and Irish just able to bring down the government if they combined. Gladstone now formed his third government, which lasted for six months in 1886. It was then that Gladstone attempted to introduce Irish Home Rule, with the disastrous results discussed above. After

Gladstone was defeated in the House of Commons, another general election was held in July 1886 which resulted in the Tories winning 316 seats, the Liberals only 190, the Liberal Unionists seventy-nine, and the Irish Nationalists eighty-five.

Salisbury now formed his second administration, which lasted until 1892. Although it could be defeated if the opposition parties combined, the Liberal Unionists – former Liberals, headed by Joseph Chamberlain and Lord Hartington who were opposed to Home Rule – never rejoined Gladstone's party, but increasingly became open allies of the Conservatives. The two groups, the Tories and Liberal Unionists, were usually referred to in the press as the 'Unionists', i.e. those favouring the continued union of Britain and Ireland. The Liberal Unionists also brought with them most of the Whig and Liberal landed aristocracy and gentry, and much of the upper middle classes, especially in London, such that by 1900 the Unionists were the normal party of Britain's Establishment, which the Conservative Party had not previously been. Salisbury's government lasted until 1892, and was marked by policies of moderate reform, including a reform of local government in London and the counties. This was the period of Queen Victoria's golden jubilee in 1887, marked by spontaneous outpourings of patriotic fervour, and by an unusual number of scandals and sensations played for all they were worth by the mass press: the divorce scandals of Sir Charles Dilke, a leading radical politician in 1885, and Charles Stewart Parnell (cited in a divorce case in 1891); the spectacular resignation of Lord Randolph Churchill, the Chancellor of the Exchequer, at the end of 1886; the death of General Charles 'Chinese' Gordon at the hands of the Mahdi (a Muslim religious and political leader) in the Sudan in 1885 and the suppression of the Mahdi's forces by Horatio (later Lord) Kitchener; and the horrifying Jack the Ripper murders in 1888, regarded as the first serial killings. Many thought that 'Victorianism' had ended well before the end of the queen's reign.

There were two more general elections in the nineteenth century, in 1892 and 1895. In 1892 Gladstone briefly returned at the head of a minority Liberal government for the fourth time. He again attempted to pass an Irish Home Rule bill, which was defeated in the House of Lords. In March 1894 Gladstone finally retired and was succeeded, for fifteen months, by Lord Rosebery, a brilliant, wealthy 'golden boy' who had become Foreign Secretary at the age of thirty-eight. Already unsympathetic to most of his colleagues, he resigned amidst much bitterness. Rosebery, a pro-imperialist moderate, never held office again, but was long regarded as a potential 'prime-minister-in-waiting'. In the general election which followed, the Unionist scored a sweeping victory. Lord Salisbury formed his third administration, making his nephew Arthur Balfour (1848–1930) First Lord of the Treasury (head of the government in the House of Commons) and bringing several Liberal Unionist leaders into the Cabinet, most notably the Duke of Devonshire (formerly Lord Hartington) as Lord President of the Council and Joseph Chamberlain as Colonial Secretary. Although seemingly a middle-ranking post, the Colonial Secretaryship became, under Chamberlain, arguably the focal point of the government, and was used by him to expand the British Empire, especially in South Africa. There, a long-running and controversial feud with the Boers in their independent republics, fanned by the discovery of gold and diamonds, led in 1899 to the outbreak of the Boer War (or Second South African War). It continued until May 1902, when Britain, after many travails, annexed the Boer republics. The last five years of the century marked the zenith of the British

Empire and of patriotic imperialism, as evidenced by the queen's diamond jubilee celebrations in 1897, whose lavishness outdid the festivities for her golden jubilee a decade earlier. Although the death of Queen Victoria in January 1901, and the succession of her eldest son Edward VII, are generally seen as marking the end of an era, in fact policies, ideologies, expectations and political conflicts continued as before.

1901–1914

In the wake of the patriotic enthusiasm aroused by the Boer War, the Unionists scored another sweeping electoral victory in the autumn of 1900, winning a general election with 402 seats to only 184 for the Liberals and eighty-two for the Irish Nationalists. At this stage, the Tories appeared impregnable, while the Liberals, racked by bitter internal divisions and without a recognised leader, appeared doomed to indefinite opposition. (Lord Rosebery was, formally, leader of the Liberal Party until early 1896 when he resigned in favour of his bitter rival Sir William V. Harcourt, who was replaced by Sir Henry Campbell-Bannerman in 1898. Campbell-Bannerman, who was sixty-four in 1900, was widely seen as a stop-gap leader until a younger, more commanding head arose.) In July 1902 Lord Salisbury retired as prime minister. Probably the dominant political leader of his time, he was replaced, without opposition, by his nephew Arthur Balfour. Balfour, a brilliant and wealthy Cambridge-educated politician and philosopher (his works on philosophy are still highly regarded), took office in circumstances possibly more favourable than virtually any recent prime minister entering office for the first time. On 31 May 1902, a few months earlier, the Boer War had ended with a British victory over the Boer republics. Yet within a year or two the situation of the Unionist Party had disintegrated beyond recognition.

There were several causes for this remarkable and sudden decline. In May 1903 Joseph Chamberlain, the Colonial Secretary who took the country into the Boer War, made one of the most important speeches of the age, in which he announced his conversion to 'Imperial Preference', the erection of a tariff wall around the whole British Empire, to exclude cheap foreign goods, and to finance measures of social reform by 'making the foreigner pay' rather than through increasing direct taxation on the well-off. Although both Germany and the United States had prospered exceedingly behind high tariff walls, so great was the force of the doctrine of free trade in Britain – it was often compared to a religion – that Chamberlain's proposals amounted to a fundamental break with the basic economic policies of Britain as they had existed during the previous sixty years. At this time, Chamberlain occupied a position in British politics arguably without parallel in the post-1832 world. He was widely regarded as the most powerful man in the Cabinet, and was probably the best-known politician in Britain, despite holding only a middle-ranking office as Colonial Secretary. Chamberlain's speech was made without seeking Balfour's approval; there has been no parallel in modern British politics to a middle-ranking Cabinet minister positing a most fundamental change of British policy without securing the approval of the prime minister and Cabinet.

Chamberlain's speech set off a tidal wave of controversy and debate. He resigned from the Cabinet in October 1903 to lead a great movement for tariff reform, and quickly organised a group of enthusiastic supporters, for whom tariff reform and imperial unity became core beliefs, as well as a Tariff

Reform League to further his cause. But he also aroused bitter hostility, leading to the resignation of several of his senior Cabinet colleagues who favoured free trade. Chamberlain's proposals also served to unite the Liberal Party, who, virtually to a man, remained strong opponents of tariffs. Balfour, the prime minister, attempted to meet Chamberlain's difficult challenge by prevarication. In October 1903 he appointed Chamberlain's elder son, Austen Chamberlain (1863–1937), as Chancellor of the Exchequer, but also appointed a strong Free Trader, Victor Cavendish, as his deputy. Balfour, a moderate but not fanatical supporter of tariff reform, was faced with a very difficult task: nevertheless, his handling of his government during the last two years of his premiership is generally viewed as inept. As noted, tariff reform immediately unified the Liberal Party, which, in conjunction with pro-free-trade elements, organised a campaign to fight Chamberlain's proposals. Central to their opposition was the contention that tariff reform would mean a tax on bread and other basic foods, which would fall most heavily on the working classes. The 'tax on bread' claim would prove fatal to tariff reform whenever it became central to the Tories' electoral proposals, as it did in 1905 and again in 1923.

Other important factors also served to undermine the Unionists' position. In 1901 there occurred the famous legal case *Taff Vale Railway Co.* v. *Amalgamated Society of Railway Servants*. The Taff Vale decision, as it became known, made it legal for a company to sue a trade union for damages and losses incurred during a strike, reversing the immunity unions had enjoyed since the 1870s and inflicting a potentially crippling blow on the trade union movement. Reversing the Taff Vale decision became a major aim of the union movement, advantaging the Liberal Party. Another major cause of Tory unpopularity was the Education Act of 1902, which had given enlarged powers to local authorities to provide secondary education. However, this brought the voluntary (i.e. religious-based) schools under the authority of local governments, using ratepayers' money, for the first time, to pay their teachers. This greatly alienated opinion among Nonconformists who launched a great campaign against the payment of rates (local taxes) to pay for what were normally Anglican schools. Nonconformist and evangelical Anglican opinion was also aroused by the growth of High Church, quasi-Catholic practice within the Church of England. In 1904–5 there also occurred a significant religious revivalist movement within the Nonconformist churches, especially in Wales. Many Nonconformists became bitterly hostile to the Tory government and supportive of a revived Liberal Party.

Nevertheless, Balfour viewed the Liberal Party as hopelessly divided, in particular between the so-called 'Liberal Imperialist' champions of Empire, whose parliamentary leaders included the future prime minister Herbert H. Asquith and Sir Edward Grey (1856–1928), and the so-called 'Little Englanders', who were more radical and generally uneasy with 'jingoist' policies. Their supporters included the leader of the Liberal Party, Sir Henry Campbell-Bannerman, and a radical solicitor from Wales, David Lloyd George, both of whom had been opponents of the Boer War. In December 1905, faced with increased unrest within his own party, and acting under the assumption that the Liberals would be unable to form a viable minority government, Balfour resigned, although he still enjoyed a working majority in Parliament.

Sir Henry Campbell-Bannerman now became prime minister, and found surprisingly little difficulty in forming a Liberal government which was both stable and able. Asquith became Chancellor of the Exchequer, Grey Foreign Secretary, and Lloyd George president of the Board of Trade. This famous government included many men who would make a lasting mark on British political life, among them the thirty-one-year old Winston Churchill (1874–1965), who was appointed Undersecretary for the Colonies. The son of Lord Randolph Churchill, Winston had entered politics as a Conservative but had become disenchanted with a range of Unionist policies, especially tariff reform, and, in 1904, joined the Liberal Party. Campbell-Bannerman then called a general election, held early in 1906. The 1906 general election resulted in a great victory for the Liberal party, entirely reversing the former political dominance of the Unionists. The Liberals won 400 seats compared with only 157 Unionists. In addition, thirty Labour MPs were elected as well as twenty-two so-called 'Lib-Lab' members officially counted with the Liberals. This phalanx of more than fifty Labour MPs was widely regarded as the most important – and, to many, unnerving – result of the election. To the anti-Tory majority in Parliament had also to be added eighty-three Irish Nationalist MPs, making an impregnable left-of-centre majority unknown since the 1832 election. While the British electoral system greatly exaggerated the actual scale of defeat suffered by the Unionists, who secured 44 per cent of the total vote, 1906 certainly marked a major climacteric in British political history.

While Campbell-Bannerman was prime minister, the Liberal government was largely Gladstonian and fiscally orthodox in its policies, and actually cut overall government expenditure. It reversed the Taff Vale decision, and in 1908 introduced the first old-age pensions (of up to five shillings – 25p – per week, perhaps £15 today, paid to those aged seventy or more), but otherwise did not differ very markedly from previous Liberal governments, and certainly did not engender radical changes. Modernisation of the army, brought about by the War Secretary Richard Haldane, was one of the few measures for which it is remembered. In April 1908 Campbell-Bannerman died, and was replaced as prime minister by H. H. Asquith. Asquith's appointment (he served until December 1916) ushered in a period of vigorous and radical measures for which the Edwardian Liberal government became famous. In particular, we associate these measures with David Lloyd George, who became Chancellor of the Exchequer, serving in the post until May 1915, and with the appointment of other reforming ministers, including Winston Churchill, who entered the Cabinet this time as president of the Board of Trade.

The Asquith government proceeded to adopt a number of quasi-collectivist measures associated with the New Liberalism, which were to be paid for by increased direct taxation of the well-off, and which were accompanied by left-wing rhetoric previously unknown. Probably the most important was the National Insurance Act of 1911, which provided unemployment insurance to manual workers in heavy industry. The trade unions were given increased rights, and were brought visibly into the affairs of governance, being frequently consulted by the government. Lloyd George, in particular, launched extravagant rhetorical attacks on the House of Lords and the aristocracy which was seen as keen to block most radical measures, most notably in a speech in Limehouse, east London, in July 1909 which was couched virtually in terms of class warfare. Aware of the growing likelihood of war in Europe, the government also greatly increased spending on the Royal Navy, which was widely seen as Britain's shield against a German attack. To finance both welfare and naval spending, in 1909 Lloyd George proposed a greatly increased budget, known as the 'People's Budget', which was to be paid for by seven new taxes, most of which were to fall on the rich and upper middle classes, especially landowners. The People's Budget also set the stage for a show-down with the House of Lords, which in November 1909 threw it out.

The Liberals now called a general election, held in January 1910, which produced an indecisive result, the Liberals gaining 275 MPs compared with 273 Tories, forty Labour, and eighty-two Irish Nationalists. While the Liberals still enjoyed a working majority, it was dependent upon the votes of the Irish MPs, whose long-standing demands for Home Rule it had ignored between 1905 and 1910. In May 1910 Edward VII died, and his son George V came to the throne. A strict martinet very different in personality from his *bon vivant* father, he nevertheless proved to be an excellent and very popular king, and was universally respected during his reign. After 1918, as one of the few surviving European monarchs of a major nation, he became a great symbol of continuity and of unity throughout the British Empire.

In order to pass the People's Budget and other legislation the Lords was likely to block, Asquith had to secure a promise from the new king to create hundreds of new peers who would give the Liberals a majority in the Upper House. He secured this promise, but only if another general election were held first. The Liberals then called a general election for December 1910, which resulted in a virtually identical result to the one held in January of that year: 272 Tories, 272 Liberals, forty-two Labour, eigty-four Irish Nationalists. In August 1911, after a terrific struggle, the government passed the Parliament Bill, which took away the right of the House of

Lords to reject money bills (such as the People's Budget) and limited the power of the Lords to delay passage of any other bill passed by the House of Commons to two years. This second proviso was enacted in order to deny the Lords the power to veto any new Irish Home Rule bill, making the passage of such a measure almost inevitable. The government did not, however, alter the composition of the Lords or further reform the Upper House, as many radicals demanded. As prime minister, Asquith created sixty-one new peers, many wealthy Liberal businessmen, finding, like all prime ministers, the patronage powers of creating honours and titles irresistibly useful. The composition of the Lords was, in fact, not altered in a serious way until 1999, when most (not all) hereditary peers lost their seats.

The three years before the outbreak of the war focused politically on the Irish question, which once again took centre stage in British political life. Dependent upon the votes of the Irish Nationalist MPs for its political survival, the Asquith government was forced to attempt to enact an Irish Home Rule bill. But, even more than in the past, this provoked the adamant hostility of the Ulster Protestants, who opposed Irish Home Rule and, at the very least, wished Ulster to be excluded from any Home Rule Act, something which the Liberals consistently refused. Yet more than before the Ulster Protestants were supported by a reinvigorated Unionist (Tory) Party. After losing three general elections, Balfour was forced to resign as leader in November 1911 (although he would continue to hold senior Cabinet positions until 1929). His replacement, a compromise choice, was a wholly unexpected one: Andrew Bonar Law, a competent, dour Canadian-born Scottish businessman with strong links to Ulster. Bonar Law served as prime minister for seven months in 1922–3 and is often referred to as the 'unknown prime minister', but he is widely regarded by historians as an unusually accomplished political leader who revivified the Unionist Party, ably served as Lloyd George's deputy from 1915–21, and as leader never lost an election. Bonar Law was emblematic of the fact that the centre of gravity in the Conservative Party had passed from the landed aristocracy – with which Bonar Law had no connection – to the business and professional middle classes, who now dominated the party. Indeed, only a handful of landed aristocrats remained in senior leadership positions in the Conservative Party, such as George Nathaniel Curzon, Lord (later Marquess) Curzon of Kedleston (1859–1925), the former Viceroy of India renowned for his superciliousness. Instead, the leadership of the Conservative Party under Bonar Law largely consisted of men drawn from the middle classes (although often educated at a major public school and Oxbridge), such as F. E. Smith, later Earl of Birkenhead (1872–1930), a brilliant, buccaneering barrister, and Sir Edward Carson (1854–1935), another celebrated barrister who was the leader of the Ulster Protestants.

Whatever their social backgrounds, nearly all Tories felt a deep sense of frustration at being excluded from power for so long. This frustration took several forms. Many Tories believed that the House of Lords had a duty to defeat the Liberals' radical legislation, and actively fought to save its power. After 1910, many gave all-out support to the Ulster Unionists, with some appearing to countenance arguably unconstitutional behaviour in defence of Ulster. Many Tories looked at Edwardian Ulster as a model for future conservatism – the nation in arms, but united for patriotic rather than seditious ends. Bonar Law, the new Unionists' leader, famously said in July 1912 that 'I can imagine no lengths of resistance to which Ulster will go in which I shall not be ready to support them and in which they will not be supported by the overwhelming majority of the British people.'

The last few years of peace were thus dominated politically by the Irish question, with the Liberal government's Home Rule Act, passed in May 1914 after the Lords had vetoed the bill for two years, due to come into force later in the year. Although Ulster was promised exemption for six years from being subject to an all-Irish Parliament, both sides were aiming for what appeared to be an inevitable armed conflict ahead. In March 1914, many army officers of Ulster Protestant background stationed at the Curragh in Ireland signed a letter stating that they would resign rather than engage in the coercion of Ulster – the so-called 'Curragh Mutiny', perhaps the only occasion in modern times when the British army appeared to 'mutiny' against Parliament. Although a compromise solution to the Irish conundrum might well have been found, the mood in some important parts of British society on the eve of the outbreak of the war was deeply troubled. A mood of discontent also enveloped many key parts of the Labour movement. In 1912, 34 million working days had been lost through strikes, the highest total in British history up to that point, including a bitter miners' dispute involving 1 million workers. The mood in the mining areas of South Wales was particularly ugly, with an undercurrent of violence which was actually compared in some newspapers to the mood in Russia in 1905 just before the first Russian revolution. The struggle for women's suffrage had also aroused major and highly visible divisions. The Women's Social and Political Union, founded in 1903 in part by Emmeline Pankhurst (1859–1928) and her daughters Christobel (1880–1961) and Sylvia (1882–1960), spearheaded a campaign of militancy which included attacks on property, picture slashing, hunger strikes, and a famous

9. British women could not vote in national elections until 1918. (Some women had the vote in local elections before then.) In the late nineteenth century, a movement to give the vote to women grew up, involving hundreds of women activists. It was divided into radical and moderate factions, and was not supported by all British women. Suffragette demonstrators became one of the most familiar aspects of Edwardian radicalism, finally triumphing as a result of the First World War.

suicide under the king's horse at the Derby. The Liberal government of these years stubbornly refused to grant women the vote in parliamentary elections. Without the First World War and its political and social consequences, it is probably unlikely that most women would have received the parliamentary vote in 1918, as they actually did. The multifaceted forces of unrest in Edwardian England have caused some historians to ask whether there was a 'Strange Death of Liberal England', as George Dangerfield put it in a famous book published in 1935.

More broadly, historians have also asked whether the New Liberalism, emphasising the deliberate use of extended state powers to mitigate social evils, was really radically different from anything in the past, and, in particular, whether it would have been strong enough to prevent what actually took place after 1918, the rise of the Labour party, now independent of the Liberal Party, as the normal left-of-centre party in British politics, with the Liberals shrinking to near-disappearance. The replacement of the Liberal Party by Labour has given rise to an extended debate among historians over whether it was in some sense inevitable, whether it was in the process of occurring before 1914, and whether the war itself, or other factors, was responsible for what occurred. Many historians believe that the next general election, scheduled for 1915 (but postponed until December 1918 because of the war), was likely to produce a Unionist majority, with Bonar Law becoming prime minister. In opposition, the Liberals could conceivably have disintegrated and given way to an irresistible Labour tide.

But in the summer of 1914, a *deus ex machina* changed literally everything. In far-off Sarajevo, the assassination of an Austrian archduke by Bosnian nationalists set off a chain reaction of war declarations and mobilisations around the Continent. On 4 August 1914 Britain declared war on Germany and, eight days later, on Austria-Hungary. In August came the retreat from Mons by the British regular army and, in October, the first Battle of Ypres, with its extraordinary casualty figures, the first of many full-scale slaughters to come. While some far-sighted observers such as Lord Kitchener expected a long war, what ensued was very different from what they had imagined. The Royal Navy effectively blockaded Germany's ports, but – contrary to what had been widely expected – played only a limited role in the fighting, which was carried out by land armies, largely in France, of incredible size and subject to nightmarish levels of casualties. Quite conceivably, had Britain's leaders known what was to come the country would have remained neutral, even at the cost of giving Germany a probable victory and hegemony on the Continent. But Germany's plans to defeat France necessarily entailed the invasion and occupation of Belgium, and it was the invasion of 'little Belgium', accomplished with much brutality, that brought a virtually united nation into the war, including those radical and Nonconformist elements which had opposed the Boer War. Having entered the war, Britain was doomed to see it out with the inevitability of a Greek tragedy. So too was most of Europe, engendering a series of conflicts and near-conflicts which, it might be argued, continued until Stalin's death in 1953, or perhaps until the collapse of the Soviet Union in 1999.

Chapter Eight

Science, Technology, Culture and Ideology

More than most periods in modern history, Britain in the years between 1832 and 1914 can be characterised by brief descriptions of its intellectual and cultural life. The mainstream of its intellectual life can be described as emphasising rationality and progress; its artistic life as emphasising Romanticism. Like all short and widely held definitional labels, while there is a great deal of positive evidence for their accuracy, one should always be well aware of their limitations.

Unlike most such cultural descriptions of an age, these characterisations remained reasonably accurate for the whole of the period from 1832 to 1914. The culture and central identities of the eighteenth century and the Regency period are generally described in terms different from that of 1832 to 1914, while the First World War is certainly almost always seen as marking a fundamental climacteric in intellectual and cultural life. Although Britain in the eighteenth century is often seen in terms of rationalism and the Enlightenment, it was not characterised by technological and scientific progress in the same way as the succeeding age, and, as J. C. D. Clark has pointed out, traditional, almost pre-modern 'church and king' modes of ideological identities remained strong until they collapsed almost completely in the period centring around the Great Reform Act of 1832. After the 1914–18 war, few could see civilisation in terms of endless progress, and any who continued to hold this view were surely disabused by the horrors of the Second World War and the opening of the Atomic Age.

It is important to emphasise that Britons – the great majority of the people of the United Kingdom – experienced actual technological change, vividly perceptible and often dramatic, during the nineteenth century, and especially in the years between 1832 and 1914. The speed of travel of important national news is a good indication of this change. News of the Battle of Trafalgar and the death of Lord Nelson, which occurred in the Atlantic Ocean off the southern coast of Spain, took from 21 October 1805 until 6 November 1805 to reach London, although every possible means of speeding the message was used by the Royal Navy. Moreover reports of the battle would have taken between three and six months to reach a remote outpost of the empire such as Sydney, New South Wales, and no power on earth was capable of shortening the delay. But when Queen Victoria died in January 1901, telegraph cables had been laid to the four corners of the world – at least to important urban centres – and news of the queen's death reached Sydney on the same day. There would still have been a time lag before the royal death appeared in (presumably 'extra') editions of Sydney's newspapers, but within forty-eight hours of the end of Victoria's reign, everyone in

Sydney could have known that her lengthy rule had ended and the British Empire had a new king. News of Victoria's death had been disseminated throughout Sydney in less than 1 per cent of the time needed to convey reports of the Battle of Trafalgar nearly a century before. Sydney – as well as London, Toronto, Dublin and Cape Town, and even cities in the tropical empire such as Bombay – of course also had a wide range of infrastructural and transport innovations utterly unknown in 1805, above all the railway, but also trams, street lighting, steamships, the telegraph, running water, indoor flush toilets, and mechanical lifts (elevators) in tall buildings. Scientific and technological change had also produced operations always conducted with anaesthetics and antisepsis (the killing of germs during and after operations), mass-produced illustrated daily newspapers with daily reports from around the world, and universal education, at least through to age thirteen, even for the poor. All of these changes bespoke obvious improvement and evolution, showing that Providence had given vast new powers to humanity, and, in particular, to white Europeans, from whom these inventions invariably emanated, demonstrating their obvious superiority to other humans and their evident fitness to rule. Who could possibly refute or deny this evidence so visible and, in the west, ubiquitous? Even those living in poverty or comparative poverty in Britain could take great pride in their worldwide empire.

The nineteenth century of course saw the development of many inventions and innovations. Most of these, at least before about 1875, were first produced in Britain; from about 1875 most were the product of the United States or Germany. Britain's role as the homeland of major inventions began in the eighteenth century with the birth of the steam engine, the spinning jenny, and other engineering innovations. The key invention developed in Britain in the nineteenth century was certainly the railway, whose chronology is common knowledge: a very early experimental railway in 1804; the Stockton to Darlington Railway, the earliest true railway, in 1825; the very important Liverpool to Manchester Railway in 1830, at whose opening the leading Cabinet minister William Huskisson was sadly killed because, standing on the line, he did not realise that, unlike a horse-drawn carriage, a railway train could not swerve off the track. The 1830s and 40s, and especially the period between 1844 and 1846, witnessed the first 'Railway Boom', when hundreds of miles of line were opened, most significantly the major London to Birmingham line, opened in 1838, the first trunk route linking London with a great provincial city. (And today, as part of the Virgin West Coast Line out of Euston Station, probably still the busiest of all trunk lines.) By 1850, over 6,000 miles of rail line had been laid, a major source of employment of both engineers and surveyors and of 'navvies': unskilled labourers worked like slaves. Unlike many other countries, all of Britain's railways were constructed with private investment capital (after securing a specific Act of Parliament, often a difficult and expensive process involving negotiation with many vested interests). Britain's railways were the source of many large engineering fortunes, like that of Thomas Brassey, who left the enormous sum of £3.5 million and whose son became an earl. As virtual monopolies, they were also a relatively secure form of investment for the upper and middle classes, who flocked to new, plausible railway investment opportunities, in Britain and later throughout the empire, the United States, and in remote foreign countries such as Argentina. By 1870 about 13,500 miles of railway had been built in the United Kingdom, a total which peaked at about 18,700 miles of rail line just before the First

World War. (After 1918, railway mileage gradually contracted following competition from road transport, and nearly one half of the entire network was closed down in the mid-1960s following Sir Richard Beeching's notorious report.) Rail passenger numbers also rose continuously and dramatically, from 30 million passengers carried in 1845 to 322 million in 1870, to 1.1 billion in 1900. Part of this increase came from the building of local urban lines, most famously the London Underground, first opened in 1863 in the form of steam-driven subsurface lines and then from 1890 in the form of electric-powered deep 'tubes'. British railways were divided into First, Second, and Third Class of accommodation; unlike American railroads, until the late nineteenth century there were no corridor carriages with perambulating conductors, but small, slam-door compartment carriages lacking toilets, dining facilities, or much in the way of security from criminal fellow passengers. Railway accidents were frequent and often horrifying, as steam-driven wooden trains – lit and heated by gas, and with highly fragile glass windows, obviously without any means of distant signalling of oncoming or stationary vehicles, and regularly travelling at night and in highly inclement weather – often proved death traps, categorically more dangerous than today's railways. Railways became a major source of labour, with locomotive drivers among the most highly paid of working-class occupations. 'Railway towns', where major lines converged and large-scale engineering works were located, such as Crewe, Swindon, Rugby and Derby, were among the great areas of urban growth; Derby's population, for instance, rose from 24,000 in 1831 to 115,000 in 1901. The great railway terminals became iconic symbols of nineteenth-century progress, with several in most large cities and thirteen in London, the last, Marylebone, built only in 1898. All of the London

10. The 'railway age' saw Britain transformed by a vast network of railway lines that criss-crossed the country. Many converged on London which, by 1900, had no fewer than thirteen major railway stations, highly symbolic of the Victorian age. One of the grandest was St. Pancras Station, opened in 1868, which was (and is) the terminus of trains to and from the East Midlands and Yorkshire. All of London's stations were built at the edges of the city as it then existed, largely for fear that the steam and sparks from the trains would start fires in central London.

terminals were built at the edge of central London, largely for fear that the steam-driven trains of the day would spark fires. Today, all but one of these terminals (Broad Street, closed in 1986), remain in use, often, after a long period of decline, busier than ever.

Britain's railways had a direct effect upon the lives of most people in the country, affecting them in dozens of ways which were universally felt. Travel time between cities declined dramatically from the days of even the fastest coaches, with, for instance, journeys from London to Edinburgh shortening from up to a week to eight hours or so. Commuting from suburbs up to forty miles or thereabouts away became possible. Goods could be transported more quickly throughout the country, as well as the mail and the news. To be sure, there were distinct limits to the range of the railway. Trains could only travel from station to station, not door to door, and (until the coming of the automobile) horse-drawn private carriages, taxis, coaches and carrying vehicles had to haul both goods and people from home or office, at least to the nearest railway station. Remote parts of Britain remained without trains, especially in northern Scotland and Wales. There, the old horse-drawn world persisted until after the First World War, as it did on most aristocratic country estates, when automobiles and trucks became ubiquitous. Nevertheless, the presence of the train in the lives and habits of most people in Britain made their lives quite different from the lives of anyone living before the railway age.

Analogous changes were also brought by the telegraph and by the press. The electric telegraph, often attributed to the American Samuel Morse (for whom the Morse code is named) was actually invented in 1837, a year earlier than Morse's device, by two Englishmen – Sir William E. Cooke (1806–79) and Charles Wheatstone (1802–75). The Great Western Railway erected telegraph lines from Paddington Station to West Drayton, thirteen miles to the west, as early as 1839. England's smaller distances and much more intensively developed railway system were tailor-made for the telegraph, which quickly became a crucial means of communication for both businessmen and the public. Since sending a telegraph was always far more expensive than mailing a letter, abbreviations

and codes soon became common in order to compress a message into as few words as possible, rather in the manner of
phone texting 150 years later (to which it is sometimes compared). Telegram messages could be sent instantaneously, but
then had to be translated from Morse code to English, written
out, and transported by a messenger to the intended recipient
– no one had an electric telegraph in their home. Tragic messages, especially deaths in the family, and happy messages,
such as the birth or marriage of a relative, meant that the telegram delivery boy was both dreaded and anticipated
– dreaded, especially in wartime, where the arrival of a telegram usually brought only tragic news. Telegrams remained
the central means of conveying news of this kind, as well as
commercial advice and information, until well into the twentieth century. From the 1870s, virtually the whole world was
linked by the telegraph, with undersea cables able to transport
messages to almost any remote country.

Although ordinary mail had existed perhaps since ancient
times, the Victorian period, led above all by England, also witnessed an astronomical increase in the Post Office and postal
service. The key motivation here was the penny postage
stamp, introduced by Sir Rowland Hill in 1841 and soon imitated in every civilised country. By the late Victorian period,
there were *eight* or *nine* mail deliveries every weekday to commercial addresses in most cities, with two or three on Sunday;
most homes received mail two or three times a day. There is a
well-known story, apparently based in fact, that a fire was
reported in mid-Victorian London by a man who *posted a letter*
with this news to the local fire station; the fire engines
responded in time to put out the fire! By the end of the nineteenth century, cheap letter and parcel postage existed for the
whole of the British Empire; the mail remained arguably the

most important means of communication until the coming of the Internet a century later.

Britain's newspaper press had existed, at least in primitive form, from the seventeenth century (although not before then), but became recognisably modern only in the nineteenth century. Greatly increased newspaper circulation became possible with the use of steam presses to print daily newspapers, beginning with the printing by steam press of *The Times* – regarded as the 'newspaper of record' – in 1814. Various legal victories for the right to publish even news damaging to the government, and the reduction of the stamp duty paid by every newspaper (finally repealed, as noted, in 1855), made possible the rise of the modern press with its 'scoops', investigative journalism, and worldwide reportage. As a result, the price of *The Times* declined from seven pence in 1836 to threepence in 1861, making it (and all other newspapers) affordable to the middle classes and even to a part of the working classes. The abolition of these 'taxes on knowledge' was an important part of the agenda of early Victorian radicalism. A virtual revolution in the press thus occurred over the next few decades. In 1850 the daily circulation of *The Times*, the best-selling daily newspaper, was only 34,000; by 1860 the circulation of *Reynold's News* had reached 350,000; and by 1901 Alfred Harmsworth's (Lord Northcliffe) popular mass circulation newspaper the *Daily Mail* had reached 1 million copies sold per day, the first newspaper in the world to reach this level. By the Edwardian period or just after, the great 'Press lords' such as Northcliffe, his brother Harold Harmsworth (Lord Rothermere), and Sir Max Aitken (Lord Beaverbrook) had gained control of much of the newspaper-reading public, giving them, in the days before competition from radio and television, enormous political power. Crucially assisted by the railways, Britain also developed a national newspaper press, with papers such as *The Times* and the *Daily Express* sold throughout the United Kingdom. this situation was quite unlike that in the United States, where there is no national newspaper press in the British sense: the *New York Times*, possibly the closest approximation to a national newspaper, is primarily sold only in New York, while even the leading newspaper of a very large city, such as the *Chicago Tribune*, is sold only in that city.

Britain also developed a major provincial newspaper press. By the early twentieth century, probably every important city in Britain had at least two (and sometimes three or four) separate daily (not weekly) newspapers, usually one supporting the Liberals and the other supporting the Conservatives, which most informed locals would buy in addition to a national newspaper. The centre of the British press, however, remained London; by the Edwardian period, there were at least *fourteen* morning newspapers published daily, and another nine daily evening papers (often read by commuters on the way home). These evening papers were not merely late editions of the morning press, but entirely separate newspapers, some, such as the *Pall Mall Gazette*, of considerable national importance. There were also eleven entirely separate national Sunday papers. Nearly all had their premises on Fleet Street in central London, and 'Fleet Street' became synonymous with the British press, a term still used, despite the relocation of today's existing newspapers to Docklands and other locales. An army of editors, subeditors, reporters, feature writers, printers, newspaper vendors and so on grew up, changing the nature of news to become synonymous with the instantaneous reportage we know today, a situation very different from that at the beginning of our period. The British press was also divided intellectually and politically, with newspapers ranging from 'heavyweights' such as *The Times* and the *Daily Telegraph* (which at the time carried verbatim reports of all speeches in Parliament) to what would now be called 'tabloids', reporting on little besides sports, murders and scandals. (One of the few sources of legal pornography in Victorian and Edwardian Britain was verbatim reports of lurid and sexually explicit divorce proceedings, which could legally escape censorship, and which formed a staple of the press, especially – for some reason – the Sunday press.) The British press was also divided politically, with Tory and Liberal-radical newspapers making their loyalties very clear. Most readers purchased a newspaper of the intellectual and political standpoint they liked best, and would normally not read one from a radically different viewpoint on the press axis. This persists today: the typical *Guardian* reader is very different from the typical reader of the *Sun*. Unlike the press in modern dictatorships, however, British newspapers never invented mendacious stories or engaged in fictitious propaganda. On the contrary, news reportage became more professional in its collection and dissemination, thanks to the formation of international news agencies such as Reuters (founded in 1855), which provided reasonably accurate accounts of events around the world. British newspaper purchasers would almost certainly not have tolerated a press which blatantly distorted the news, however slanted a newspaper editorial might be.

The number of book publishers greatly increased during the nineteenth century, adding enormously to the literature of the imagination (discussed below). Many of these well-known publishers – Macmillan, Nelson, Heinemann – were 'self-made men', often of Scottish background. But many works only reinforced the rationalism and penchant for facts and accurate data found in other spheres. Encyclopaedias (long predating the nineteenth century) probably reached their zenith with the universally praised 1910 edition of the *Encyclopaedia Britannica*. Reference works which provided wide-ranging factual information proliferated, often updated on an annual basis, such as *Who's Who* (from the mid-nineteenth century, but in its current form from 1897), *The Statesman's Year Book* (from 1841), *Whitaker's Almanac* (from 1869), *Pears Shilling Cyclopedia* (from 1897) and many other works. *Burke's Peerage and Baronetage* and *Burke's Landed Gentry*, both dating from the 1830s and 40s, giving (ostensibly) accurate information on the families and genealogies of the upper classes, were also characteristic of the Victorian period, although they had predecessors and continue to the present time. Perhaps most remarkable of all were the city and country directories, giving the names, addresses and occupations of literally everyone living in that area, and normally revised on an annual basis. Although there were predecessors to these works in the eighteenth century, they became more remarkable in the Victorian period, when local directories were compiled for virtually every locale in Britain. The labour involved in compiling, revising and printing these extraordinary works must have been almost incalculable, and presumably entailed the employment of hundreds of staff. Even beyond this were the censuses. These were first compiled in 1801, and on a ten-year basis thereafter until the present (with the exception of 1941, when the Second World War precluded the compilation of a census). The earliest named census dates from 1841, and thus an officially compiled database giving the names, ages, addresses, occupations and relationship to the head of the household of everyone in Britain (recently made available, to 1911, on the Internet) provides salient data on the entire British population.

Nothing like it, and certainly nothing of an official nature, had been compiled on a continuing basis before. Impressive information on a vast array of topics was published annually in the 'Blue Books', the reports of the various departments of the government, and are invaluable to historians.

Nearly all these were compiled by civil servants or by highly intelligent and extraordinarily energetic amateurs, and seldom by academics. Very few of the seminal figures of the Victorian intelligentsia were employed at universities, whose purpose, until the early twentieth century or even later, was to instil a time-honoured classical curriculum, based around the Greek and Latin classics, Christian divinity and mathematics, to another generation of elite leaders and gentlemen. There were some exceptions, especially at Cambridge, and some great scientific innovators did hold university posts, such as William Thomson (Lord Kelvin) and James Clerk Maxwell, but most notable intellectuals had little or no connection with universities after graduation (if they were university graduates, which was not universally the case). Many were gentlemen of wealth and leisure, such as Charles Darwin, who inherited a fortune from his grandfather Joseph Wedgwood, the pottery manufacturer, and from his father Robert Waring Darwin, a wealthy doctor. After graduating from Cambridge and embarking upon his celebrated voyage on the *Beagle*, Darwin lived as a country gentleman in Kent. He apparently never set foot in Cambridge between graduating in 1830 and visiting it again in 1869, and had no connection with his alma mater or any other university. Similarly, the majority among the famous Victorian intellectual figures and writers – John Stuart Mill, Alfred Russel Wallace, Herbert Spencer, the early Fabians, Charles Dickens, Alfred Tennyson, Benjamin Disraeli, Thomas Hardy and (of course) all women cultural figures until the very end of the nineteenth century – were unconnected with any university. They participated in debates and discussions via institutions such as the illustrious scientific body the Royal Society and other learned societies (most of which were in London), in the press and journals, and through their published works. Itellectual output in the twentieth and twenty-first centuries has been very different, increasingly focused among university academics, although a high-brow intelligentsia unconnected with the universities also continues to exist.

Major scientific discoveries were thus often made by gifted amateurs such as Michael Faraday (1791–1867), a key contributor to the science of electromagnetism, who was the son of a blacksmith and received no education past the age of fourteen, when he was apprenticed to a bookbinder. Faraday served as assistant and even valet to Sir Humphry Davy, yet eventually became president of the Royal Society, whose first president was Sir Isaac Newton. Faraday's contribution to the study of electricity and chemistry was so great that Albert Einstein kept a picture of Faraday in his study. Although Faraday's career was highly unusual, it was the case, as noted, that few British scientists emerged from the ranks of university academics, as the majority would certainly be today. This was also particularly true of civil engineers, who often received little education beyond their apprenticeship. For instance, Thomas Brassey, the greatest (and richest) of all British railway builders, was the son of a farmer in Cheshire and was apprenticed to a land surveyor at sixteen. Like Faraday, he was fortunate in meeting and being favoured by a successful engineer – in this case the famous Thomas Telford – who recognised his great ability. This mode of success was surprisingly common in nineteenth-century Britain.

Culture

The centrality of rationality in British life extended in part – but only in part – to what is nominally denoted by the term 'culture'. It might be useful in beginning this discussion to outline those aspects of high culture in which the British made virtually no impact during the nineteenth century. Perhaps most striking is classical music, where no British composer of the first rank (or even the second rank) appeared between Handel (who, of course, was born in Germany), who died in 1759, and the wave of notable British composers, especially Edward Elgar (1857–1934) and Ralph Vaughan Williams (1872–1958), whose works first appeared in the late Victorian period. Some great European composers, including Haydn, Mozart and Mendelssohn, frequently visited England and are, to a certain extent, associated with it, but it is a fact that no great British composer emerged for over 140 years. No work by a British composer in this period has entered the classical repertoire. When the 'English School' of composers emerged in the late nineteenth century, it did so without real precedent and was heavily influenced by Continental Romanticism and also, in many cases, by British folk music. Compared with the musical compositions from Germany, Italy, Russia or France, classical music in Victorian Britain was plainly inferior. In many respects this is curious, as the relative wealth of Britain meant that there were pianos and other instruments in most homes, while England produced many notable musicians and musical groups such as Manchester's famous Hallé Orchestra, founded in 1858. Arguably, the lack of a tradition of aristocratic patronage after the collapse of the Italian Opera in London in the mid-eighteenth century was a factor in this void, as well, possibly, as the puritanism and mistrust of Continental modes of enjoyment among much of the middle class. Moreover, the phrase often used by Continentals about England, that it was 'a land without music', is clearly a great exaggeration. Nevertheless, the absence of great composers is a strange gap in British culture.

Even more striking, perhaps, is the absence of notable British drama between the time of Richard Brinsley Sheridan (1751–1816) in the late eighteenth century and the plays of Oscar Wilde (1854–1900), John Millington Synge (1871–1909) and George Bernard Shaw (1856–1950) in the late nineteenth century – again, roughly the same gap as with British classical music. A number of Victorian farces and comedies, such as Dion Boucicault's *London Assurance* (1841), John Maddison Morton's *Box and Cox* (1847), and Brandon Thomas's *Charley's Aunt* (1892) are still remembered (and occasionally still performed), but of serious drama of the first rank there was little or nothing. The late Victorian period also saw the celebrated comic operas of William Schwenck Gilbert (1836–1911) and Arthur Sullivan (1842–1900), who produced fourteen musicals between 1871 and 1896, which are, of course, probably more frequently performed than any other works of their time. As with the absence of great British classical music, the lack of great drama is surprising, given the plethora of theatres in London and the provinces which flourished at the time, and the visibility of acting as a profession. This period also saw the apotheosis of Shakespeare as the British national dramatist and poet, installed as the demigod of English literature.

The mainstream of Victorian English high culture in literature was represented by novels, other forms of fiction, and by poetry. The great novelists of Victorian England – above all Charles Dickens (1812–70), and also William Makepeace Thackeray (1811–63), Wilkie Collins (1824–89), Anthony

Trollope (1815–82), the Brontë sisters Anne (1820–49), Charlotte (1816–55), and Emily (1818–48), George Eliot (Mary Ann Evans, 1819–80), Elizabeth Gaskell (1810–65), Benjamin Disraeli (1804–81), and the later writers George Gissing (1857–1903), Thomas Hardy (1840–1928) and their contemporaries, are universally regarded as the best-known and most accurate depicters of the Victorian age. They built on an earlier tradition of English novelists, such as Henry Fielding (1707–54), Laurence Sterne (1713–68), Mary Shelley (1797–1851), and, most famously, Jane Austen (1775–1817) and Sir Walter Scott (1771–1832), which was already a century old when the Victorian era began. The great nineteenth-century novelists were inevitably influenced by the major international themes of nineteenth-century European literature, especially Romanticism and its emphasis on the heroic individual. In many respects, the Victorian English novel represented a reaction from the rationality of British scientific culture and industrial innovation – directly in the works of Dickens, Gaskell and Hardy, indirectly in the works of the writers who simply ignored what was around them and centred their work on the aristocracy (known only at second or third hand) or on historical novels of the past. The late Victorian period witnessed a widening of the genres among the writers of fiction, with the emergence, for example, of the uniquely British tradition of the classical detective story, best known, of course, in the works of Sir Arthur Conan Doyle (1859–1930), inventor of Sherlock Holmes, who has been termed one of the three most famous characters in all of fiction (Hamlet and Don Quixote are said to be the others). H. G. Wells and others (imitating Edgar Allan Poe in America and Jules Verne in France) introduced the science-fiction story in such works as *The War of the Worlds* (1898) and *The Time Machine* (1895). Yet another genre exemplified, if not originating, in

Victorian literature, was children's literature, where such classics as *Alice's Adventures in Wonderland* (1865) and its sequel *Through the Looking Glass* (1871) by Lewis Carroll (Charles Lutwidge Dodgson, 1832–98); *Tom Brown's Schooldays* (1857) by Thomas Hughes (1822–96), the famous novel of life at Rugby School; and the nonsense poems and stories of Edward Lear (1812–88) are among the best-known Victorian works of the imagination.

Literature and popular writing was one area where women became both successful and well known. There was no bar, de facto, or *de jure*, against women writers, and writing for money was one of the main areas open to middle-class women who lacked career structures. (Nevertheless, Mary Ann Evans deliberately used the masculine pseudonym 'George Eliot' so that the reader would not prejudge her as a 'woman writer'.) Jane Austen, the Brontë sisters, the poet Elizabeth Barrett Browning (1806–61) and others became fully accepted as authors in the mainstream British literary canon. Women did probably write a disproportionate number of romantic novels, and, in the first half of the twentieth century, became pre-eminent authors of detective novels, possibly the most popular form of literary entertainment among the English middle classes. Despite the realistic possibilities apparently open to women, there was, strangely, arguably no woman writer of the first rank between George Eliot and Virginia Woolf (1882–1941), despite their eminence in the Victorian era.

That literary culture often paralleled scientific culture in Victorian Britain is also shown, at least to a certain extent, by the writings of the most famous historians of the period, such as Thomas Babington Macaulay (1800–81). Macaulay's incredibly vivid and engaging histories and essays were the personification of the 'Whig interpretation of history', whose dominant theme was the evolution of Britain from barbarism and autocracy to superior semi-democracy (but with the Whigs firmly in charge) in his own time. It highlighted with approval the rational liberal development of the recent British past (although it may be seen as oversimplifying the multiform dimensions of Britain's political, social and economic history). Carlyle, in contrast, wrote in a much more difficult style, which was linked to the (for Britain) highly unusual tradition of German idealism, and attacked many aspects of modern commercial life. It also represented a search for 'heroes' and dominant personalities throughout history which is seen by many later observers as presaging twentieth-century fascism. On the other hand, a newer, more recognisably modern historiography also appeared, which based all viable history in historical documents and historical evidence, used as dispassionately and accurately as possible, as is followed today by all mainstream historians. This relatively new view of how to write history was emphasised in the works of such notable Victorian historians as the medievalists William Stubbs (1825–1901) and Edward Augustus Freeman (1823–92), both of whom – unlike Macaulay or Carlyle – were senior Oxford University academics.

Even more than Victorian fiction, Victorian poetry built on a long-established and very distinguished tradition, which had produced Spenser, Shakespeare and Milton. It flourished, in particular, in the period just before the Victorian era, with Lord Byron (1788–1824), Percy Bysshe Shelley (1792–1822), John Keats (1795–1821), William Wordsworth (1770–1850) and Samuel Taylor Coleridge (1772–1834) the most important and renowned figures. All of these are invariably grouped as Romantic poets, major exemplars of 'Romanticism', the predominant cultural movement throughout Europe at the time.

Briefly, Romanticism is generally seen as emphasising the individual artist and his (or her, although most Romantics were men) individual emotional experience, and represented a revolt against the orderliness of the classical forms which dominated the literature of Europe and Britain in the eighteenth century. It strongly appreciated the power and majesty of nature, and the experience of the 'sublime' this engendered. Initially, most figures in the Romantic movement were also politically radical. Byron, for instance, died in Greece at the age of thirty-six, engaged in fighting for Greek independence from Ottoman Turkey, a goal favoured by many classically trained, well-educated Britons. Wordsworth, Coleridge and their contemporaries strongly supported the French Revolution in its initial phases ('Bliss it was in that dawn to be alive, / But to be young was very heaven', Wordsworth described it). But many early Romantics became appalled at the excesses of the Reign of Terror in revolutionary France, and by the rise of Napoleon, becoming, after their youth had passed, arch-conservatives. Coleridge became one of the doyens of intellectual Burkean conservatism. Robert Southey (1774–1843), a close associate of Coleridge, originally a radical and one of the progenitors with him of a utopian community in America, became an almost violent anti-radical, but combined his hatred of 'the rabble' with an equally fierce criticism of conditions for the working classes in factory towns; he thus advocated a kind of 'One Nation Toryism' later taken up by Disraeli. (Southey, who was Poet Laureate from 1813 until 1843 – he was succeeded by Wordsworth – also coined the word 'autobiography'.) His most enduring work, oddly enough, is *The Story of the Three Bears* (1837).

After this great burst of poetic creativity, as in other spheres there was something of a diminution in outstanding British poetry until the very end of the Victorian period, the most important exception being the great figure of Alfred Tennyson (1809–92), Poet Laureate from 1850 until his death. Very much in the Romantic tradition, Tennyson's verse also expressed the growing 'crisis of faith' caused by Darwinism and other recent theories. Tennyson was also the first (and so far only) poet to be awarded a peerage, in 1884. Other outstanding mid-Victorian poets included Robert Browning (1812–89), his wife Elizabeth Barrett Browning (1806–61), Matthew Arnold (1822–88) and Edward FitzGerald (1809–83), whose translation, with much poetic licence, of The Rubaiyat of Omar Khayyam (1859 and subsequent editions) remains one of the most popular of all English-language poems.

The late Victorian and Edwardian period also saw some notable English poets whose works to a certain extent represented new departures, such as the Catholic religious poet Gerard Manley Hopkins (1844–89) – virtually unknown in his lifetime – Rudyard Kipling (1865–1936), whose possibly ambiguous verse is often taken as a full-blooded championing of British imperialism, Thomas Hardy, a highly esteemed poet as well as a novelist, A. E. Housman (1859–1936) and Algernon Charles Swinburne (1827–1909), whose pseudo-decadence (he was known in some circles as 'Swineburne') was more hinted at than blatant. English verse, indeed, could not break free of traditional forms, language and subject matter – let alone deal openly with sexuality or other taboo topics – until after the First World War. Nor, perhaps, did it wish to, with most notable poets seeking respectability after youthful wild oats, and nor would its audience necessarily wish it to either.

British art and architecture flowed from much the same streams of the imagination as other forms of culture at the time, emphasising the Romantic in contrast to the classical.

Landscape artists such as John Constable (1776–1837) and J. M. W. Turner (1775–1851) had, like other Romantics, stressed both the power and exoticism of nature, even in mundane England. Nineteenth-century British painters emphasised these themes, but also the Romanticism which drew on the past, and on literary and biblical themes, most famously in the Pre-Raphaelite movement (William Holman Hunt (1827–1910), Dante Gabriel Rossetti (1828–82), and John Everett Millais (1829–96) among others), in ultra-realistic and minutely detailed works. But academic painting and portrait painting were seldom at war with established society, and many artists became extremely successful. Sir Frederic Leighton (1830–96), for instance, served as president of the Royal Academy from 1878 until his death, and was the first (and so far only) painter to receive a peerage, on the day before his death. Victorian architecture wished to be Romantic, but the realities of engineering and cost accounting were always adversely present. The most characteristic style of Victorian architecture, the Gothic Revival, was most famously exemplified by the Houses of Parliament (Sir Charles Barry (1795–1860) assisted by Augustus Pugin (1812–52), completed 1852), but also lay behind such archetypically Victorian works as the St Pancras Railway Station and the Midland Hotel (1868) and Tower Bridge (1894), designed to look old, components of an 'invented tradition' in stone. But most Victorian buildings were necessarily utilitarian and, to many later eyes, simply hideous, even frightening. Victorian structures were increasingly large and grandiose, such as the truly remarkable Forth Bridge (Sir John Fowler and Sir Benjamin Baker, opened 1890), whose 8,300-foot span appears to have been constructed by an advanced technology from outer space. Ships, in particular, became ever larger and more powerfully driven by steam and propeller, culminating, before 1914, in the 'dreadnought' class battleships and the ill-fated *Titanic* (1912). Comparing the *Titanic* with even the most advanced wooden sailing ships of a century before seemingly demonstrates at a glance the incredible technological advances of the Victorian era. (Yet it sank.) But there were still many who protested at the century's utilitarianism, for instance John Ruskin (1819–1900) and William Morris (1834–96), founder of the Arts and Crafts Movement. The Victorian period also saw some authentically novel modes of art, most notably photography, pioneered between 1826 and 1840, which rapidly overtook painting as the main medium of portraiture and, then, the actual depiction of major events as they occurred. British Victorian photographers were often distinguished by their artistic substance, as in the works of Julia Margaret Cameron (1815–79; she was the great-aunt of Virginia Woolf). The first important historical event to be photographed is said to have been the great Chartist rally on Kennington Common, photographed by William Kilburn in April 1848. By the second half of the nineteenth century, the appearance of virtually every leading British politician and public figure was known through his photograph. Photography was increasingly instrumental in forming the common depictions of the colonial world, of foreign scenes, as well as of the families of ordinary people, and thus changed visual depictions forever.

An interesting point about Britain's leading intellectual figures of the Victorian and Edwardian periods is that many of the most famous of them became affluent and successful; whatever the pattern might have been on the Continent, surprisingly few died in poverty in garrets and cellars. Although Charles Dickens wrote extensively about early Victorian poverty – so much so that we use the term 'Dickensian' to describe urban poverty of the time – he left £80,000 (about £9 million today), plus a small landed estate not included in this figure at his death. Charles Darwin inherited a fortune and left around £200,000 at his death. Several became peers or achieved other official honours. Most, in other words, fully participated in bourgeois society and were seldom in revolt from it. This was the norm even in the most unexpected cases. While Karl Marx, who of course lived in London for most of his adult life, left only £500, his collaborator and benefactor Friedrich Engels was a very successful umbrella-cloth manufacturer in Manchester who left £80,000 and was noted for giving expensive parties and for his love of fox hunting, normally associated with the landed gentry. Needless to say, not all British writers and artists were rich, and success often depended upon good luck and honest agents. Many struggled continuously. For instance, Fergus Hume (1859–1932), an English-born writer who grew up in New Zealand and then lived in Melbourne, Australia, was the author of the 1886 mystery novel, set in Melbourne, *The Mystery of a Hansom Cab*. Virtually forgotten today, it sold 500,000 copies around the world, more than any other Victorian mystery novel, and directly inspired Arthur Conan Doyle's *A Study in Scarlet*, the first Sherlock Holmes story, published the next year. Sadly, the impecunious Hume had sold the rights to his book for only £50, and spent the rest of his life – he settled in England in 1888 – writing over a hundred additional novels, none of which is remembered today, even to experts in Victorian fiction. He died in almost complete obscurity in Essex in 1932. Hume's career was an example of late Victorian and Edwardian 'Grub Street', the world of impecunious hack novelists, dramatists and journalists, little known in their lifetime and forgotten today. While few actually starved (as was apparently not unknown in eighteenth-century

Britain), none achieved real success. Nevertheless, it is also true that remarkably few challenged the established order of society in an adversarial way.

The 1890s and the Edwardian period saw something of a broadening of the genres and subject matter regarded as permissible for writers and artists in the Victorian period. We associate these years with *The Yellow Book* of Aubrey Beardsley (1872–98), with its emphasis on the 'decadent' and erotic, with the flamboyance of Oscar Wilde, and with the British socialism of the early Fabians. Yet there were distinct and very perceptible limits to what was allowable, as the downfall of Oscar Wilde clearly showed. The cultural bohemianism of this period had little impact on wider society, especially on what was regarded as public behaviour in high society and official circles. These high walls of the permissible of course disguised hypocrisy on a grand scale, as the career of the arch-womaniser the Prince of Wales (later King Edward VII) illustrates. Any frank or explicit discussion of sexuality was taboo, and in particular of any sexual practice outside of marriage. When the pioneering sexual researcher Havelock Ellis (1859–1939) published *Sexual Inversion* in 1897 (co-authored with the poet John Addington Symonds (1840–93)), the first English-language medical textbook on homosexuality (Ellis apparently coined the term), a bookseller who stocked the work was prosecuted for obscenity, despite its formal, scientific nature. It is often noted that Charles Dickens never overtly depicts the prostitution and vice which permeated London, about which he must surely have known. Victorian and Edwardian novels thus seldom or never fully explored the kind of psychological themes we take for granted, more often focusing on the effects of outward society upon the individual. Any real change in this only occurred after the First World

War, while strong barriers of legal censorship and self-censorship remained in place until the 1960s. Britain produced much less of a bohemian 'underground' than most other European countries. Art nouveau, if not modernist forms, did appear, with such figures as the great Scottish architect Charles Rennie Mackintosh (1868–1928), but cultural figures detached from the mainstream were notably rare. Something like the Armory Show of 1913 in New York, which introduced 'modern art' to the United States, even before the First World War, had no real equivalent in Britain. Indeed, even during the interwar period, modern artists aroused great hostility in many circles (as they did, often even more fanatically elsewhere, especially in totalitarian countries). Wealthy collectors of modern art such as Samuel Courtauld (1876–1947) were always much rarer in Britain than elsewhere, and the late nineteenth century began the process of frequent sales of art collections owned by aristocrats.

Ideology

It seems clear from all of this that the predominant ideology of Britain in the period from 1832 through 1914 was a moderate but quite pervasive liberalism, and that no ideology which radically dissented from it – whether from the political right or left, or from religious or secular sources – was likely to gain more than a minor following. Perhaps the most clear-cut evidence for this was the absence of a radical right which wished to undo the effects of the Reform Act of 1832, either from unreconstructed aristocrats or right-wing intellectuals. Nor did any such right-wing opposition to reformist democracy develop during the early twentieth century, in a way which might have foreshadowed a British fascism or twentieth-century nationalistic authoritarianism. Indeed, many of the major reforms of the early part of the period 1832–1914 were actually instituted by the Whig government, which was headed by enormously wealthy hereditary land-owners. The Conservative Party, dominated by wealthy landowners until the Edwardian period (when businessmen largely supplanted them), always acquiesced in these reforms. No component of the British aristocracy or landed gentry ever advanced, overtly or covertly, a plan to reverse the move towards democracy after 1832. During the Edwardian period, a 'radical right' (as it is sometimes termed by historians) emerged, appalled by some aspects of the Liberal government which came to power in 1905. But its agenda centred around ensuring the unity of the British Empire by erecting a high tariff wall around it; opposition to Home Rule in Ireland; the possible introduction of military conscription; and a measure of 'social reform' aimed at improving the (apparently degenerating) health of the British working classes. Again, it is difficult to see any parallel between it and any kind of proto-fascist ideology except in its strong British nationalism (widely shared by much of the Liberal Party). A number of right-wing intellectuals and writers – such as Thomas Carlyle and, much later, the advocates of the eugenics movement in the Edwardian period – can be viewed as comprising a kind of extreme right, but the mainstream of British conservatism owed its origins to Edmund Burke, and advanced a view of society as an 'organism' which could only be made worse by radical changes engineered by intellectuals and social theorists. British conservatism's mainstream evolved during the later Victorian period to encompass Disraeli's redefinition of the British right to centre on 'imperialism and social reform'. To this, Joseph Chamberlain and his followers added, in 1903, the erection of a high tariff barrier around the empire. This vision fully supported the supremacy of the British Empire, but also of its increasingly democratic institutions. It was always also an essentially secular vision, supporting the Protestant Christian religion but seldom in a central way. It always maintained that the White race was plainly superior to the others, but this notion was almost universally supported at the time and had few dissenters.

Much the same pattern can be found on the British left. There was a notable absence of any kind of doctrinaire social-ist agenda or belief system, or even of socialist parties of any importance. Although Karl Marx lived and wrote in London after 1849 (while Engels also lived in England from 1842 to 1844, and after 1849) neither had any significant impact on the British left. The political group they helped to found in London in 1864, the International Workingmen's Association (also known as the First International), later held conferences in various European cities, represented a wide variety of pro-gressive views, and had little or no attraction to British intellectuals or working-class leaders. For instance, its 1869 conference at Basle, Switzerland, was attended by seventy-five delegates, but only six were from Britain. The First International was so divided that it actually disbanded in 1876, and was revived as the Second International only in 1889. When he died in London in 1883, Marx was not unknown, but virtually no one would have believed that his doctrines would become the (at least nominal) basis of a political movement that in the twentieth century ruled over one third of the world's popula-tion. As is well known, Marx and Engels were extremely pessimistic about the realistic possibility of a socialist revolu-tion in Britain (or the United States), given the reluctance of the British upper classes to resist democratic reforms by force, the existence of a worldwide empire as a 'safety valve' for working-class discontent, the relatively high wages paid to many British skilled workers, and the lack of a genuine tradition of militancy among Britain's trade unions.

Instead, until the 1880s or 90s the British left espoused a 'radical' programme (as it was generally known), aimed at movement towards political democracy, the removal of hereditary privileges and of 'Old Corruption', free trade and religious and political liberty. It eschewed any legislation which was anti-capitalist or collectivist in nature, much less overt socialism. Thus, the Chartist programme of the 1830s and 40s, embodied in its charter of 1838, for instance, demanded such reforms as universal male suffrage, the secret ballot, payment for Members of Parliament (who, apart from government ministers, were unpaid until the early twentieth century), and annually elected Parliaments. It thus had no economic or social component to its demands. Its rival and successor as the main left-wing activist movement, the Anti-Corn Law League (founded in 1839), demanded the removal of tariff restrictions on the importation of grain into Britain, a move which would benefit workers (through cheaper bread) and manufacturers (who could pay less as the cost of living for their workers declined). It did not contain any *positive* demands for economic or social legislation to directly benefit the poor. Many skilled workers (and those in the lower middle classes) also emphasised the virtues of 'self-help' through regular savings, membership in friendly societies, personal sobriety, and other similar lifestyle aspects. This was often combined with church or chapel membership, a regular component of both working-class and middle-class life throughout the nineteenth century. This 'radical' agenda continued to dominate the British left's programme until the 1880s. In 1885, Joseph

Chamberlain (still a powerful radical Liberal MP) and his colleagues drew up a 'Radical Programme', which advocated the disestablishment of the Church of England, manhood suffrage, and the payment of MPs, all familiar from traditional radicalism. But it also included, perhaps for the first time on the mainstream left, measures aimed at the redistribution of property, especially a higher rate of taxation on large landed estates, and also the encouragement of local governments to undertake schemes of housing and local improvement (as Chamberlain had famously pioneered in Birmingham).

Although Chamberlain and many of his colleagues left the Liberal Party the following year, the agenda of the party itself now moved to the New Liberalism aimed, for the first time, at achieving measures of social reform such as old-age pensions. These came to fruition when David Lloyd George was Chancellor of the Exchequer from 1908 to 1915. They were accompanied, from the 1890s, by higher rates of income tax and death duties. Yet these measures should certainly not be exaggerated. In 1913, after eight years of Liberal rule, the income tax on millionaires' incomes stood at only about 10 per cent; after the First World War the top marginal rate of income tax was never lower than 40 per cent and was often much higher. The Liberals had no agenda of nationalising any industry, even those like coal mining where there was a considerable demand for public ownership. Many of the Liberals' key supporters continued to be wealthy industrialists, businessmen, and even landowners. It was not a socialist party, and indeed differed little in this respect from the Conservatives, apart from its staunch advocacy of free trade.

There *were* socialist groups and organisation which emerged from the 1880s on, most famously the Fabian Society, founded in 1884, whose middle-class intellectual leaders included such luminaries as Beatrice and Sidney Webb, George Bernard Shaw, Graham Wallas and H. G. Wells. It advocated slow, steady progress towards a rational, socialist, planned society. But it was anything but radical in many of its desiderata, advocating the control of society by an intellectual elite (composed of themselves), and supportive of the Boer War, as likely to increase the dominance of the British Empire. The early Labour Party, founded in 1900, is generally seen as the trade-union-based auxiliary of the Liberal Party, and did not actually become a genuinely separate political party, with an explicit socialist, collectivist agenda, until 1918. In fact, one would be hard pressed to identify any real socialist party or group in late Victorian England, the exceptions being the Social Democratic Federation, founded by the writer H. M. Hyndman in 1884, and the Independent Labour Party, founded in 1893. To be sure, there were many violent strikes and demonstrations in Britain in this period, for instance the Trafalgar Square riot of 19 November 1887 (known at the time as 'Bloody Sunday') in which 10,000 protestors, demonstrating for socialist and Irish Nationalist causes, came into conflict with 2,000 police and 400 troops; and the serious rioting throughout south Wales, especially in Tonypandy in the Rhondda Valley, in 1910–11, over conditions in the coal mines (vigorously suppressed by Winston Churchill, then Home Secretary). What was almost entirely lacking, however, was either a mainstream explicitly socialist party of significance, such as prominently existed in France and Germany, or a Marxist-based intellectual critique of British capitalism. As well, anarchist and syndicalist revolutionary men and movements, which plagued almost all of mainland Europe at this time, were also notably absent from the British scene, except among radical Irish Nationalist and Fenian groups. On both the right and left of British politics, there was a virtual consensus on the acceptance of moderate, step-by-step reforms which, once in place, would not readily be challenged; along with this went a concomitant acceptance of the main institutions of Britain, including the monarchy and the empire. This consensus proved strong enough to survive the Great War, the rise of a strong Labour Party, and the descent of much of Europe into right- and left-wing totalitarianism.

As noted in the discussion of nationality in Chapter Five, this predominant ideology resulted in a narrative of British history and identity that emphasised a British triumphalism which deserved to have been triumphant *because* it was progressive and rational, in contrast with the histories of other nationalities which suffered from deficiencies of backwardness, permanently oppressive government and religions, perpetual unrest or general chaos. It was difficult to dissent from this prevalent British narrative, congruent with the 'Whig interpretation of history', in part because it melded together the right-wing desideratum of patriotic nationalism with the left-wing desideratum of progress and liberty. Britain's history contained few if any real tragedies in modern times, unlike the history of, say, France, its traditional rival, but seemed to be a perpetual move towards liberty, enlightenment and progress. It was difficult to construct a rival ideology. As noted, a part of the left emphasised the long tradition of the 'freeborn Englishman', held captive by the 'Norman yoke' of aristocratic rule. On the ideological right, any reconstruction of previous 'church and king' Toryism proved difficult to maintain in an increasingly democratic and secular age. The validity of Britain's institutions, especially the monarchy and the empire, to some extent proved a replacement for the old Toryism, but Burkean–Disraelian conservatism, as it emerged in nineteenth-century Britain, proved to be quite different. In the late Victorian and Edwardian periods, a reunified Catholic or Anglo-Catholic narrative also appeared, from the pens of such writers as Hilaire Belloc (1870–1953) and G. K. Chesterton (1873–1936), which glorified pre-Reformation Catholic Britain and its institutions. Such ideologies, however, remained distinct minority viewpoints. The combination of British patriotism, liberty and progress proved virtually irresistible to intellectuals and to ordinary persons alike.

Britain's predominant ideological trends were also reflected in the underlying and parallel philosophical movements which prevailed in Britain and in the other English-speaking countries, but not in mainland Europe. The mainstream British philosophical school has for centuries been generally known as empiricism, whose basis is that (apart from mathematics and logic) nothing can be known for certain, and that our knowledge derives from empirical evidence and experience: there are no inherent truths which it is possible for the human mind to know a priori. British empiricism is normally contrasted with the mainstream of Continental philosophy, known as Idealism, ultimately derived from Plato, which has held that there are indeed inherently knowable truths and inferences about truths. Idealism as postulated by a Continental philosopher such as Hegel is often seen as providing justification for authoritarianism and oppression, and for doctrines of historical necessity such as Marxism, where the individual is of no importance. In contrast, British empiricism is generally associated with liberalism and tolerance, its main proponents – John Locke (1632–1704), George Berkeley (1685–1753), David Hume (1711–76), John Stuart Mill (1806–73) – are often viewed as providing the underpinning of British liberalism. Akin to empiricism was utilitarianism, the doctrine in philosophy associated with Jeremy Bentham (1748–1832), James Mill (1773–1836) and John Stuart Mill, that public institutions and laws were to be scrutinised and assessed as to whether they were conducive to providing 'the greatest happiness of the greatest number'. Utilitarianism was significant in shaping measures of political and legal reform during the nineteenth century. In the late nineteenth century, Britain saw the brief emergence of its own Idealist school of philosophers, such as F. H. Bradley (1846–1924) and J. M. E. McTaggart (1866–1925), although this school proved short-lived and certainly steered clear of justifying any authoritarian doctrines. Indeed, one leading British philosopher influenced by idealism, T. H. Green (1836–82), is often seen as providing some of the pillars of the New Liberalism associated with the post-1890 Liberal Party, which emphasised an increased role of the state in providing for the poor. The twentieth century has certainly seen no radical departure from this long-standing British philosophical mainstream, with logical positivism, an extreme version of empiricism, being among the dominant trends.

Education and leisure

Although 'progress' was its watchword, nineteenth-century Britain was never so much 'advanced' as it claimed to be. One reason for this was education and its provision, which reflected both the deep divisions in social class opportunities and the general preference for the local and piecemeal over the national and centrally directed. Britain (apart from Ireland) always had higher rates of literacy than perhaps any other major European state. In 1800, probably 85 per cent of adult men and 75 per cent of adult women in England had very basic literacy skills, compared with, say, 20 per cent (at most) of Russians, at the other end of the scale. Nearly all children learned to read and write in local dame and Sunday schools or by other means, although only a small minority proceeded beyond the age of ten or so. In 1819, about 1.1 million children attended a school in England (including Sunday schools), about 55,000 in Wales and 239,000 in Scotland (figures which may include some double counting). Precise statistics are difficult to obtain, but perhaps one third of all children aged between five and thirteen were attending any of these schools at any one time, although most children attended a school at some time. The 1833 Factory Act provided for the education of children working in textile factories but, basically, nothing was done at a national level until the passage of the 1870 Education Act (known as 'Forster's Act', for in Gladstone's Cabinet W. E. Forster MP (1818–96), vice president of the Privy Council Committee on Education, was chiefly responsible for the measures), which allowed school boards to be established throughout England and Wales, and excused poorer parents from paying fees. The difficult and divisive question of religious education at school – whether it should be primarily Anglican or non-denominational – was resolved by allowing state schools to provide religious instruction not 'distinctive of any particular denomination'. In 1880, education for children aged between five and ten was made compulsory, and further measures extended the range and comprehensiveness of education for those aged thirteen or younger. The religious divide between Anglicans and Nonconformists still proved toxic, as with Balfour's Education Act of 1902. The number and percentage of children attending school rose continuously, with 5.5 million children attending school in the United Kingdom in 1900. The Achilles heel of the system was that virtually no one below the middle classes attended school past the age of thirteen or so. In 1902, only 9 *per cent* of children in England, Wales and Scotland were still at school at the age of fourteen, and only 1 *per cent* at sixteen. For all practical purposes, education beyond the elementary level was closed to all but the luckiest or ablest of working-class children. Their parents, it should be noted, often regarded their employment from the earliest possible age as an economic necessity, and could simply not afford the fees of secondary or higher education. It might also be noted that a significant culture of working-class 'autodidacts' – men and women who read voraciously, often with the assistance of the network of public and commercial lending libraries which was growing up – also flourished, despite (or because of) the lack of formal educational opportunities. This working-class autodidactic culture certainly lasted until the Second World War or later, meaning that, for instance, many early working-class Labour MPs were as learned and well read as upper-class MPs who had attended a public school and a university.

Many saw, and see, in the near-comprehensive lack of educational opportunities for anyone below the middle classes one of the main reasons why Britain increasingly fell behind Germany and the United States, especially in the new technology of the late Victorian and Edwardian periods. At the apex of the educational hierarchy, the number of 18–21-year-olds attending a university remained minute. In 1910, Oxford and Cambridge universities each had about 3,600 undergraduates with about 1,200 new students matriculating (formally entering) each year, in addition to about 200 women undergraduates, not officially counted in these figures. In 1900, about 20,000 students were enrolled in full-time tertiary education in *all* of Britain's universities, including London University and the provincial 'redbricks', with another 5,000 enrolled in a teacher-training school. At this time there were about 2.5 million men, and the same number of women, aged between eighteen and twenty-one in the United Kingdom: thus probably less than 1 per cent of eligible men and a smaller fraction of eligible women, attended any tertiary institution. The microscopic Oxbridge-educated coterie dominated Britain's political elite throughout the entire period from 1832 to 1914. Of the nineteen members of Lord Salisbury's Unionist Cabinet which took office in 1895, eleven attended Oxford and three Cambridge (with one a graduate of Trinity College, Dublin; the remaining four had not attended a university, although three were educated at a public school and the fourth was a law graduate of the Inner Temple). Of the nineteen members of Sir Henry Campbell-Bannerman's Liberal Cabinet, formed in 1905, and despite the Liberals' growing base in the middle and working classes, seven attended Oxford and four Cambridge (with one each at Edinburgh University and Sandhurst; four attended no university, including David Lloyd George and John Burns). This pattern of Oxbridge political dominance has continued, despite the enormous growth in tertiary education, to this day: of the thirteen prime ministers who have held office since 1945, nine (among them three Labourites) attended Oxford University (none, surprisingly, attended Cambridge; Sir Winston Churchill was at Sandhurst and Gordon Brown at Edinburgh University).

Popular culture

The nineteenth century was a time when the institutions commonly thought of as characteristic of the British working classes became set in place; often their development was much later than might be thought. The first fish-and-chips shop in

Britain probably dates from only about 1860 (previously, meat pies were the norm); the first purpose-built music hall (in Bolton, Lancashire) from 1840; Blackpool illuminations from 1879. Blackpool, the pre-eminent northern working-class seaside resort, had a population of only about 1,000 in 1811 and only about 4,000 in 1861; by 1911 its permanent population had risen to 61,000. It was also during this period, especially the mid to late Victorian era, that modern sports took recognisable shape in Britain, as they did elsewhere in the western world (for instance, professional major league baseball in the United States dates from 1871–6). Prior to the nineteenth century, competitive sport in Britain meant horse racing, boxing and cricket, with the Marylebone cricket club founded in 1787 and Lord's Cricket Ground in 1813. A successful boxer such as Daniel Mendoza (1764–1836) was nationally known by the 1790s. The classic British horse races, such as the Epsom Derby, also date from the late eighteenth century and early nineteenth century, and were some of the few events at which the social classes, from dukes to dustmen, could temporarily mix freely. (Gambling on races was allowed, exclusively at racetracks, from 1845.) In cricket, the distinction between 'gentlemen' and 'players' (the former, mainly public school and university men, were unpaid, at least officially; 'players' were openly paid and regarded as distinctly inferior socially) dates from 1806 and persisted until 1962. (Today, it would simply be inconceivable that a talented cricketer would not be paid but would rely on his private income.) The modern apparatus of competitive cricket dates from the second half of the nineteenth century: *Wisden*, the cricketing yearbook, first appeared in 1864; the first Test match (between England and Australia) was held in 1877. The great cricket sensation of his time, Dr W. G. Grace (1848–1915), began his career in the

11. England's 12 Champion Cricketers on board a ship at Liverpool bound for America 1859. Although cricket was played in England from around 1550, it became a national sport in the eighteenth century, and was the summer sport in England throughout the Victorian age and beyond. It also became the national summer sport in much of the British Empire. By the late nineteenth century, many of today's popular sports had emerged in something like their present form.

mid-1860s and reached his peak between about 1870 and 1890. Universally known and an iconic figure with his black beard and enormous bulk, he was certainly one of the first British sportsmen to be as familiar as the prime minister or any other public figure.

The 1870s also saw the emergence of football, dominated by the working classes and centred in the north of England and in Scotland. The Football Association dates from 1863 and the earliest FA cup from 1871. (The Rugby Football Union dates from 1871; Rugby League from 1895.) Professionalism – the payment of small sums to team members – was accepted around 1885, although for the next ninety years or more salaries remained unbelievably low by today's standards, and most professional footballers necessarily had day jobs throughout their entire career. The growth of working-class-oriented sports initially appalled many Christian ministers, especially when Sunday play was threatened, but it was encouraged by the middle classes, even if not necessarily controlled by them, when it seemed likely that intense loyalty to a local team would become an all-pervasive feature of male working-class life in the industrial towns and urban slums, which ensnared the passions of most local workers and youths who might otherwise have concentrated their minds on the wretchedness of their condition, a powerful form of what Marxists term 'false consciousness'. Intense loyalty of this kind to a team has, since the late nineteenth century, pervaded virtually all societies and most social-class milieus around the world. In England, if Methodism prevented a working-class revolution during the Industrial Revolution, one might suggest that sport has had a similar effect in the years since 1880.

The late Victorian period also arguably saw a broadening of the nature and acceptability of leisure activity of all kinds throughout nearly all of British society. Sunday observances as a strict day of rest and religious devotion almost certainly peaked in the mid-nineteenth century and then steadily declined, although it should be remembered that large shops and supermarkets in Britain could not open on Sundays until 1994, and then only with restrictions. By 1914 most London museums were open on Sunday afternoons from about 2.30 to 6.00; they had not been allowed to open on Sundays before the late nineteenth century. Boroughs with a population of 10,000 or more were given the legal right to establish a public library in 1850. By 1857 there were 133 free libraries, and all local government units were allowed to establish public libraries in

1892. From about 1900 Andrew Carnegie, the Scottish-born American multimillionaire (allegedly the second richest man in the United States, after John D. Rockefeller) used his fortune to build over 125 public libraries in England, Scotland and Wales, which each stocked thousands of works of fiction and non-fiction, reference books and newspapers, becoming familiar, indeed ubiquitous, focal points of literacy and culture throughout Britain.

Was the nineteenth century a time of gain for the happiness or standard of living of the average person? This is obviously a difficult question to answer. Arguably the two most important gains for humanity of the nineteenth century were medical: the development of anaesthetics in the 1840s and of antisepsis around thirty years later. Both were strongly associated with British physicians – antiseptics, for instance, with Joseph Lister (1827–1912). In 1800, although inoculation and other important medical breakthroughs had been discovered, medicine was probably closer to what it had been during the Dark Ages than to what it would be in our time. The discovery of the germ theory of disease by Louis Pasteur and others, and the remarkable improvements in surgery and other life-saving techniques, were among the most important of humanitarian achievements of the nineteenth century; often these were pioneered in Britain. But although, for instance, infant and childhood mortality declined between 1800 and 1900, it was still tragically high by today's standards. In other areas there was little or no concern for matters of health and safety that we now take for granted. For example, the scaffolding on building sites consisted of planks of wood simply tied together by rope; accidental deaths and injuries on building sites, and in mines and factories, were vastly more frequent than today. Open fires were everywhere, in homes, in

locomotives and steamers, in factories, and fires and confla-
grations were much more common. No one knew of the
dangers of smoking which, by the Edwardian period, was
almost ubiquitous among men. Crossing a busy street, with
no traffic lights (these date only from the 1920s) and horse-
drawn vehicles coming from all directions, may not have been
much less hazardous than crossing a battlefield.

All houses, needless to say, lacked central heating, at least
until the early twentieth century. Double-glazing was
unknown, and British mansions were notorious for their
draughtiness. The homes of the poor were often miserable
beyond description, with no indoor toilets or running water.
(It might be noted that there were apparently no public single-
sex toilets in any city prior to the Great Exhibition of 1851;
anyone following a call of nature, it seems, had to ask to use a
shop's backyard privy.) There were no lifts (elevators) in any
British public building or hotel prior to 1861, and no escalators
prior to the Edwardian period. All houses, even the mansions
of the very rich, were by our standards silent, lacking radio or
television or virtually any labour-saving consumer goods,
dependent for their running on an ample supply of servants.
In the absence of electronic media, many people owned pianos
and made their own music, read, or in all likelihood went out
in the evening far more than today; pubs, theatricals, talks and
lectures of all kinds, and religiously based meetings flourished, as did political party meetings. Until the Edwardian
period, outdoor noise was the noise of horses, carts and carriages, and evidence of horses was everywhere. Anyone
transported back in time to 1832, or even to 1910, would be
astonished at the sheer differences in all the background phe-
nomena to ordinary living and ordinary lives, and would
probably be appalled and repelled by what they found, even

those who regard the past as better than the present. (1910 was the first year in which the number of automobiles used as taxi-cabs in London exceeded the number of horse-drawn hansom cabs.)

Despite all this, it is probably the case that most people, in all likelihood the great majority, regarded the period from 1832 to 1914 as one of extraordinary progress and improvement, and were proud to be British, a nationality which seemed singularly favoured by God and which ruled so much of the world. Plainly, no one could see into the future or predict either the further improvements to standards of living and lifestyles of the average person which lay ahead, or the catastrophes of two world wars and the Depression. Most were certainly grateful for who they were and what had been achieved; the historian ought to leave it at that.

Chapter Nine

Foreign Policy, Wars
and the Empire

Foreign Policy and Wars

To an unusual extent, Britain's foreign policy has been determined, continuously and across the centuries, by a number of overriding and persisting principles, which were certainly operative in the nineteenth century. Probably the most important principle underlying Britain's foreign policy was the maintenance of the balance of power in Europe, and especially continuing opposition to a European hegemonic power which would dominate the Continent. Over the centuries, Britain opposed Spain, the Hapsburg realms, France, Germany and Russia in order to prevent a single dominant power from gaining control of Europe. With the defeat of France in 1815, Britain was fortunate in that no single power emerged, for most of the next century, whose aim seemed to be Continental domination. After Napoleon's defeat, France never tried it again, and indeed generally grew closer to Britain in its foreign policy aims, allying itself with Britain during the Crimean War and entering into a formal alliance with Britain early in the twentieth century. Only occasionally, as over the 'Fashoda Incident' (the name given to an attempt by French troops to gain control of the White Nile, thus excluding Britain from the Sudan) in East Africa in 1898, did the two countries seriously quarrel. One reason for France's lack of Continental ambitions was that it was relatively less populous than it had been in previous centuries, when it was probably the most populous nation (apart from Russia) in Europe, and, by 1850 or so, had a considerably smaller population than did Germany. As well, France failed to industrialise to the same extent as Britain, Germany, and the United States, and could no longer aspire to Continental domination. Like Britain, it increasingly saw its future in its vast colonial empire second in size only to the British Empire. France's notorious political instability, where monarchies (of various types) and republics, punctuated by revolutions, succeeded each other with abandon, also certainly deterred any European ambitions.

Before the mid-nineteenth century neither Germany nor Italy were unified nations. From about 1870, both became unified, and Germany in particular was increasingly feared for its ambitions to dominate. Previously a collection of smaller states, from 1870 Germany was unified under the leadership of Bismarck, and that year soundly defeated France in the Franco-Prussian War. The new Germany, with its capital at Berlin, also became the dominant German-speaking power, treating Austria-Hungary (with its twin capitals at Vienna and Budapest) as a subservient ally. Initially, many in Britain were not averse to Germany's unification and central role, viewing it as a Protestant power to which it was linked by interrelated monarchies. With reasonable goodwill, Britain and Germany might have become allies rather than enemies. However, Germany's insistence after the 1890s on developing a formidable ocean-going navy, despite having few colonies scattered around the globe, was viewed by most British policymakers as a direct threat to the Royal Navy, to Britain's policies of freedom of the seas, and, potentially, to the British Empire. In addition, what many historians have seen as Germany's 'special path' to modernity – in which a reactionary and aggressive Prussian landowning aristocracy was linked to a formidable industrial and heavy-industry sector, determined to crush true democracy, made most British opinion-makers increasingly uneasy. Increasingly, too, Germany viewed its future in gaining 'living space' to the east, in the vast realms of tsarist Russia, which, if successful, would have given it Continental domination. Although war between Britain and Germany was certainly not inevitable, what many in Britain viewed as German bloody-mindedness and intent at aggression made it much more likely than it could have been. The growth of formal alliances among the European powers, which by 1914 saw Germany and Austria-Hungary ready to fight France and Russia, made a catastrophic conflict the likely product of any international miscalculation, as occurred after the assassination of Franz Ferdinand, the heir to the Hapsburg throne, in June 1914.

The final European great power was Russia, truly formidable in its size and potential strength, but largely backward and underdeveloped under the tsarist regime. Britain (and France) fought Russia during the Crimean War, and greatly feared possible Russian expansion into the Near East and India, but by the early years of the twentieth century had become a de facto ally of Russia in opposition to Germany, despite the near-universal dislike of its autocratic government. There were other European powers as well – Italy, nearly unified after 1870s, with ambitions in the Mediterranean area that might have conflicted with Britain's long-established interests, and the rapidly declining Ottoman Empire, occupying a crucial geographical area but propped up in large part by Britain, which feared a Russian, German or French takeover of its decaying empire. Outside of Europe were two emerging potential great powers. Japan, which had resoundingly and surprisingly thrashed Russia in the Russo-Japanese War of 1904–5, had become the first formidable non-white nation in centuries, in large part by sedulously imitating the west without abandoning its Japanese heritage. Across the Atlantic was potentially the greatest power of all, the United States, which by 1914 was already unquestionably the strongest economic and industrial nation in the world, but one entirely cut off from European power politics by its long-established policy of isolationism. But the commonalities that united Britain, its white empire, and the United States – especially the common descent of its elites, a somewhat similar ideology of liberal capitalism, and above all the English language – would bring these nations together in war and peace as arguably the most potent and significant single factor in twentieth-century international politics.

Britain's long-standing policy of maintaining the balance of power in Europe was chiefly carried out by indirect rather than direct means: only occasionally did Britain intervene militarily in European conflicts. In the century after 1815 there were few European conflicts, and these were relatively brief and decisive, such as the Franco-Prussian War of 1870. Britain did participate directly in the Crimean War of 1854–6, but this was the only exception in the century after the end of the Napoleonic Wars. When Britain did intervene, it was traditionally as an ally of another European power, its aim to decide the conflict and prevent the emergence of a European hegemon. Thus, Britain fought with Prussia and Russia against Napoleon, with France, Russia (to 1917), and the United States (in 1917–18) against the kaiser's Germany, and in the Second World War, initially (1939–40) as an ally of France. When France surrendered to Nazi Germany in June 1940, it fought alone for a year until first the Soviet Union (from June 1941) and then the United States (from December 1941) entered the war as its powerful allies. During the Cold War, Britain also opposed Soviet expansionism in alliance with the United States and western Europe.

With these exceptions, Britain eschewed direct military participation on the Continent. It did not have a large standing army, its professional army normally being involved in wars and administration throughout the empire, especially in India. Virtually alone among the great powers, Britain did not have peacetime military conscription, its army consisting almost always of volunteers and professional officers, augmented by part-time local militia and territorials. The Royal Navy was always regarded as the 'senior service', performing a vital role in protecting the empire and the international sea routes, with Nelson arguably a greater hero than Wellington. Despite its military disadvantages, the British army was always respected and feared by its adversaries, and was seldom underestimated. Most remarkably for a nation without a real standing army, Britain has never lost a war (the only exception being the American Revolution, fought against its kinsmen), and saw off Napoleon, the kaiser, Hitler, and Stalin's successors, despite the fact that France, Germany and Russia were imposing military powers.

Besides the maintenance of the balance of power in Europe, Britain had a number of other long-standing and fundamental foreign policy objectives. One was the policy of ensuring freedom of the seas for international shipping, with, above all, the maintenance of the sea routes from Britain to its empire, especially India, the most important colony. For this reason, Britain maintained a navy stronger than that of any other power, and down to the 1930s or even beyond, would brook no rivals in naval warfare. Along with this went the maintenance of the British Empire itself, which included the increasingly independent white Dominions as well as its growing non-white empire in the Third World. There were, as well, areas of the globe, such as China and South America, where British trade was so increasingly important that, while certainly not components of the British Empire, the Royal Navy always kept a watchful eye, and on occasion intervened directly.

Another continuing facet of British foreign policy is more difficult to define precisely, although it was almost always there. During the century from 1815 through 1914, Britain was the 'liberal' great power. Rather like the United States in the century since then, it used its influence to oppose the worst aspects of repression and reaction by the other European powers. Britain itself voluntarily abolished slavery in 1833 and did its best to suppress slavery and the slave trade thereafter, whenever it had a choice in the matter. In its Third World colonies, it suppressed the worst and most barbaric features of native society, such as suttee (widow-burning) and thuggee (gangs of religiously motivated mass murderers) in India, and human sacrifice and cannibalism in Africa and the Pacific. In 'heathen' societies it oversaw the growth of Christianity, widely regarded as a civilising force as well as the Word of God, and introduced western medicine and western education, at least for a small elite among the natives. In some respects, this attempted co-option of local elites proved to be a Frankenstein's monster, engendering western-educated local leaders who hated British colonialism and led the struggle against British imperialism. In

India, for instance, Jawaharlal Nehru, India's first prime minister and one of the most important leaders of the drive to India's independence, from a wealthy Brahmin background, was educated at Harrow School, the elite British public school where Winston Churchill was educated, and later at Oxford University. Mohandas Gandhi, the prime mover of the drive to Indian independence, was educated at University College London and then trained as a barrister at the Inner Temple (one of the Inns of Court in London where all would-be barristers must enrol and learn to practise law), despite his appearance as an impoverished rural native, while Muhammad Ali Jinnah, the leader of Pakistan's independence movement and Pakistan's first head of state, was also a barrister trained at Lincoln's Inn (another of the Inns of Court in London) who practised for many years at the British bar before returning to British India. Such men as these – and there were many others of similar backgrounds and views – emerged from their British or western educations with a determination to free their nations from British imperialism.

Although Britain was the 'liberal' great power, it seldom acted with the crusading spirit of the United States in the twentieth century. By definition, its own leaders seldom if ever sought to undermine the British Empire itself and lacked both the will and resources to embark on a global programme of 'making the world safe for democracy', as the United States often appeared to do from the First World War onwards. Many British people were, however, active in achieving international liberal ends. For example, many (like Byron) became involved in the struggle for Greek independence from Turkish rule, having wallowed in the Greek classics at school and university, while the force of British liberalism made it impossible for Britain officially to recognise the South (the Confederate states of America) as an independent nation during the American Civil War, although many British conservatives would have preferred this course: support for the Union and a deep hostility to slavery, which underpinned the *raison d'être* of Southern independence, made this impossible for the British government. Before and during the First World War, most British liberals were unhappy with tsarist Russia as an ally of Britain and France, autocratic Russia being widely regarded as 'the prison of nations' and a brutal and repressive oligarchy. During the twentieth and twenty-first centuries, Britain continued with this role of promoting liberal values, generally as second in command (as it were) to the United States, which became seemingly committed to a mission of engendering liberal democracy around the world. In the period between about 1870 and 1914, Britain often did see itself as having a 'civilising mission' in its empire and beyond, taking up 'the White Man's Burden' (as Rudyard Kipling put it) of bringing western civilisation to the natives of the tropical world. For many, this sense gave a higher purpose to British imperialism and helped to justify it among British opinion-leaders.

During this period from 1832 to 1914, Britain fought two major wars – 'major' compared with the other wars it fought, but relatively minor compared with the two world wars of the twentieth century: – the Crimean War of 1853–6, and the Boer War of 1899–1902. (The latter was technically the Second Boer War, the first having been fought in 1880–1.) The Crimean War was fought in alliance with France, governed at this time by Emperor Napoleon III, ironically the nephew of the great Napoleon Bonaparte (Napoleon I) against whom Britain had fought two generations earlier in a titanic struggle. The war had the effect of preserving the independence of the Ottoman Empire for another sixty years, and preventing Russia from gaining a foothold in the Mediterranean Sea or the Middle East south of the Caucasus, areas that increasingly came to be dominated by Britain (in Egypt and, after the First World War, in what then became Palestine, Transjordan and Iraq), France and Italy. Although it was fought with notorious military incompetence (it was probably the only major war fought by the British in modern times which did not produce a well-known military leader; arguably the most famous senior commander of the war, Lord Raglan, is known only for ordering the ill-fated Charge of the Light Brigade), it was also quite a remarkable feat of military logistics, as Britain sent its forces, numbering 26,000 men, to the north coast of the Black Sea.

The Boer War was fought for very different reasons – not to maintain the balance of power in Europe, but to expand the British Empire. It took place at the time of the very zenith of the 'new imperialism', its aim to add the Boer republics of Transvaal and the Orange Free State to the British Empire. (Many of the war's critics argued that its real aim was to add the vast diamond and gold mineral wealth of South Africa to the British Empire.) Seemingly, any conflict between Great Britain and two mini-states consisting of Dutch farmers on the rural African plains was truly a fight between Goliath and David, but at first it also seemed that the biblical account would repeat itself, for the Boers initially gained the upper hand, especially during 'Black Week' (10–15 December 1899), when 3,000 British soldiers were killed during a string of Boer victories. Eventually, however, the British managed to transport 300,000 troops to South Africa, an incredible feat at the time, and little by little gained the advantage. One turning point came with the relief of Mafeking on 17 May 1900, after a 217–day siege by the Boers. The senior British commanders in the Boer War, such as Lord Roberts and Lord Kitchener, became national heroes, although, unlike Marlborough, Nelson and Wellington, they are largely forgotten today. While fought against two minor states 6,000 miles away, the costs of the Boer War were astronomical – £222 million, an incredible amount at the time – and 5,800 British soldiers killed. Many reasoned that if Britain could virtually go bankrupt fighting against two Lilliputian nations, any real war between Europe's great powers was surely impossible, since it would bankrupt all the nations involved. This argument was put most famously in 1910 in a celebrated book by Norman Angell (published as a pamphlet the year before), *The Great Illusion*, which argued that Europe's economic interdependence made a major war so mutually destructive as to be impossible. Unfortunately, the events of 1914–18 disconfirmed Angell's thesis.

Apart from these significant wars, Britain also fought in a large number of minor wars in distant parts of the world, for instance, in Burma (1824–6, 1852–3 and 1885–98), in Afghanistan (1839–42 and 1878–81), against Persia (1856–7), against the Ashanti on the Gold Coast of West Africa (1873–4), against the Zulus (1878–9) and the first war against the Boers (1880–1) in South Africa, in Egypt (in 1882), the Sudan (in 1884–5 and 1896–9), among others. Nearly all of these were fought to expand the outer borders of the British Empire or to suppress local threats to it. A partial exception were the Opium Wars of 1839–42 and 1856–60, fought to stop the Chinese government from ending Britain's lucrative but deadly opium trade, which did not actually lead to further British annexations. Only a few of these wars made more than a limited impression in Britain, but there were exceptions. The Indian Mutiny of 1857–8, fought to retain control of parts of central India after a revolt by Hindus and Muslims, led to the ending of the East India Company and formal control of India by the

British government. In 1884–5, General Charles George Gordon was sent to Sudan to suppress the victorious forces of the Sudanese Mahdi, but his forces were cut off and he was killed at Khartoum, two days before General Sir Garnet Wolseley arrived with further armed forces. Word of Gordon's death led to a widespread feeling of hostility towards Gladstone's government, which had apparently allowed this humiliation to occur.

These remote, colonial wars were thus generally popular, although the long, indecisive wars fought in Crimea in 1853–6 and against the Boers in 1899–1902 led to backlashes of significance. The Boer War, in particular, was bitterly attacked by a part (not all) of the left, including many socialists and radical Liberals, as fought against two small nations by the forces of 'finance capitalism', based in the City of London and its allies in the aristocracy. Further disquiet on the left was aroused by the erection by the British of 'concentration camps' where Boer women and children were herded as a part of the war effort. (These 'concentration camps', as they were called at the time, obviously had nothing in common with those in Nazi Germany, although they are referred to by the same name.) In 1901 Sir Henry Campbell-Bannerman made his famous denunciation of these camps: 'When is a war not a war? When it was carried on by the methods of barbarism in South Africa.' Yet these dissenters represented only a minority of British opinion, most of which strongly supported the British war effort and were enthusiastically patriotic. In the 1900 general election, fought in the middle of the Boer War, the Unionists gained an overwhelming victory, and anti-war, 'pro-Boer' spokesmen were genuinely unpopular – as David Lloyd George, at this point a radical Liberal anti-war MP, found out when he was almost lynched by an irate mob after attacking the British war effort.

Britain entered the twentieth century and the period leading to the outbreak of the First World War with a largely
unrealistic view of what was likely to transpire if war erupted
in Europe. It was widely believed that in any Continental war,
Britain's small professional army (numbering about 153,000
men in 1890; the Royal Navy numbered 69,000 men at the
time) would be an adjunct to the vastly larger French army,
while the main tasks of Britain in the war would fall upon the
Royal Navy, which would blockade Germany and hopefully
rout the German navy in a decisive sea battle, as Nelson had
done against the French in 1805.

Nevertheless, Britain's land army did undergo a number of
crucial reforms just before the outbreak of the war in 1914
which put it in a significantly better condition to fight than
before. In 1902 a Committee of Imperial Defence was created
to co-ordinate the empire's military response. In 1904 the
office of commander-in-chief, held from 1856 until 1895 by
the Duke of Cambridge, and then by Lord Wolseley and Lord
Roberts, was abolished, and the office of chief of the General
Staff created. This more professional head of the army was
held before 1914 by three younger generals. Additionally, a
General Staff, common in the armies of Germany and other
European powers, was also created. Under Richard Haldane,
the new Secretary of State for War in the Liberal government
which took office in 1905, a British Expeditionary Force, especially created for any conflict on the Continent, was established
and a Territorial Army of reserves who trained periodically
during the year, but were able to be called to duty in an emergency, replaced the old more amateurish system of local
militias. The Royal Navy had also been beefed up, with the
construction of new 'dreadnought' class battleships a high

priority. These changes were brought about as much by the allegedly pro-pacifist Liberal government of 1905–15, but were largely endorsed by the Conservatives. Britain thus entered the European conflict in August 1914 in a fairly strong military position, seemingly much stronger than a decade before. But the sheer scale of the Great War, in which 6.5 million soldiers and sailors took part and 720,000 perished (along with another 200,000 troops from the empire) was simply beyond the imagination of even the most pessimistic observers of the European scene. Part of the reason for the stalemate and for the monstrously high rate of British casualties lay with the leaders of the British army, who became widely known, especially after the war, as 'butchers' and blundering incompetents. But the stalemate was also the result of the nature of the war as it developed from 1914, with endless, deadly offences on the western front and the introduction of new weapons, such as the fighter plane and the tank, with which old professional soldiers were unprepared to deal. As well, Britain was fighting Germany, an unusually powerful and professional military power, and had always to play second fiddle to the French. In the end, after more than four years of brutal conflict, Britain did emerge victorious, and with an empire larger than before. But economic power had now shifted permanently to the United States, its great and powerful ally across the Atlantic whose entry into the war in April 1917 turned a likely German victory into an Allied one. Nor did the Great War unfold in the way most observers before 1914 believed it would: although the Royal Navy's blockade of Germany was vital to the victory, there was no 'knockout blow' à la Nelson at Trafalgar, only the indecisive Battle of Jutland in 1916. Nevertheless, given its lack of military spirit and very late military reforms, Britain did fairly well in the First World War, and was more successful than its preparations for war suggested it would be in a conflict of the kind which occurred in 1914–1918.

The empire

In 1832, Britain already had a great, worldwide empire, although not one as great as it would subsequently become and not one which was central to its national identity. It had control of what is today Canada, Australia, New Zealand, much of India, the Cape of Good Hope in South Africa, parts of the coastal areas of Africa, and other colonies and possessions around the globe from Malta to Mauritius to British Guiana. The 'old' British Empire – often termed the 'First British Empire' – dated from Elizabethan times and is usually seen as having ended with the independence of the American colonies in 1783. It was largely based in rule from London, with little regard for its local inhabitants, and was hallmarked by the existence as local rulers of autonomous trading companies such as the East India Company. New South Wales in Australia was founded in 1788 as a dumping ground for English convicts. Britain's colonial rule was, however, not immune from the liberal trends of the age. Slavery was abolished throughout the British Empire in 1833, a year after the Great Reform Act provided a more progressive basis for British politics. In 1852, Benjamin Disraeli famously remarked that Britain's colonies – apparently he meant colonies settled by Europeans such as Canada, not those in the tropical world – were 'a millstone around our neck'. What was lacking in the first half of the nineteenth century and beyond was a *raison d'être* for the existence of the empire.

There were, however, two trends in the long period from

the defeat of Napoleon in 1815 to the emergence of an explicit
ideology of imperialism in the 1870s which were significant
for the future of the empire. First, it continued to expand,
almost through absent-mindedness, as wits later termed this
phase. In the single decade 1841–51 Britain formally acquired
New Zealand (initially settled previously), the Gold Coast,
Natal in South Africa, the Punjab and Sind regions of India,
and Hong Kong, all places which would later prove major
components of the British Empire at its zenith. It also began
the process of giving democratic rights to the white inhabitants
of those colonies settled by Britons and other Europeans. This
development is often seen as having been initiated by the
Durham Report of 1839, concerning the future of upper and
lower Canada (Quebec and the English-speaking areas of
eastern Canada) which recommended, among other things,
the introduction of responsible government with the creation
of legislative assemblies elected by the people (i.e. adult males
with property qualifications), and with power being held by
the party which elected the most members. Britain would
retain final power through a Governor General, but the
inhabitants would be given wide local powers. British immigration would be encouraged, and the customary and
antiquated basis of the law in French-speaking Canada would
be replaced by modern British law. The Durham Report was
named for its author, John Lambton, 1st Earl of Durham
(1792–1840), a wealthy Whig aristocrat and former Whig
Cabinet minister, known as 'Radical Jack' for his advanced
views (he was one of the authors of the Great Reform Act of
1832). That an aristocratic former Cabinet minister and one
of the richest men in Britain (he owned extensive collieries in
County Durham) could put forward a programme of radical
democracy for the European-settled colonies indicated how

much the political atmosphere had changed with the Great Reform Act. As a result of the Durham Report, the Canadian Act of Union merged the two parts of Canada and responsible government was established by the British Parliament for all of British North America. The Constitution Act of 1867 established the Dominion of Canada which embraced all of British North America (except for Labrador and Newfoundland) by 1873. The first Canadian prime minister, Sir John Macdonald, took office in 1867, and Canada became established as an unusually stable, generally prosperous democracy. Britain's establishment of Canada as a unified democracy was also motivated by two other factors: fear that the United States, Canada's immediate and powerful neighbour to the south, might interfere with Canada's British loyalties or even invade it; and the necessity to curb any tendency towards unrest or disunion in Quebec, the French-speaking province whose capital, Montreal, was one of the largest cities in North America. Prior to 1867 (and again in the twentieth century), Quebec was marked by considerable unrest. The settlement in Canada did keep the Canadian provinces in place, with Quebec granted a considerable degree of local self-rule. This mixture of general democracy and local self-rule proved to be a winning formula to ensure Canada's loyalty to the British Crown; it entered both world wars as a key ally of Britain. From 1815 through 1850, no fewer than 800,000 immigrants, the majority (60 per cent) from Britain, settled in Canada, many from Scotland or rural England. By 1911, Canada's population had risen to 7.2 million.

Although Canada's experience was unique, in particular because of its pre-existing French-speaking population, its evolution was replicated in Australia, New Zealand, and to a lesser extent in South Africa, the other areas of extensive white settlement. Australia's initial role as a vast outdoor prison for English convicts gave way, by the 1820s, to extensive free settlement from Britain, with many immigrants from Scotland, Wales and Ireland, as well as from England. Victoria, whose capital is Melbourne, broke away from the older New South Wales in 1851 and was always a colony of free settlers rather than of convicts. Melbourne was first settled by Europeans only in 1835. It experienced vast population growth due in part to a local gold rush which began, coincidentally, in 1851. By 1901 its population had increased to 494,000, and the city was renowned for its outstanding architecture and modern infrastructure of trains and trams. South Australia and New Zealand were settled by Europeans in part through the theories of Edward Gibbon Wakefield (1796–1862), who recommended the planned emigration of British settlers who would be required to pay for their land, and build a prosperous colony similar to the one they left behind. Local self-government, similar to that granted to Canada, came to the Australian colonies and New Zealand in the mid-nineteenth century, with Australia becoming a federated Dominion (known as the 'Commonwealth of Australia') in 1901 and New Zealand in 1907. The situation in South Africa was more complicated, with Britain gaining final control of the Cape of Good Hope in 1806, but of Natal in 1849, and of the Orange Free State and Transvaal only at the end of the Boer War in 1902. The Europeans in these colonies were mainly Boers, descendants of Dutch settlers from the seventeenth century, who had little love for the British. Their defeat in the Boer War made them grudgingly accept British rule, while the Liberal government's granting of Dominion status to South Africa in 1907 won over many. A prime example was Jan Christian Smuts (1870–1950), a leading Boer military commander in

1899–1902, who later served as prime minister of South Africa for fourteen years and became so pro-British that he was actually made a member of the British Cabinet in 1917–19, although he was not a member of either of the British Houses of Parliament. (Smuts was also the principal author, in 1945, of the United Nations Charter.) The South African situation was also complicated by the fact that up to 90 per cent of the population consisted of its indigenous Africans, themselves divided among many separate tribes. Although the whites in South Africa never contemplated anything like equality for its black majority, it is probably fair to say that British rule proved more just for the indigenous peoples than the subsequent rule of the Boer-dominated National Party, with its policy of strict apartheid. British rule elsewhere in the colonies with a European majority was also arguably fairer for their indigenous peoples – Native Americans in Canada, the Maoris in New Zealand, the Aborigines in Australia – than, say, in the United States, whose treatment of its Indians was often brutal and savage, and which legally imposed strict segregation on its black population in the Southern states until the 1960s, a century after slavery was abolished.

Several of the white colonies became pioneers of social and economic radicalism, and were internationally known for their apparent radicalism. In 1893 New Zealand became the first nation in the world to give women the vote, while in the same year a local woman, Elizabeth Yates, was elected mayor of a town near Auckland, the first time a woman was elected to municipal office in the British Empire. In 1907 came the so-called Harvester Judgement (named for the Sunshine Harvester Company, a large agricultural machinery manufacturing firm near Melbourne) in which a court ruled that, regardless of its ability to afford high wages, a firm had to pay a living wage, enough to keep a family in relative comfort, to its employees. The Australian Labor Party was founded in 1891, one of the first social democratic parties in the world, became electorally significant in several Australian colonies by the mid-1890s, and formed a minority government in Queensland in 1899, a quarter-century before the Labour Party came to power in Britain. Much other evidence of progressive tendencies in the white colonies can be found. With this, however, all of the white colonies remained bastions of bourgeois respectability, and their progressive ideology always revolved around excluding most non-British immigrants, especially (in Australia) excluding Asians and Pacific Islanders as sources of cheap labour.

The white colonies thus remained thoroughly loyal to Britain. One of their main purposes was to act as a 'safety valve' for radicalism and unrest in Britain by offering a safe place where impoverished and marginalised Britons could migrate, and hopefully become rich and thus loyal Tories and imperialists. Magwitch, the frightening convict sent to Australia in Dickens's *Great Expectations*, who eventually becomes Pip's unsuspected benefactor, was a literary creation probably grounded in reality. It is a fact that when war came in 1914, all of the white colonies enthusiastically joined in to defend the mother country. It is also a fact that no white British possession ever imitated the thirteen American colonies of 1776 and attempted to break away from British rule. Indeed, even today, a century after the First World War, Canada, Australia and New Zealand retain the British monarch as their head of state, while even post-Apartheid South Africa quickly rejoined the Commonwealth from which it was expelled in 1961.

The non-white empire

The great majority of inhabitants of the British Empire lived in the non-European world. In 1911, the population of the United Kingdom was 45.3 million; of Canada 7.2 million; of Australia 4.5 million; of New Zealand 1.1 million; the white population of South Africa about 1.3 million (out of a total population of 5.5 million). But the population of British India was 320 million; of Britain's possessions in Africa about 40 million, with another 2 million or so in the West Indies, Malaya, and other possessions around the globe. While much of India and other parts of this enormous empire had come under the control of Britain before the mid-nineteenth century, vast regions, especially in Africa, became British after 1850, during the 'scramble for Africa' and expansion in other parts of the world known as the 'new imperialism'.

Even by about 1870, the European powers had barely penetrated the African continent, apart from Arab North Africa, beyond the coastline and the Boer settlement in South Africa. Many African explorers and missionaries, such as Dr David Livingstone, had begun the exploration and (in European eyes) civilising of the African interior, but the colonisation of Africa's interior took place mainly after the late 1870s. Britain had major rivals in the continental carve-up in the form of France, Germany, Belgium and Portugal. In 1882, Britain occupied Egypt in North Africa; it remained a British protectorate until 1922 and, unofficially, until 1952. By 1914, Britain had gained control of what became known as Basutoland (now Lesotho, 1884); Bechuanaland (now Botswana, 1885); British Somaliland (now part of Somalia, 1887); British East Africa (1895, later known as Kenya); the interior of Gambia (1888); the interior of the Gold Coast (now Ghana); Nigeria (united under British

rule in 1906–7); Northern Rhodesia (now Zambia, 1889);
Nyasaland (now Malawi, 1891); Southern Rhodesia (now
Zimbabwe, 1889); the Anglo-Egyptian Sudan (now Sudan and
South Sudan, 1899); Swaziland (1903); Uganda (1894); and
Zanzibar (now part of Tanzania, 1890). The reasons for this
extraordinary, sudden expansion have been much debated by
historians and are probably many and varied. For religious and
ethical reasons, the British (and other European powers) intervened to suppress the most horrifying and barbaric tribal
practices, end slavery, and bring Christianity and western education to the heathens. The success of African missionaries
was keenly followed by thousands of Anglican and other
Protestant congregants in Britain, motivated by religious and
charitable considerations. But Britain also derived some economic gains from tropical Africa, rich as it was with minerals,
useful plants, crops and animals. Britain also needed, above all,
to control the sea routes to India which, after the other
European powers intervened in Africa, meant acquiring the
interiors as well as the coastal regions of the continent in order
to forestall its rivals. Prestige was also a major factor: Britain
had the greatest of all empires, on which 'the sun never set',
and could not permit any other European power to exceed the
size and mightiness of its realms. In the days before there were
macroeconomic measurements of national wealth and power,
a world map with millions of square miles seen as belonging
to a European power had much the same role as publicity
given to a nation's GNP has today. Britain's vast empire,
usually coloured pink on the map (and often exaggerated by
the Mercator projection on world maps by the imposing size
of northern Canada) was a fundamental source of pride.
Governance of the British Empire also created an ever-
larger workforce of local administrators, army personnel,

merchants, teachers and missionaries which provided employment for those from all ranks of the British social scale, and
especially for those at the top. Peers, baronets and knights normally served as governors of the colonies; upper-class younger
sons often comprised the local officer corps; young British
Oxbridge graduates could 'jump the queue' and become pro-
fessors in Adelaide at twenty-eight, or specialist doctors with
large practices in Cape Town years before this was likely in the
mother country. The Marxist theory of imperialism saw
the need for higher rates of profit, declining badly in Britain
itself, as the prime motivating factor behind the 'new imperialism'. Probably all of these factors were important, with,
arguably, national prestige and power the most important.

India was central to the British Empire. Its centrality was
most visibly noted in 1876 when Queen Victoria, at Disraeli's
behest, was created Empress not of Africa, or Canada, or
Australia, but of India. Britain's possessions in India did expand
during the nineteenth century, adding a range of border
regions such as Upper Burma in 1886, but had already been
mainly set in place before the mid-nineteenth century. Britain's
Indian realms were of two kinds: areas directly administered
by the British Crown, and the so-called princely states, where
the local hereditary ruler continued in place, subject to British
control. The areas directly administered by Britain had been
governed, prior to 1858, by the East India Company, but had
been taken over by the Westminster Parliament in that year,
directly following the suppression of the Indian Mutiny. At the
apex of British rule was the Viceroy of India, the effective
supreme ruler of the subcontinent, normally a senior British
politician (who was almost always awarded a marquisate, the
second highest title in the British aristocracy, upon his retirement). The Indian provinces ruled directly by Britain – Madras,

Bombay, Bengal, the United Provinces, Punjab and Burma –
all had their own British governors, many of whom were
British aristocrats or senior politicians. The other component
of the British Raj ('reign' in Hindustani, the name generally
used for Britain's rule in India) were the many princely states
(over 600 in number, many very small) which were indirectly
ruled by Britain, although in 1858 they lost their right to maintain private armies and other privileges. The four largest
princely states – Hyderabad, Mysore, Baroda and Jammural
Kashmir – retained maharajas as their local rulers who were,
often, phenomenally wealthy and maintained elaborate royal
courts.

British India was thus not a single geopolitical unit (unlike,
say, China, Japan or Egypt), but an incredibly complex hodge-
podge of local states, which was also bitterly divided by
religion (between Hindus, Muslims, Sikhs, Jains and Buddhists
in Burma and Ceylon, as well as small minorities of Christians,
Jews and Zoroastrians), by caste among the Hindus, ranging
from Brahmins to Untouchables, by education and socioeconomic status from sophisticated and well-educated elites in
the big cities to tens of millions of illiterate peasants and primitive hill tribes, and by gender and ethnicity. British rule in
India was, for many decades, relatively successful because it
was widely seen as neutral, disinterested and, in a broad sense,
committed to India's development. Britain brought a range of
local infrastructural improvements such as the railway, the telegraph, western education and medicine, and entry to the
worldwide economic system for its merchants, in exchange
for its continuing rule. Most educated Indians probably
regarded British rule as, in some sense, relatively beneficent –
and, at the time, more neutral and beneficent than any likely
Indian ruler – until the Amritsar Massacre of 1919, when

Indian nationalism grew enormously and, eventually, irresist-ibly. The Indian National Congress, the main vehicle for advancing Indian self-government, was founded in 1885 as a medium for dialogue among educated Indians. From the first, it was bitterly divided between radicals and moderates and, in particular, between Hindus and Muslims, with Muslims per-ceiving it as Hindu-dominated, an impression which led eventually to the creation of Pakistan in 1947. The congress did not, however, become a mass movement explicitly aimed at Indian independence until after the First World War.

Britain also ruled in India, as elsewhere in its empire, by retaining local rulers where possible and local customs where these were not blatantly barbaric. Although it applied brute force whenever this was necessary, it also appealed to the trad-itional Indian sense of ceremony and to its traditional culture. British rule was maintained by a remarkably small cadre of local administrators, no more than a few thousand in the early twentieth century, by an army consisting in 1913 of only 77,500 British troops and 159,000 Indian troops, and a few thousand other police and officials, these to rule a country of 345 million. This could not have been readily accomplished without the tacit or indeed active co-operation of most of the people of the subcontinent, bearing in mind that the British could and did use an iron hand to maintain their rule where this seemed necessary. As with so many other institutions throughout the world, it was the First World War and its out-come that began the major assault on British rule in India, which conceivably might have continued for another century had it not occurred. In 1914, there was little or nothing to sug-gest that British rule in India would end completely only thirty-three years later.

The third area of British expansion was in the Pacific Ocean and the Pacific Rim. Neither Britain nor any other European power could colonise the vast expanse of China, but Britain did, in 1843, gain Hong Kong, the lucrative commercial gateway to trade with China, which remained the last significant British colony when it was ceded to China in 1997. In the Pacific the British obtained such island territories as Fiji (in 1874) and the New Hebrides (as a condominium with France, in 1906; the New Hebrides became known as Vanuatu when it gained independence in 1980). The Pacific was probably the most important area where British missionaries brought Christianity to the local 'heathens', their success exceeding even their efforts in Africa. Missionary activity in the Pacific was not, however, without its distinct hazards. Rev. John Williams (1796–1839), probably the most important Congregationalist missionary of the early nineteenth century, was (along with another missionary, James Hirst) killed and eaten by cannibals in the New Hebrides in 1839, while the last occasion when a missionary was killed and eaten in Fiji was as late as 1876.

This list by no means exhausts an account of the growth of the British Empire in this period. Britain also added the strategically important island of Cyprus in the Mediterranean to its realms in 1878, and a range of other economically or tactically key important areas such as the Straits Settlements (later Malaya) in 1867, and Singapore (held by the East India Company from 1824, but part of the Straits Settlements from 1867, famously founded by Sir Stamford Raffles (1781–1826) in 1818), as well as British North Borneo (1893), and the virtually unexplored Papua (the south-eastern portion of the island of New Guinea; it was administered by Australia from 1906, and became part of the independent nation of Papua New Guinea in 1975).

Although Britain plainly sought economic and military benefits from its vast empire, within its lights it almost always attempted to do justice and bring the benefits of western civil-isation to these areas. There are no parallels, in the nineteenth-century British Empire, to the apparently cata-strophic loss of life in the Congo Free State, a personal possession of the Belgian king, from 1885 to 1908, often described, accu-rately or not, as genocide, or the massacres in German South-West Africa (now Namibia) carried out by the German military against the Herero and Namaqua peoples in 1904 to 1907, where genocide appears to be an accurate term for what occurred. On the contrary, the British authorities nearly always attempted to protect the indigenous population; where mas-sacres (on a much smaller scale) occurred, as in Queensland, Australia, these were mostly carried out by local frontier settlers geographically and culturally beyond central control.

Support for the empire was, in general, ubiquitous across the political spectrum. This may seem surprising, in view of the close association of the political left with anti-imperialism (however defined), and the later willingness of the political right to abandon the imperial idea. But the second half of the nineteenth century saw the empire emerge, almost consensu-ally, as a primary motivating factor in British life. On the political right, from 1872 – when, in a notable speech, Benjamin Disraeli postulated imperialism and social reform as the proper ideals of a Conservative government – the imperial idea grew and became ever more central to Conservative ideology. This viewpoint climaxed under Joseph Chamberlain, the radical-turned-Liberal Unionist, who, as Colonial Secretary from 1895 to 1903, viewed the maintenance of a worldwide empire as the primary definitional test of Britain remaining a great power in the twentieth century; Chamberlain saw an imperial tariff, linking all of the empire into a single economic unit and replacing the dominant ideology of free trade, as the central step towards this goal. On the left, more surprisingly, much of this sentiment was echoed by the Fabian Society. Far from being anti-imperialists, in 1900 the society published *Fabianism and the Empire* (written by George Bernard Shaw), which – like Chamberlain on the right – saw the twentieth century as belonging to great empires, and which supported the British in the Boer War. To be sure, many radical Liberals opposed the Boer War and military expansion of the British Empire, but they seldom if ever opposed the existence of the empire per se, and many of their primary constituents, such as religious Nonconformists, supported the empire for the opportunities it presented to missionaries, or Liberal business-men, who supported the empire for obvious economic motives. Attacks on the very existence of the British Empire did not really emerge until after the First World War, fanned by Bolshevism, domestic socialists with agendas more radical than the previous generations, and, especially, by indigenous anti-colonialists, particularly western-educated Indians such as Gandhi and Nehru. As well, the apparent weakening of Britain as a great power after the First World War, with the perception that imperialism was a form of capitalist exploitation, and the weakening of the Nonconformist missionary instinct, under-mined much former support for the continuation of the empire. It was also the case that the rise of Keynesianism and of the common use of macroeconomic statistics now univer-sally employed, like the gross national product, served as a substitute for measuring British power by the colour pink on the world map. But prior to 1914 extreme anti-imperialist sen-timent hardly existed at all. It is interesting to note that the first (and possibly only) 'Anti-Imperialist League' was founded in the United States in opposition to the Spanish-American War, when America acquired Cuba, Puerto Rico and the

Philippines as colonies. No such parallel body existed in Britain, certainly not one with any public visibility. Ending Britain's tropical empire would, at the time, have meant the reversion of India, Africa, and the Pacific to their previous state of barbarism, without the civilising influence that British control invariably brought with it. Few British humanitarians failed to note this at the time.

Although there were pro-empire societies and organisations in Victorian and Edwardian Britain, such as the Imperial Maritime League, these were remarkably marginal and few compared with the vast number of voluntary societies of all descriptions in Britain at the time. Support for the empire was, in contrast, almost automatic and subconscious, and emanated from unofficial sources without formal approval or support. For instance, the *Boy's Own Paper*, published weekly from 1879 on, emphatically depicted the empire as the pinnacle of civilisation, lauding the creators of the empire such as Clive of India as heroic figures, and natives as barbaric. Popular novels and consumer items such as biscuit tins depicted the empire in a similar light. To reiterate, there was virtually nothing at the time from the left to champion anti-imperialism. Anti-imperialist novels such as E. M. Forster's *A Passage to India* (1924) or the essays and early novels of George Orwell, did not appear until after the First World War, and would have had little popular traction before 1914 if they had appeared. Britain entered the Great War in 1914 consensually supportive of the British Empire and its uplifting, civilising mission.

The empire probably benefited all the inhabitants of the United Kingdom but, in particular, provided opportunities for the Scots and Scots-Irish of Northern Ireland, who emigrated throughout the empire in considerable numbers and with

considerable success. These groups were certainly disproportionately important in the settlement of Canada, Australia and
New Zealand, forming a large number of the political and
economic elites of these parts of the 'New Britannia'. Irish
Catholics also emigrated in large numbers to both the white
empire and the United States, but probably achieved less success than the Protestant groups. The empire has often been
termed a 'safety valve' for Britain, to which potential radicals
and revolutionaries could emigrate (or be sent). Almost
uniquely of European states, Britain did not experience a revolution in 1848, when virtually all of Europe erupted in radical
violence, and later did not produce a significant Marxist party.
It seems unarguable that the existence of the empire, to which
millions of Britons emigrated, was a major factor in Britain's
relative stability.

Britain emerged from the First World War with its empire
even larger than in 1914. As a result of the victory over
Germany, it gained Tanganyika, thus making possible the
long-held dream of a 'Cape to Cairo' railway, uninterruptedly
from Africa's north to south, as well as a string of other former
German colonies. As a result of the victory over Turkey, it
gained what became known as Palestine, Transjordan and
Iraq, and crucially assisted both Arab nationalism and, by
promulgating the Balfour Declaration in 1917, the Zionist
dream of a Jewish state in Palestine. In the interwar period –
and contrary to popular belief – the British Empire was
arguably still the most powerful geopolitical unit in the world.

Probably the most important achievement of the British
Empire, however, was the spread of the English language
around the world, so that by the last third of the twentieth
century it had become the universal language of diplomacy,
commerce and scholarship. Much of the credit for this, of

course, was due to the political and economic influence of the
United States after the Second World War, but Americans
speak English because America, too, had once been a British
colony. But the spread of English to the four corners of the
world was primarily due to the size and extent of the British
Empire. This achievement, the evolution of English as the universal language, is likely to outlive both the British Empire and
Britain's status as a great power by centuries.

12. The British Empire was, famously, so large that 'the sun never set' on it, and stretched
across the globe, as this map illustrates. By the First World War, it contained about one-
quarter of the world's population. In an age when a nation's might and power was often
measured by how much territory it controlled (rather than by Gross National Product, a
concept not yet developed) the British Empire was extraordinarily impressive and deeply
reassuring to most British people.

Chapter Ten

Some Counterfactuals

It is plausible to imagine several alternative political histories for Britain in this period. The most obvious, perhaps, is a refusal by the House of Lords to concede parliamentary reform in 1831–2, leading to a revolution which would have swept away much more of the British 'old regime' than actually occurred. Many contemporary observers such as Macaulay expected a revolution to occur had the Reform Act not been passed by Parliament, a revolution perhaps involving insurrection repressed by violence. France experienced a revolution in 1830 which overthrew the Bourbon monarchy, and it is possible that something similar might have occurred in Britain. Such a revolution might have established a British republic, although this is probably less likely than the enactment of much wider modes of democratic government, perhaps including manhood suffrage and the disestablishment of the Anglican Church. Whether the British Establishment would have lost control of the situation so comprehensively as to have allowed a sweeping revolution to have occurred is, however, arguable: Whigs as well as Tories were united in opposing anything like what we would term democracy. It is also possible that a working-class revolution might have occurred, although it is safe to say that the whole of established society would have opposed it, and any revolutionary violence would certainly have been ruthlessly suppressed.

A more intriguing possibility is that the Whig-dominated Age of Reform might not have occurred at all, but that Britain might have continued indefinitely as a Tory-led, unreformed, neo-mercantilist state where 'church and king' Anglicanism also continued to predominate. Such a possibility is not as fanciful as it might seem: support for parliamentary reform, which hardly existed in the early 1820s, grew suddenly and dramatically just before 1832, while Britain had experienced industrial and commercial growth in a regulated economy with tariff protection. Even in 1839, John Stuart Mill acknowledged in a perceptive article in the *London and Westminster Review* how strong were the forces *opposed* to free-trade liberalism which, he claimed, included almost the whole of the landed classes, the older professions, the Church of England, and a range of trades such as 'the shipping interest, the timber interest, the West Indies interest' where foreign competition was still prohibited. The modernisation process did indeed occur in societies which did not experience the liberalism associated with Britain's Age of Reform, most strikingly in Germany between 1848 and 1918, whose so-called 'special path' to modernity combined particularly rapid industrialisation (behind high tariff walls) with the continued ascendancy of premodern elites, and the military in pursuit of largely nationalistic ends: economic growth based on self-sufficiency rather than free trade; a more narrow elite based on continuing Anglican and landowning domination without modification by liberal values. Nevertheless, such a possibility

was far less likely in Britain than in Germany. Britain's powerful
Whig aristocracy was pervaded by liberalism in a way which
had no parallel in Germany; the fact that Britain had already
experienced industrialisation and much urbanisation had itself
created both an urban-industrial elite and an industrial working
class generally permeated by radical and liberal values.
Germany had no parallel to Britain's large Nonconformist
religious minority or to Scottish Presbyterianism; Britain
seemingly had no parallel to the Prussian tradition of
militarism or to the German habit of obedience, although it
can certainly be argued that Britain's military traditions, as
well as that of 'church and king' Toryism, offered more in the
way of similarities than Whig and liberal historians might
credit. Britain was already a unified nation state (albeit
composed of three separate kingdoms), while German unity
was defined and imposed in 1864–71 by Bismarck, the
Hohenzollern monarchy and the Prussian Junkers, along with
their own historical values.

Just as for the earlier part of the nineteenth century, it is
possible to imagine and consider a number of alternative scenarios in the political history of later nineteenth-century Britain
which did not occur but might have. Perhaps the most plausible is the electoral triumph in the 1880s of a radical Liberal
government with a large majority which would have enacted
the Radical Programme of advanced Liberalism, a programme
which would potentially have included the abolition or thorough reform of the House of Lords, universal manhood
suffrage, the disestablishment of the Church of England, 'land
reform' giving farmers the right to buy out the estates of the
great landowners and abolishing the 'strict settlement' of
land, measures giving local governments much wider powers
to enact 'municipal socialism', and a scaling back of British

involvement in the empire. At its most extreme, ending the monarchy and establishing a British republic might conceivably have been considered, although Queen Victoria's return to carrying out public duties in the 1870s after an extended period of mourning following the death of Prince Albert in 1861 probably ruled this out as a realistic possibility. By the 1880s, a major portion of the Liberal Party, especially that portion associated with Joseph Chamberlain, was favourable to these measures. Such a programme would have encountered fierce resistance, with, for instance, the House of Lords being viewed by both conservatives and moderates as a bulwark against socialism, while the Church of England would certainly never have agreed to give up its legal establishment. Had such a programme been enacted, however, Britain would probably have looked much more like the United States of America, a republic with no established church and wide measures of local autonomy rather than central rule.

This Radical Programme is also notable for what it did not contain: it did not propose to enact 'socialism' in the sense this is commonly understood, with public ownership, at a national level, of key industries, and high rates of taxation on the rich. Increased direct taxation on the rich (but at much lower rates than anything known since 1914) did become part of the agenda of the left at a slightly later date, with the Harcourt Death Duties of 1894 (higher levels of taxation on wealthy estates passing at death, enacted by Chancellor of the Exchequer Sir William Harcourt) and higher rates of income tax enacted by the Asquith government in 1909–14, but were not a part of the mainstream radical agenda before then. At that time, many, perhaps most, influential radicals were wealthy businessmen, especially northern manufacturers, who opposed 'confiscatory' levels of taxation. Socialism in the

sense known in the twentieth century was hardly known in
Britain at all at this time. Until much later, the trade unions
had no socialist agenda, and nationalisation did not really
become a debatable issue in the mainstream until the rise of
the Labour Party in 1918–22. Had the Radical Programme of
the 1880s been enacted, however, it might have set the stage
and provided the conditions for a socialist programme earlier
and more extreme than actually occurred in twentieth-
century British politics. It might also have opened the door for
aspects of the radical agenda which are mainly forgotten
today, such as the temperance movement which, at its most
extreme, wanted to outlaw all alcoholic beverages (as was
actually done in the United States between 1919 and 1933).

In fact, however, the Radical Programme was not enacted.
The Liberal Party was still controlled by relative moderates
until the Liberal Unionist split of 1886. Gladstone, liberalism's
leader, was concerned with other things, especially Ireland; he
was a deeply religious Anglican and something of a partisan
of the Whig aristocracy who was unlikely to enact such a
sweeping programme. The man who was most likely to enact
it, Joseph Chamberlain, paradoxically left the Liberal Party in
1886 and, by the mid-1890s, was a key member of the Tory
Cabinet. By 1900 the Radical Programme itself looked distinctly old-fashioned, with the extreme left now in favour of
measures of collectivism to enact social reform and a strong
Liberal imperialist wing within the Liberal party that cham-
pioned the empire. Politically, the Liberals were never in a
position to enact their programme between 1884 and 1906,
when new issues came to dominate the political scene. Ireland
and Irish Home Rule moved to the centre of British political
life, and many wealthy industrialists and businessmen had
moved into the Unionist (i.e. Conservative) Party.

At the centre of British political life in this period was Ireland, and it is also worth considering what might have happened had Ireland been successfully 'pacified' – as Gladstone put it – by a Home Rule bill enacted in 1886. A successful solution to the Irish question would necessarily have required the Catholic south and Protestant Ulster to co-operate harmoniously over the range of areas in local government delegated to Ireland under Gladstone's proposals. This possibility is not far-fetched, and it is likely that a Home Rule Ireland would have seen growing links and co-operation between politicians of both religions in such mundane realms as railways, harbours, civic improvements, public health and so on. Successful co-operation would obviously have diminished mutual hostility and increased mutual respect. One might assume, too, that it would have weakened the forces of extreme nationalism in southern Ireland later responsible for the creation of the Irish Republic. On the other hand, such a rosy scenario may well be far too optimistic. Even within the areas of legislation reserved for an Irish Home Rule Parliament, there was ample room for mutual conflict in such areas as education (with its continuing sectarian dimensions) and, more importantly, the overall division of an Irish budget among the communities. A 'normal' Irish political system, based largely on class, might have emerged, although it is difficult to see the rural-based poor of the south and the Protestant urban proletariat of Ulster ever realistically coming together. More broadly, it is difficult to see southern Irish nationalists being genuinely satisfied with this situation as a permanent settlement. They would, almost inevitably, surely demand wider measures of self-government. The 1916 Easter Uprising might well have occurred despite Gladstone's best efforts.

Because the war began so suddenly in 1914 and resulted in

a fundamental break in European history, it is seemingly easier to reflect on what might have occurred for the 1900–14 period than for the earlier decades surveyed in this chapter. In reality, it is more difficult to arrive at plausible alternative scenarios for this period than before. Had the war not broken out, it seems very likely that some kind of violent civil war would have been fought in Ireland later in 1914 once Irish Home Rule finally became law. This conflict would have been led by Ulster's Protestants, who enjoyed almost unanimous support in their own community and among Tories in other parts of Britain, and who were armed and desperate. Had conflict erupted in Ireland in 1914–15, its consequences are simply too unclear for an obviously plausible scenario to be posited; it would have depended on the reaction of the Catholic south, of the Liberal government, and of the British army. It is likely that extreme nationalists in the south would have been greatly strengthened by an armed uprising in Ulster, leading, perhaps, to a similar division of Ireland to that which actually occurred in 1922. Much would have depended on the government in power in Westminster. A general election was due to be held in 1915. Most historians believe that the Unionists under Bonar Law would have won such an election. The party had consist-ently been winning by-elections, while most of southern Ireland's MPs would have been excluded from the Westminster Parliament under the Home Rule Act due to take effect. Bonar Law was a remarkably able party leader who easily took the Tories to a predominant position at both the 1918 and 1922 general elections, the only ones he contested as party leader. Had the Tories been in power from 1915, it seems certain that more would have been done to mollify Ulster, probably lead-ing to a backlash in the south.

The Tories lost power in 1905. They did not return to

government for ten years, until they joined the Asquith-led wartime coalition in 1915. While they were the largest single party in Parliament following the 1918 general election, the Conservatives did not form another government in their own right until October 1922, seventeen years after the last exclusive Conservative government resigned in December 1905. Had the Tories been in power in the years 1905–15, would events have been much different? On one level, probably not: Britain entered the First World War under a Liberal government, a government which spent millions on building an advanced navy equipped with dreadnought battleships and which reformed the army. If the Tories had been in power during this period, probably much the same course of events would have occurred. After the First World War, some critics blamed the Liberal government for not making crystal clear beforehand to Germany that Britain would have immediately declared war if Germany launched an aggressive attack on Belgium or any other country, a warning which, it was claimed, might have deterred German aggression. While it is possible that Germany militarism might have been deterred by outspoken British firmness, it is probably more likely that it would have made no difference: Britain's army was too small in 1914 to have had any real effect on the actions of Germany's high command. For British military (as opposed to naval) power to have successfully deterred Germany's sweep through Belgium on the way to encircling Paris, the British army would have had to have been vastly larger, a standing army of hundreds of thousands backed by an even larger, well-trained reserve force, on Continental lines.

For Britain to have had such a force in place in 1914 would have required a fundamental change not merely in British military thinking (which *always* viewed the Royal Navy as primary) but in the essence of British liberalism itself, for it would certainly have required the introduction of universal male conscription, with men obliged to perform reserve training for several months a year until they were perhaps fifty. Some voices in the Unionist Party indeed wanted such a development, along with other right-wing collectivist measures, especially the enactment of Chamberlain's tariff reform proposals to unify the British Empire. Such a view was by no means dominant in the Unionist Party during the period 1904–15, and would almost certainly have proven to have been electorally disastrous. Nevertheless, it is just possible that a thorough going right-wing programme, including conscription, would, if enacted, have made Germany's leaders regard the launching of a war against France in 1914 as too costly to contemplate, leading to an armed truce which might have continued indefinitely. Such a right-wing programme would also almost certainly have been harsher against trade union and labour militancy than was the Liberal government of 1905–14 which, thanks largely to Lloyd George's influence, did its best to accommodate labour demands and to end strikes and workplace militancy on a negotiated basis. Especially in the coalfields and docks, Britain would probably have seen more labour unrest than actually occurred, had such a right-wing programme been in place. On the other hand, a central claim made by the advocates of tariff reform is that a tariff would have produced lower levels of unemployment than did free trade: if these claims proved accurate, one assumes that labour unrest would have lessened. Over Ireland, it goes without saying that a Unionist government would have been unsympathetic to Home Rule. Presumably, therefore, militant Protestant Unionism in Ulster would not have arisen in the same form as it actually did in 1900–14, although extreme

Catholic Irish nationalism was likely to have been stronger and more visible. Whether the course of Irish history as we know it – comprising the 1916 Easter uprising, the Irish Civil War of 1918–22, and the emergence of the Irish Free State – would have been radically different, is much more arguable, for its essence was the rise to centrality of just such an extreme Catholic Irish nationalism, sweeping away the relative moderation of Home Rule.

The most widely discussed 'what if?' question in recent British political history, however, concerns the long-term fate of the Liberal Party, specifically whether Labour would inevitably have replaced it as the predominant party of the left, as happened after 1918–22. Labour was indeed making many gains at the expense of the Liberals (and Tories) at the local level in the period 1900–14, and a class-based politics was clearly emerging, at least in many heavily industrialised areas. Yet there are reasons for supposing that Labour would not have replaced the Liberals if war had not broken out. The war itself was the principal cause of the political realignment which followed, engendering the wartime split between Asquith and Lloyd George, the 'coupon' election of 1918 which marginalised Asquith's followers, and the decision of Labour's leaders in 1918, especially Arthur Henderson, to form a genuinely separate party with a radical and socialist constitution. The war also engendered great social and economic changes which worked to the Liberals' disadvantage and to Labour's advantage such as the decline of Nonconformity and a considerable growth in trade union membership. The Representation of the People Act 1918 gave the vote to all adult males (including perhaps 40 per cent of the adult male population still without a vote) and to women over thirty, measures which advantaged both Labour and the Tories, but not the Liberals. The war moved all of European politics to the left, at least temporarily, with Bolshevism in power in Russia. Presumably, in the absence of a war, none of this would have occurred – although most women would inevitably have been given the vote – and certainly not the range of events which all worked to Labour's advantage. It is quite possible, even likely, that the Liberal Party would have remained the normal left-of-centre party in Britain indefinitely (with, for instance, Winston Churchill quite possibly becoming Liberal prime minister around 1930, rather than Tory prime minister in 1940!), probably and ironically espousing a position not much different from that of Tony Blair and New Labour at the end of the twentieth century.

Had there been no First World War, too, Europe's empires and traditional societies would presumably have remained intact. The lives of up to 10 million soldiers killed in the war would have been spared, and neither Communism nor fascism would, presumably, have come to power anywhere. Lenin, Stalin, Mussolini and Hitler would be unknown to history. It is at seminal junctures such as that of the 1914–18 war that 'counterfactual' history is both most imaginative and most likely to be inaccurate, since the whole of contemporary history from August 1914 until today would have been utterly different and essentially incalculable. For example, three men who served as front-line soldiers in the First World War (Attlee, Eden, Macmillan) eventually became prime ministers of Britain. But how many among the 720,000 British dead in the war would otherwise have lived to become prime minister, giving us a list of prime-ministerial names very different from that we know? Or was the First World War inevitable in some form? Europe consisted of two armed camps, needing only a spark to ignite, and if this was not supplied in Sarajevo in 1914 it might well have been provided somewhere else in 1915 or 1916, with perhaps roughly similar results. Or, in such a conflict, would Germany have managed to win quickly – as she was not able to do in August 1914 – and become Europe's hegemon for generations? We can posit a series of seemingly plausible possibilities, but hindsighted plausibility leaves no room for accident, happenstance, or the simply unknowable. By definition the plausible, or a range of plausibilities, leaves no room for the unexpected.

That the British economy generally did well throughout the nineteenth century was due in part to its successful multiplicity of functions, which to a certain extent were fortuitous developments. Had any of these been thwarted, it is possible that Britain's economy would have been very different and much less productive. For instance, it is entirely possible that France under Napoleon or his successors might have emerged as the leader of the Industrial Revolution, or that London's role as the world's greatest financial centre might have been taken instead by Amsterdam, Paris or Hamburg. Britain's economic ascendancy was also based on its links with the empire, the so-called 'unofficial empire' in Latin America and the Far East, and the United States, which in turn rested on Britain's control of the seas. None of this was preordained, but was largely the result of fortunate circumstances.

Could Britain have developed otherwise than it did between about 1830 and 1914? There are grounds for answering that question in the negative. The forces which challenged the growth of constitutional democracy were, arguably, never strong enough to have prevented what occurred, while the economic forces of industrialisation and commerce were already in place by the early nineteenth century. There were, of course, points at which history might have turned but did not, although these probably always reflected contingencies rather than more basic trends. As has been noted, it was *possible* that, for instance, a genuinely revolutionary situation might have arisen in 1830–2 had not the Reform Act been passed: certainly many Liberals such as Macaulay feared that a violent revolution was possible had the Lords not given way and enacted reform. Here larger considerations weighed against such a dramatic outcome: the 'safety valve' of empire and foreign emigration was already in place, as was the moderating force of Methodism, while the British Cabinet in 1830–2 was in the hands of Whig liberals, not ultra-conservative Tories. Similarly, it is possible that the long tragedy of Ireland might have been avoided had the pre-1801 Irish Parliament remained in place, or, many decades later, that Ireland's centrally divisive role in late Victorian and Edwardian politics might have been avoided had Gladstone succeeded in enacting Home Rule in 1886. By 1914–18, it is possible Catholic Ireland, its reasonable demands satisfied, might have produced a majority patriotic to the United Kingdom, while Protestant Ulster might have learned to coexist and co-operate with the Catholic south. It is arguable that the forces of extreme nationalism in the south, Sinn Fein and the IRA, would have remained tiny fringe groups or never existed at all. Against this, however, it must be said that no attempt to appease Catholic Ireland had ever diminished the forces of Irish nationalism in the long term, and it is possibly unrealistic to imagine that a successful Home Rule Act would have been any different.

It is also worth asking what Britain would have been like in the twentieth century had there been no First World War. Probably its class system, institutional structure and pre-1914 party politics would have remained intact for many decades, and probably the British Empire would have lasted longer than it did and, indeed, might well still exist. It is unlikely, although not impossible, that Labour would have replaced the Liberal Party as the major left-of-centre party, although it seems certain that the trade unions would have played a major role in British politics. It is perhaps rather difficult realistically to see a pacific 1914–18 as having led to a British future radically or fundamentally different from what actually ensued. Although Britain plainly changed in many ways as a result of the First World War, it emerged in the interwar years arguably less altered than any European society: Britain's government and institutions were virtually identical in 1935 to what they had been in 1910. To be sure, there was some change: southern Ireland was independent (although nominally still a British dominion); women had the vote; Labour had replaced the Liberals. But, in terms of formal and institutional change, that was it. Whereas throughout central and eastern Europe all the old landmarks were gone and society had altered fundamentally, Britain came through the Great War with surprisingly little changed and its major institutions intact – sadder, certainly; not necessarily wiser; but victorious and intact.

The years since the Great War of 1914–18 saw, at least for the period until about 1980, a great increase in the power, roles and economic resources of the central government, far beyond what would have been imaginable to most observers in our period. It saw the equally unimaginable reality of the end of the British Empire and a second catastrophic world war, as well, especially after the 1960s, as sweeping social changes, such that the assumptions of British politics and society of the period 1832–1914 would arguably seem infinitely remote.

Bibliography

The standard works on the history of Britain in the period covered in this work are *The New Oxford History of England* volumes: Boyd Hilton, *A Mad, Bad, and Dangerous People? England 1783–1846* (Oxford, 2006); K. Theodore Hoppen, *The Mid-Victorian Generation, 1846–1886* (Oxford, 1998), and G. R. Searle, *A New England? Peace and War, 1886–1918* (Oxford, 2004). These have not necessarily displaced the relevant volumes in the old *The Oxford History of England* series, which are much more straightforward: Sir Llewellyn Woodward, *The Age of Reform, 1815–1870* (Oxford, 1962) and R. C. K. Ensor, *England 1870–1914* (Oxford, 1936). Elie Halévy's *A History of the English People in the Nineteenth Century* (6 vols., London, 1924), by the great French historian, has in many respects never been superseded, especially its celebrated first volume, *England in 1815*. Harold Perkin's two-volume history of modern Britain, *The Origins of Modern English Society, 1780–1880* (London, 1969) and *The Rise of Professional Society: England Since 1880* (London, 1989) are a valuable attempt to chart the whole picture, as is – from a very different perspective

– E. J. Hobsbawm's *Industry and Empire* (London, 1968). There are many general textbooks in the field, with R. K. Webb's *Modern England: From the Eighteenth Century to the Present* (New York, 1969) standing out. A more recent work is Richard Price, *British Society, 1680–1880* (Cambridge, 1999). Extremely useful reference works, with tables and lists, include Chris Cook and Brendan Behan, *British Historical Facts, 1830–1900* (London, 1975) and its updated version, Chris Cook, *The Routledge Companion to Britain in the Nineteenth Century, 1815–1914* (Abingdon, 2005); another general guide, by leading historians, is Chris Williams, ed., *A Companion to Nineteenth Century Britain* (Oxford, 2004). An invaluable work with statistics and data on all aspects of demographic and economic history is B. R. Mitchell and Phyllis Deane, *Abstract of British Historical Statistics* (Cambridge, 1971). Valuable general social histories include F. M. L. Thompson, ed., *The Cambridge Social History of Britain* (3 vols., Cambridge, 1990); Edward Royle, *Modern Britain: A Social History, 1750–1985* (London, 1987); José Harris, *Private Lives, Public Spirit: Britain 1870–1914* (London, 1993); Susie L. Steinbach, *Understanding the Victorians: Politics, Culture and Society in Nineteenth-Century Britain* (Abingdon, 2012); and F. M. L. Thompson, *The Rise of Respectable Society: A Social History of Victorian Britain, 1830–1900* (London, 1998). A useful collection of essays on major topics is Kelly Boyd and Rohan McWilliam, eds., *The Victorian Studies Reader* (Abingdon, 2007).

General accounts of the growth of the population and of demographic change include E. A. Wrigley, *Poverty, Progress, and Population* (Cambridge, 2004) and E. A. Wrigley and R. S. Schofield, *The Population History of England, 1541–1871* (Cambridge, 1989). Asa Briggs, *Victorian Cities* (London, 1963) remains a classic account. Another general study is Tristram Hunt, *Building Jerusalem: The Rise and Fall of the Victorian City*

(London, 2004). There are many histories of London, such as Peter Ackroyd, *London: The Biography* (London, 2001) and Roy Porter, *London: A Social History* (London, 2000). Histories of major provincial cities include Alan Kidd, *Manchester: A History* (Manchester, 2006); Andrew Miles, *The Hurricane Port: A Social History of Liverpool* (Edinburgh, 2011); and Eric Hopkins's two-volume work, *Birmingham: The First Manufacturing Town in the World, 1760–1840* (London, 1989) and *Birmingham: The Making of a Second City, 1850–1939* (Stroud, 2001).

There exist many accounts of the British economy in this period, which saw the later phases of the Industrial Revolution and Britain's role as both 'the workshop of the world' and the 'clearing house of the world'. One might start with Walt Rostow's famous *The Stages of Economic Growth: A Non-Communist Manifesto* (Cambridge, 1960), which introduced the concept of a 'take-off into self-sustained growth' during the Industrial Revolution. The notion of a rapid 'take-off' has been challenged by more recent historians such as N. F. R. Crafts in *British Economic Growth During the Industrial Revolution* (Oxford, 1985), which actually revived an older perspective of non-rapid British economic growth associated with economic historians of a previous generation like Sir John Clapham. Peter Cain and Tony Hopkins highlighted the importance of 'gentlemanly capitalism' and the City of London in *British Imperialism, 1688–2000* (revised edn, London, 2001); see also C. H. Lee, *The British Economy Since 1700: A Macroeconomic Perspective* (Cambridge, 1986). A large-scale general collection of essays is Roderick Floud and Paul Johnson, eds., *The Cambridge Economic History of Modern Britain* (Cambridge, 2004); see also the essays in Patrick O'Brian and Roland Quinault, eds., *The Industrial Revolution and British Society* (Cambridge, 1993) and Maurice W. Kirby and Mary B. Rose, eds., *Business Enterprise in Modern Britain: From the Eighteenth to the Twentieth Century* (London, 1994). General economic histories of modern Britain include Peter Mathias, *The First Industrial Nation* (London, 1975) and Martin Daunton's two-volume work, *Progress and Poverty: An Economic and Social History of Britain, 1700–1850* (Oxford, 1995) and *Wealth and Welfare: An Economic and Social History of Britain, 1851–1951* (London, 2011). Recent general studies include Pat Hudson, *The Industrial Revolution* (London, 1992); Joel Mokyr, *The Enlightened Economy: Britain and the Industrial Revolution 1700–1850* (London, 2011), and Robert G. Allen, *The British Industrial Revolution in Global Perspective* (Cambridge, 2009). There are also many histories of individual components of the British economy. For instance, there are literally hundreds of books on the railways, by an army of enthusiasts. A good general guide is Edgar Jones, *The Penguin Guide to the Railways of Britain* (Harmondsworth, 1981). The rural sector is surveyed in such works as Mark Overton's *The Agricultural Revolution in England: The Transformation of the Agrarian Economy, 1500–1850* (Cambridge, 1996). The City of London has long been under-researched, but see David Kynaston, *City of London: The History* (London, 2012), based on his previous four-volume history, and R. C. Michie, *The City of London: Continuity and Change Since 1850* (London, 1992).

General surveys of social classes include Harold Perkin's two-volume work, noted above. On the upper classes, see F. M. L. Thompson, *English Landed Society in the Nineteenth Century* (London, 1963); David Cannadine, *The Decline and Fall of the British Aristocracy* (New Haven, 1990); and W. D. Rubinstein, *Men of Property: The Very Wealthy in Britain Since the Industrial Revolution* (revised edn, London, 2006). The alleged consequences of the 'gentrification' of the aristocracy are examined in Martin J. Weiner's well-known *English Culture and the Decline of the Industrial Spirit, 1850–1980* (London, 1981) and the rejoinder by W. D. Rubinstein, *Capitalism, Culture and Decline in Britain, 1750–1990* (London, 1991). Works examining components of the upper classes include Yossef Cassis, *City Bankers, 1890–1914* (Cambridge, 1994); Anthony Howe, *The Cotton Masters, 1830–1860* (London, 1984); and Richard Trainor, *Black Country Elites* (Oxford, 1993). Middle-class professions have been explored, although not to the extent they merit, in such works as Daniel Duman, *The English and Colonial Bars in the Nineteenth Century* (London, 1983); A. G. L. Haig, *Victorian Clergy: Ancient Profession Under Strain* (London, 1984); and M. Jeanne Peterson, *The Medical Profession in Mid-Victorian Britain* (Berkeley, 1978). A well-known work on middle-class inheritance is Leonore Davidoff and Catherine Hall, *Family Fortunes: Men and Women of the English Middle Classes, 1780–1850* (revised edn, London, 2002). Many recent monographs have surveyed the middle classes from the perspective of cultural history, such as Simon Gunn, *The Public Culture of the Victorian Middle Class: Ritual and Authority in the English Industrial City, 1840–1914* (Manchester, 2000) and Albert D. Pionke, *The Ritual Culture of Victorian Professionals: Competing for Professional Status, 1838–1877* (Farnham, 2013). Geoffrey Crossick's *The Lower Middle Class in Britain, 1870–1914* (London, 1977) remains a classic study. On the working classes, one should start with E. P. Thompson's celebrated work *The Making of the English Working Class* (London, 1963) – which, paradoxically, discusses only the pre-factory artisanal working classes. Thompson (1924–93) never went on to examine (from his perspective) the Victorian factory and mining proletariat. General accounts of the nineteenth-century working classes include John Benson, *The Working Class in Britain, 1850–1939* (London, 1989) and D.

G. Wright, *Popular Radicalism: The Working Class Experience, 1780–1880* (London, 1988). Aspects of the working-class world are surveyed in Joanna Bourke, *Working Class Cultures in Britain, 1890–1960: Gender, Class and Ethnicity* (London, 1994) and Jonathan Rose, *The Intellectual Life of the British Working Classes* (New Haven, 2010). Robert Roberts's *The Classic Slum: Salford Life in the First Quarter of the Century* (new edn, Harmondsworth, 1990) is a valuable autobiography. John Foster's *Class Struggle and the Industrial Revolution: Early Industrial Capitalism in Three English Towns* (London, 1974) is a Marxist examination, in detailed terms, of local class relationships. A more mainstream study is Dennis Smith, *Conflict and Compromise: Class Formation in English Society, 1830–1914* (London, 1982) about Birmingham and Sheffield. The 'standard of living' debate is surveyed in Arthur J. Taylor, *The Standard of Living in Britain in the Industrial Revolution* (London, 1975). Studies of the relief of poverty in Britain, most significantly the New Poor Law of 1834, include David Englander, *Poverty and Poor Law Reform in Nineteenth-Century Britain, 1834–1914: From Chadwick to Booth* (London, 1998) and Anthony Brundage, *The English Poor Laws, 1700–1930* (Basingstoke, 2001).

Studies of religion in Victorian Britain, centring on the Anglican Church but more wide-ranging, include Owen Chadwick, *The Victorian Church, 1829–1901* 2 vols., London, 1966 and 1970); Gerald Parsons et al., eds., *Religion in Victorian Britain* (5 vols., Manchester, 1988–97); and Kenneth Hylson-Smith, *The Churches in England From Elizabeth I to Elizabeth II, Volume One: 1788–1833* (Edinburgh, 1988) and *Volume Two: 1833–1998* (London, 2011). On aspects of the Church of England, see Edward Carpenter, *Cantuar: The Archbishops in Their Office* (London, 1971); Boyd Hilton, *The Age of Atonement: The Influence of Evangelicalism on Social and Economic Thought,*

1795–1865 (Oxford, 1988); Peter B. Nockles, *The Oxford Movement in Context: Anglican High Churchmanship, 1760–1857* (Cambridge, 1996); and John Shelton Reed, *Glorious Battle: The Cultural Politics of Victorian Anglo-Catholicism* (London, 1998). On Newman, a central figure, see Ian Ker, *John Henry Newman: A Biography* (Oxford, 2009). Nonconformity is considered in such works as David Bebbington, *The Nonconformist Conscience: Chapel and Politics, 1879–1914* (London, 1982) and *idem, Evangelicalism in Modern Britain: A History From the 1730s to the 1980s* (London, 1989). K. D. M. Snell and Paul S. Ell look in a detailed way at the 1851 religious census and other surveys in *Rival Jerusalems: The Geography of Victorian Religion* (Cambridge, 2000). Edward Norman, *The English Catholic Church in the Nineteenth Century* (London, 1984) and *idem, Anti-Catholicism in Victorian England* (London, 1968) discuss a minority religion and its impact, as does W. D. Rubinstein, *A History of the Jews in the English-Speaking World: Great Britain* (London, 1996). On the 'crisis of faith' and its impact, see Susan Budd, *Varieties of Unbelief: Atheists and Agnostics in English Society, 1850–1960* (London, 1977). On the impact on politics of religion, see David Hempton, *Religion and Political Culture in Britain and Ireland: From the Glorious Revolution to the Decline of Empire* (Cambridge, 1996). The role of religion in working-class identity is studied in Hugh McLeod, *Religion and the Working Class in Nineteenth-Century Britain* (Basingstoke, 1984). An interesting biography which sheds light on the continuing legal powers and role of the Church of England is S. M. Waddams, *Law, Politics and the Church of England: The Career of Stephen Lushington, 1782–1873* (Cambridge, 1992). Recent general studies include Frances Knight, *The Nineteenth-Century Church and English Society* (Cambridge, 1999); Julie Melnyk, *Victorian Religion: Faith and Life in Britain* (Westport, 2008); and Herbert

Schlossberg, *Conflict and Crisis in the Religious Life of Late Victorian England* (New Brunswick, 2009).

British national identity has not been well researched, but see Linda Colley, *Britons, 1707–1837: Forging the Nation* (London, 1992) and *idem, Acts of Union and Disunion: What Has Held the UK Together and What is Dividing It* (London, 2014). Studies of English national identity have increased in recent years, and include Robert Colls, *Identity of England* (Oxford, 2012); Krishan Kumar, *The Making of English National Identity* (Cambridge, 2003); and Peter Mandler, *The English National Character: The History of an Idea From Edmund Burke to Tony Blair* (New Haven, 2006). See also Philip Mason, *The English Gentleman: The Rise and Fall of an Idea* (London, 1993) and, its working-out in mid-Victorian politics, Jonathan Parry, *The Politics of Patriotism: English Liberalism, National Identity and Europe, 1830–1886* (Cambridge, 2006).

On Scotland, its history and identity, see Christopher Harvie, *Scotland and Nationalism: Scottish Society and Politics 1707 to the Present* (London, 2004); and Murray Stewart Leith and Daniel P. J. Soule, *Political Discourse and National Identity in Scotland* (Edinburgh, 2012). Excellent general histories of modern Scotland include the three-volume work by T. M. Devine, *The Scottish Nation: A Modern History; Scotland's Empire: The Origins of the Global Diaspora;* and *To the Ends of the Earth: Scotland's Global Diaspora* (all Harmondsworth, 2012), which examine the spread of the Scots throughout the empire; S. G. Checkland and Olive Checkland, *Industry and Ethos: Scotland 1832–1914* (Edinburgh, 1989); David Ross, *Scotland: History of a Nation* (Edinburgh, 2013); and T. C. Smout, *A Century of the Scottish People, 1830–1950* (London, 2010). Callum G. Brown, *Religion and Society in Scotland Since 1707* (Edinburgh, 1997) examines an important aspect of Scottish identity. John Keay and Julia Keay, *The Collins Encyclopedia of Scotland* (London, 2000) is a useful reference work.

On Welsh identity, see Gwyn A. Williams, *When Was Wales? A History of the Welsh* (Harmondsworth, 1985) and the unusual but cogent Dorian Llywelyn, *Sacred Place, Chosen People: Land and National Identity in Welsh Spirituality* (Cardiff, 1999). On modern Welsh history, see Kenneth O. Morgan, *Rebirth of a Nation: A History of Modern Wales 1880–1980* (Oxford, 1982); D. Gareth Evans, *A History of Wales: 1815–1906* (Cardiff, 2011); and Russell Davies, *Hope and Heartbreak: A History of Wales and the Welsh 1776–1871* (Cardiff, 2005). Kenneth O. Morgan, *Wales in British Politics, 1868–1922* (Cardiff, 1991) examines the move of the Welsh electorate to the Liberals and then to Labour. John Davies et al., eds., *The Welsh Academy Encyclopedia of Wales* (Cardiff, 2008) is a recent reference guide.

Most works about identity and history in Ireland survey both what is now the Republic of Ireland and Northern Ireland, as well as other communities within Ireland such as the Anglo-Irish. The standard recent survey, consisting of many essays by expert historians, is W. E. Vaughan, ed., *A New History of Ireland, Volume V: Ireland Under the Union, 1801–1870* and *Volume VI: Ireland Under the Union, 1870–1921* (both Oxford, 1989). Good one-volume histories about this highly contested subject include Alvin Jackson, *Ireland 1798–1998: Politics and War* (Oxford, 1999); R. F. Foster, *Modern Ireland 1600–1972* (Harmondsworth, 1990); F. S. L. Lyons, *Ireland Since the Famine* (London, 1985) and *idem, Culture and Anarchy in Ireland, 1890–1939* (Oxford, 1989), which examines the outlook of the various communities on the island, and Paul Bew, *Ireland: The Politics of Enmity, 1789–2006* (Oxford, 2007). Specific accounts of the rival nationality claims include Robert Kee, *The Green Flag: A History of Irish Nationalism* (Harmondsworth, 2000);

James Loughlin, *Ulster Unionism and British National Identity Since 1885* (London, 2003); and Eugenio F. Biagini, *British Democracy and Irish Nationalism, 1876–1906* (Cambridge, 2007). Brian Lalor, *Encyclopedia of Ireland* (Dublin, 2003) is a useful work.

There is by now a vast literature on feminism and the position of women in Victorian and Edwardian society, much of it written since the 1970s. General works include Sheila Rowbotham, *Hidden From History* (London, 1977); Jane Lewis, *Women in England, 1870–1950: Sexual Divisions and Social Change* (Hemel Hempstead, 1984); and Susie Steinbach, *Women in England 1760–1914* (London, 2004). On the struggle for political rights, see Susan Kingsley, *Sex and Suffrage in Britain 1860–1914* (London, 1990) and Martin Pugh, *The March of Women: A Revisionist Analysis of the Campaign for Women's Suffrage, 1866–1914* (Oxford, 2002). On the family and gender relations, see Lucy Bland, *Banishing the Beast: English Feminism and Sexual Morality, 1885–1914* (London, 1995); Michael Mason, *The Making of Victorian Sexual Attitudes* (Oxford, 1994); Pat Jalland, *Women, Marriage and Politics 1860–1914* (Oxford, 1986); and Robert B. Shoemaker, *Gender in English Society, 1650–1850: The Emergence of Separate Spheres?* (Harlow, 1998). Other aspects of women and Victorian society are surveyed in Angela John, ed., *Unequal Opportunities: Women's Employment in England, 1800–1918* (London, 1986); Elizabeth Roberts, *Women's Work, 1840–1940* (Basingstoke, 1988); Ronald Hyman, *Empire and Sexuality: The British Experience* (Manchester, 1990); and Judith R. Walkowitz, *Prostitution and Victorian Society: Women, Class and the State* (London, 1980). The masculine dimension in gender relations has also been studied, in such works as Catherine Hall, *White, Male and Middle Class: Explorations in Feminism and History* (Cambridge, 1992); John Tosh, *A Man's Place: Masculinity and the Middle-Class Home in Victorian England* (New Haven, 2007); and the well-researched work by Henry French and Mark Rothery, *Man's Estate: Landed Gentry Masculinities, 1660–1900* (Oxford, 2012). On Victorian sexuality more widely, see Ronald Pearsall, *The Worm in the Bud: The World of Victorian Sexuality* (Harmondsworth, 1983); Michael Mason, *The Making of Victorian Sexuality* (Oxford, 1995); and, more provocatively, Linda Dowling, *Hellensism and Homosexuality in Victorian Oxford* (Ithaca, 1996).

On the unreformed Parliament and political world, see J. C. D. Clark's influential *English Society, 1660–1832* (second edn, Cambridge, 2000) and the essays at the beginning of the relevant volumes of the *House of Commons* series of biographies of MPs and constituency studies. The nature of the unreformed political system is studied in Frank O'Gorman, *Voters, Patrons, and Parties: The Unreformed Electorate of Hanoverian England, 1734–1832* (Oxford, 1989). On the pre-1832 parties, see Brian Hill, *The Early Parties and Politics in Britain, 1688–1832* (London, 1996) and Austin Mitchell, *The Whigs in Opposition, 1815–1830* (Oxford, 1967). On the movement to parliamentary reform, see Eric J. Evans, *Parliamentary Reform in Britain c.1770–1918* (London, 1999) and Michael Brock, *The Great Reform Act* (London, 1973). A view of the nature of politics from the perspective of modern cultural history is found in James Vernon, *Politics and the People: A Study in English Political Culture, c.1815–1867* (Cambridge, 2009). Studies of leading political figures of the Reform Act period include E. A. Smith, *Lord Grey, 1764–1845* (Oxford, 1990); Peter Jupp, *British Politics on the Eve of Reform: The Duke of Wellington's Administration, 1828–30* (London, 1998); Wendy Hinde, *George Canning* (London, 1993); and John Prest, *Lord John Russell* (London, 1972).

There are many studies of British politics between 1832 and

1867. Starting at the very top, Matthew Dennison, *Queen Victoria: A Life of Contradictions* (London, 2013) shows the continuing importance of the monarchy in politics. Most prime ministers and other political notables have been the subject of recent biographies. On Melbourne, see L. G. Mitchell, *Lord Melbourne, 1779–1848* (Oxford, 1997) and Philip Ziegler, *Melbourne* (London, 1976). Peel's life has been examined many times, for instance by Richard A. Gaunt in *Sir Robert Peel: The Life and Legacy* (London, 2010). David Brown's *Palmerston* (New Haven, 2012) and *idem, Palmerston and the Politics of Foreign Policy, 1846–1855* (Manchester, 2002) survey this colourful figure. J. B. Conacher's *The Aberdeen Coalition, 1852–1855* (Cambridge, 1968) is a detailed study of this episode. Probably the least-known head of government in this period has been given his due in the two-volume work by Angus Hawkins, *The Forgotten Prime Minister: The 14th Earl of Derby* (Oxford, 2007). The two giants have received the most coverage. Notable biographies of Gladstone include Philip Magnus, *Gladstone: A Biography* (London, 1963); H. C. G. Matthew, *Gladstone, 1809–1898* (Oxford, 1997); and Roy Jenkins, *Gladstone* (London, 1995). The standard biography of Disraeli remains Robert Blake, *Disraeli* (London, 1966); see also John Vincent, *Disraeli* (Oxford, 1992); and William Kuhn, *The Politics of Pleasure: A Portrait of Benjamin Disraeli* (London, 2006). The famous clashes between the two have been discussed in Richard Aldous, *The Lion and the Unicorn: Gladstone vs. Disraeli* (London, 2007) and in Dick Leonard, *The Great Rivalry: Gladstone and Disraeli* (London, 2013). General considerations of this period include the well-known work by W. L. Burn, *The Age of Equipoise: A Study of the Mid-Victorian Generation* (London, 1967) and an examination of his ideas in Martin Hewitt, ed., *The Age of Equipoise? Reassessing Mid-Victorian Britain* (Aldershot, 2000). Broad considerations of the political world in this era include Norman Gash, *Reaction and Reconstruction in English Politics, 1832–1852* (Oxford, 1965) and *idem, Politics in the Age of Peel* (Brighton, 1977); Ian Newbould, *Whiggery and Reform, 1830–1841: The Politics of Government* (Stanford, 1990); H. J. Hanham, *Elections and Party Management: Politics in the Time of Disraeli and Gladstone* (Brighton, 1978); and William Thomas, *The Philosophic Radicals* (Oxford, 1979). Important movements and events in the period include Malcolm Chase, *Chartism: A New History* (Manchester, 2007) and Margot Finn, *After Chartism: Class and Nation in English Radical Politics, 1848–1874* (Cambridge, 2004); Norman McCord, *The Anti-Corn Law League, 1838–1846* (London, 1958); F. B. Smith, *The Making of the Second Reform Bill* (London, 1967); and Maurice Cowling, *1867: Disraeli, Gladstone and Revolution* (Cambridge, 1967). On the Crimean War, see Clive Ponting, *The Crimean War: The Truth Behind the Myth* (London, 2005) and Trevor Royle, *Crimea: The Great Crimean War, 1854–1856* (London, 1999). The attitudes of Tories towards protection – an issue which split the party in 1846 – is examined in Anna Gambles, *Protection and Politics: Conservative Economic Discourse 1815–1852* (Woodbridge, 1999). On the nascent far left, see Royden Harrison, *Before the Socialists: Studies in Labour and Politics, 1861–1881* (Aldershot, 1994).

On late Victorian politics, two important reference-type works are Michael Kinnear, *The British Voter: An Atlas and Survey Since 1885* (London, 1981) and Henry Pelling, *The Social Geography of British Elections, 1885–1910* (London, 1967). Kinnear's atlas – which continues to cover general elections in the 1970s – shows how every constituency voted at every election. Pelling's work, based heavily on contemporary local newspapers, examines every constituency in detail. They both show how British electoral politics in this period became increasingly class-based, with patterns that persist to the present. On the Conservative Party, see Robert Blake, *The Conservative Party From Peel to Thatcher* (London, 1985) and a more recent account by John Charmley, *A History of Conservative Politics Since 1830* (Basingstoke, 2008). The great Conservative leader of this period has (after long neglect) a good biography in Andrew Roberts's *Salisbury: Victorian Titan* (London, 1999), and Michael Bentley, *Lord Salisbury's World: Conservative Environments in Late Victorian Britain* (Cambridge, 2011). See also Robert Rhodes James, *Lord Randolph Churchill* (London, 1959) and one of many studies of arguably the most important figure in British politics at this time, Travis L. Crosby's *Joseph Chamberlain: A Most Radical Imperialist* (London, 2011). On the Liberal Party, see Robert Ingham and Duncan Brack, *Peace, Reform and Liberation: A History of the Liberal Party in Britain, 1679–2011* (London, 2011); Jonathan Parry, *The Rise and Fall of Liberal Government in Victorian Britain* (New Haven, 1993); Terry Jenkins, *The Liberal Ascendancy, 1830–1886* (London, 1994); and Leo McKinstry, *Rosebery: Statesman in Turmoil* (London, 2005). On the Liberal Unionists, see Ian Cawood, *The Liberal Unionist Party: A History* (London, 2012). From a cultural historical perspective, there is David Craig and James Thompson, eds., *Languages of Politics in Nineteenth-Century Britain* (Basingstoke, 2013). The crucial subject of Irish Home Rule is discussed in many works. A good general survey is Alan O'Day, *Irish Home Rule, 1867–1921* (Manchester, 1998). On Parnell, see F. S. Lyons, *Charles Stewart Parnell* (Dublin, 1978) and Paul Bew, *Enigma: A New Life of Charles Stewart Parnell* (Dublin, 2012); and Bew's *Coercion and Conciliation in Ireland, 1890–1910: Parnellites and Radical Agrarians* (Oxford, 1987). The small but eventually influential network of English intellectual socialists is examined in Norman and Jeanne Mackenzie, *The Fabians* (New York, 1977) and in Royden Harrison, *The Life and Times of Beatrice and Sidney Webb: 1858–1905, The Formative Years* (Basingstoke, 2000).

There is a vast literature on politics and political conflict during the Edwardian period. On the two kings (Edward VII and, from 1910, George V), see Jane Ridley, *Bertie: A Life of Edward VII* (London, 2013) and Kenneth Rose, *George V* (London, 2000). Possibly the best-known and most provocative assessment of the period is George Dangerfield, *The Strange Death of Liberal England* (originally New York, 1935; reissued and edited by Paul Bew, London, 2012), although it is highly partisan. Bernard Semmel, *Imperialism and Social Reform* (New York, 1960) remains illuminating on the background ideology of the period. John Ramsden, *The Oxford Companion to 20th-Century British Politics* (Oxford, 2002) and Chris Wrigley, ed., *A Companion to Early Twentieth Century Britain* (Oxford, 2009) are useful reference works. On the Conservative Party – in power from 1895 until 1905, but then doomed to a decade of frustrating opposition – see R. J. Q. Adams, *Balfour: The Last Grandee* (London, 2013) and *Bonar Law* (London, 2009); Martin Pugh, *The Tories and the People, 1880–1935* (Oxford, 1985); Matthew Fforde, *Conservatism and Collectivism, 1886–1914* (Edinburgh, 1990); Frank Coetzee, *For Party or Country: Nationalism and the Dilemmas of Popular Conservatism in Edwardian England* (New York, 1990); and E. H. H. Green, *The Crisis of Conservatism: The Politics, Economics and Ideology of the British Conservative Party, 1880–1914* (London, 1995). On the Liberals, see Paul Adelman, *The Decline of the Liberal Party, 1910–1931* (Harlow, 1995) and G. R. Searle, *The Liberal Party: Triumph and Disintegration* (London, 1992). On the Liberals' leaders, see John Wilson, *CB: The Life of Sir Henry*

Campbell-Bannerman (London, 1973); Roy Jenkins, *Asquith* (London, 1964); John Grigg, *Lloyd George: The People's Champion, 1902–1911* (Harmondsworth, 2002) and *idem, Lloyd George: From Peace to War, 1912–1916* (London, 1985); and Travis L. Crosby, *The Unknown Lloyd George* (London, 2014). On the New Liberalism, see Peter F. Clarke, *Lancashire and the New Liberalism* (London, 1971). On the nascent Labour Party, see Ross McKibbin, *The Evolution of the Labour Party, 1910–24* (Oxford, 1975); K. E. Brown, ed., *Essays in Anti-Labour History* (London, 1970); and Martin Pugh, *Speak For England! A New History of the Labour Party* (London, 2010). For background, see Andrew Miles and Mike Savage, *The Remaking of the British Working Class, 1840–1940* (London, 1994). Crucial issues of the period are discussed in such works as Paul Bew, *Ideology and the Irish Question: Ulster Unionism and Irish Nationalism, 1912–1916* (Oxford, 2007); Ronan Fanning, *Fatal Path: British Government and Irish Revolution, 1910–1922* (London, 2013); Alan Sykes, *Tariff Reform and British Politics* (Oxford, 1979); Maroula Joannou and June Purvis, eds., *The Women's Suffrage Movement: New Feminist Perspectives* (Manchester, 2009); and Jon Tetsuro Sumida, *In Defence of Naval Supremacy: Finance, Technology, and British Naval Policy, 1889–1914* (London, 1993). The rather forgotten Boer War is examined in Dennis Judd and Keith Surridge, *The Boer War: A History* (London, 2013).

An enormous literature exists on all aspects of culture in Britain in the period from 1832 to 1914, especially literary culture. On music, see Robert Stradling and Meirion Hughes, *The English Musical Renaissance, 1840–1940: Constructing a National Music* (Manchester, 2001); Rosemary Golding, *Music and Academia in Victorian Britain* (Farnham, 2013); Michael Ainger, *Gilbert and Sullivan: A Dual Biography* (Oxford, 2002); Byron Adams, *Edward Elgar and His World* (Princeton, 2007);

and Alain Frogley and Aidan J. Thomson, eds., *The Cambridge Companion to Vaughan Williams* (Cambridge, 2013).

General works on literature and culture in this period include Jon Klancher, *Transfiguring the Arts and Sciences: Knowledge and Cultural Institutions in the Romantic Age* (Cambridge, 2013); Marilyn Butler, *Romantics, Rebels and Reactionaries: English Literature and Its Background, 1760–1830* (Oxford, 1981); J. A. Sutherland, *Victorian Fiction: Writers, Publishers, Readers* (London, 1995); Kate Flint et al., *The Cambridge History of Victorian Literature* (Cambridge, 2012); and John Plunkett et al., *Victorian Literature: A Sourcebook* (Basingstoke, 2012).

Nearly all leading writers of this period have full-scale modern biographies. Among these are: Nicholas Roe, *John Keats* (New Haven, 2013); Fiona McCarthy, *Byron: Life and Legend* (London, 2003); Paula Byrne, *The Real Jane Austen* (London, 2014); Richard Holmes, *Shelley: The Pursuit* (London, 2005); Juliet Barker, *The Brontës* (London, 2010); A. N. Wilson, *The Laird of Abbotsford: A View of Sir Walter Scott* (Oxford, 1980); W. A. Speck, *Robert Southey: Entire Man of Letters* (New Haven, 2006); Hunter Davies, *William Wordsworth* (London, 2009); A. S. Byatt, *Unruly Times: Wordsworth and Coleridge in Their Times* (London, 2008); Robert E. Sullivan, *Macaulay: The Tragedy of Power* (Cambridge, Mass., 2010); Claire Tomalin, *Charles Dickens: A Life* (London, 2011); D. J. Taylor, *Thackeray* (London, 1999); John Morrow, *Thomas Carlyle* (London, 2007); John Batchelor, *Tennyson: To Strive, To Seek* (London, 2012); Stefan Collini, *Matthew Arnold: A Critical Portrait* (Oxford, 2008); Margaret Foster, *Elizabeth Barrett Browning: A Life* (London, 2012); Iain Finlayson, *Browning* (London, 2005); Karoline Leach, *In the Shadow of Dreamtime: The Myth and Reality of Lewis Carroll* (London, 2009); Kathryn Hughes,

George Eliot: The Last Victorian (London, 1998) and Jenny Uglow, *George Eliot* (London, 2008); Paul Delany, *George Gissing: A Life* (London, 2009); Rikki Rooksby, A. C. *Swinburne: A Poet's Life* (Farnham, 2007); Claire Tomalin, *Thomas Hardy: The Time-torn Man* (London, 2012); Richard Ellman, *Oscar Wilde* (Harmondsworth, 1988) and Neil McKenna, *The Secret Life of Oscar Wilde* (London, 2004); Andrew Lycett, *Rudyard Kipling* (London, 1999); Michael Sherbourne, *H. G. Wells: Another Kind of Life* (London, 2012); Andrew Lycett, *Conan Doyle: The Man Who Created Sherlock Holmes* (London, 2008); Michael Holroyd, *Bernard Shaw: A Biography* (London, 1998); Ian Ker, *G. K. Chesterton: A Biography* (Oxford, 2011); Hermione Lee, *Virginia Woolf* (London, 1997). On the Bloomsbury Group, the seminal work is Michael Holroyd, *Lytton Strachey* (two vols., New York, 1968; new edn New York, 1994); Nigel Jones, *Rupert Brooke: Life, Death and Myth* (London, 1999).

On the press and Fleet Street, see Stephen E. Koss, *The Rise and Fall of the Political Press in Britain* (London, 1990); Hannah Barker, *Newspapers and English Society, 1695–1855* (London, 1999); Dennis Griffiths, *Fleet Street: Five Hundred Years of the Press* (London, 2006); Mark Hampton, *Visions of the Press in Britain, 1850–1950* (Urbana, 2005); and S. J. Taylor, *The Great Outsiders: Northcliffe, Rothermere and the Daily Mail* (London, 1996). On the key institution of the Post Office, there is Martin Daunton, *Royal Mail: The Post Office Since 1840* (London, 1985) and Duncan Campbell-Smith, *Masters of the Post: The Authorized History of the Royal Mail* (London, 2012).

On British philosophy, especially in the nineteenth century, see R. S. Woolhouse, *The Empiricists* (Oxford, 1988); W. J. Marder, ed., *The Oxford Handbook of British Philosophy in the Nineteenth Century* (Oxford, 2014); and David Boucher and Andrew Vincent, *British Idealism: A Guide for the Perplexed*

(London, 2012). The development of British science in this period is analysed in Bernard Lightman, *Victorian Science in Context* (Chicago, 1997); Jonathan Conlin, *Evolution and the Victorians: Science, Culture and Politics in Darwin's Britain* (London, 2014); and Peter Harman and Simon Mitton, eds., *Cambridge Scientific Minds* (Cambridge, 2002). Cambridge has generally supported science as an academic discipline and scientific research far more than Oxford. On the great achievements of British engineering, see the (identically titled) L. C. T. Rolt, *Victorian Engineering* (Harmondsworth, 1974) and Alan Evans, *Victorian Engineering* (London, 1987).

For detailed histories of Oxford and Cambridge universities in this period and the great changes in their structures and self-definition, see M. G. Brock and M. C. Curthoys, eds., *A History of the University of Oxford, Volumes VI and VII: The Nineteenth Century* (Oxford, 2000); Peter Searby, *A History of the University of Cambridge, Volume 3: 1750–1870* (Cambridge, 1997); and Christopher N. L. Brooke, *A History of the University of Cambridge, Volume 4: 1870–1990* (Cambridge, 1993). A briefer history is G. R. Evans, *The University of Oxford: A New History* (London, 2013). On London University, see F. M. L. Thompson, ed., *The University of London and the World of Learning, 1836–1986* (London, 1990). An account of a redbrick university is *Redbrick University: A Portrait of University College, Liverpool and the University of Liverpool, 1881–1981* (Liverpool, 1981). On women at university, see Carol Dyhouse, *No Distinction of Sex? Women in British Universities, 1870–1939* (Bristol, Pa., 1995). On the role of the universities in affecting membership in Britain's elites, see R. D. Anderson, *Universities and Elites in Britain Since 1800* (Cambridge, 1995).

On the public schools, an excellent account of each one and its history is Brian Gardner, *The Public Schools* (London,

1973). Many public schools have their official histories, but few are searching or critical. An exception is Christopher Tyerman, *A History of Harrow School, 1324–1991* (Oxford, 2000). Sociologically based studies of the backgrounds and careers of ex-public school boys include T. J. H. Bishop and Rupert Wilkinson, *Winchester and the Public School Elite* (London, 1967) and W. D. Rubinstein, *Capitalism, Culture and Decline in Britain, 1750–1990* (London, 1991). More general works on education and on non-elite education include Patrick Scott and Pauline Fletcher, eds., *Culture and Education in Victorian England* (Lewisburg, 1990); David Ian Allsobrook, *Schools For the Shires: The Reform of Middle Class Education in Mid-Victorian England* (Manchester, 1986); Jane McDermid, *The Schooling of Girls in Britain and Ireland, 1800–1900* (New York, 2012); and David F. Mitch, *The Rise of Popular Literacy in Victorian England* (Philadelphia, 1992).

There are many studies of famous artists and architects of this era. More general works include Lionel Lambourne, *Victorian Painting* (London, 2003) and Elizabeth Prettejohn, *The Art of the Pre-Raphaelites* (London, 2000); Roger Dixon and Stefan Muthesius, *Victorian Architecture* (London, 1978); Derek Avery, *Victorian and Edwardian Architecture* (London, 2003); Michel J. Lewis, *The Gothic Revival* (London, 2002); and Geoffrey K. Brandwood, *Living, Leisure, and Law: Eight Building Types in Victorian England, 1800–1914* (London, 2010).

On museums and libraries, see Barbara J. Black, *On Exhibit: Victorians and Their Museums* (Virginia, 2000); Giles Mandelbrote and K. A. Manley, eds., *The Cambridge History of Libraries in Britain and Ireland, Volume II, 1640–1850* (Cambridge, 2006); and Peter Hoare, ed., *The Cambridge History of Libraries in Britain and Ireland, Volume III, 1850–2000* (Cambridge, 2014).

Various aspects of social history are treated in the

following works – a by no means exhaustive list: Kelley Graham, *Gone to the Shops: Shopping in Victorian England* (Westport, 2008); Barry J. Faulk, *Music Hall and Modernity: The Late Victorian Discovery of Popular Culture* (Ohio, 2014); Judith Flanders, *Consuming Passions: Leisure and Pleasure in Victorian Britain* (London, 2007); Richard Crone, *Violent Victorians: Popular Entertainment in Nineteenth-Century London* (Manchester, 2012); Norman Longmate, *The Workhouse* (London, 2003); Pat Jalland, *Death in the Victorian Family* (Oxford, 1996); and James Stevens Curl, *The Victorian Celebration of Death* (Stroud, 2000).

There are several wide-ranging histories of the evolution of British sport. These include Derek Birley, *Sport and the Making of Britain* (Manchester, 1993); Richard Holt, *Sport and the British* (Oxford, 1989); and Mike Huggis, *Victorians and Sport* (London, 2007).

Accounts of British ideologies in this period may be found in Gareth Stedman Jones and Gregory Claeys, eds., *The Cambridge History of Nineteenth-Century Political Thought* (Cambridge, 2013); Ben Eggleston and Dale E. Miller, eds., *The Cambridge Companion to Utilitarianism* (Cambridge, 2014); David Paterson, *Liberalism and Conservatism, 1846–1905* (London, 2001); and Mark Bevir, *The Making of British Socialism* (Princeton, 2011).

Wide-ranging histories of the British Empire in this period include Andrew Porter and William Roger Louis, eds., *The Oxford History of the British Empire, Volume Three: The Nineteenth Century* (Oxford, 1999); Philippa Levine, *The British Empire: Sunrise to Sunset* (Harlow, 2007); Piers Brendan, *The Decline and Fall of the British Empire, 1781–1997* (London, 2008); Lawrence James, *The Rise and Fall of the British Empire* (London, 1998); Bernard Porter, *The Lion's Share: A History of British Imperialism, 1850 to the Present* (originally 1975; revised edn Harlow, 2012);

Robert Hyam, *Understanding the British Empire* (Cambridge, 2010); and John Darwin, *The Empire Project: The Rise and Fall of the British World Empire* (Cambridge, 2009) and *idem, Unfinished Empire: The Global Expansion of Britain* (London, 2013). Aspects of the British Empire of relevance to this work include several volumes in the *Oxford History of the British Empire* series, such as Robert Bickers, ed., *Settlers and Expatriates: Britons Over the Seas* (Oxford, 2010); John M. Mackenzie and T. M. Devine, eds., *Scotland and the British Empire* (Oxford, 2011); Kevin Kennedy, ed., *Ireland and the British Empire* (Oxford, 2004); and Philip D. Morgan and Sean Hawkins, eds., *Black Experience and the British Empire* (Oxford, 2006). Briefer histories of the white empire include Margaret Conrad, *A Concise History of Canada* (Cambridge, 2012); Stuart Macintyre, *A Concise History of Australia* (Cambridge, 2009); and Philippa Mein Smith, *A Concise History of New Zealand* (Cambridge, 2012). Accounts of British India include Douglas M. Peers and Nandini Gooptu, eds., *India and the British Empire* (Oxford, 2012); Lawrence James, *Raj: The Making and Unmaking of British India* (London, 1997); and Richard Holmes, *Sahib: The British Soldier in India* (London, 2006). The classic but controversial study of the British expansion into Africa is Ronald Robinson and John Gallagher, *Africa and the Victorians: The Official Mind of Imperialism* (originally 1961; revised edn London, 1982). See also Thomas Packenham, *The Scramble for Africa* (London, 1991); Leonard Thompson and Lynn Berat, *A History of South Africa* (New Haven, 2014); and Martin Meredith, *Diamonds, Gold, and War: The Making of South Africa* (London, 2007). An interesting collection of essays on one influential interpretation of imperialism is Shigeru Akita, ed., *Gentlemanly Capitalism, Imperialism and Global History* (Basingstoke, 2002).

On British foreign policy, useful works include John Aldred,

British Imperialism and Foreign Policy, 1846–1980 (Oxford, 2004); Muriel E. Chamberlain, Pax Britannica? British Foreign Policy, 1789–1914 (London, 1989); and A. L. Friedberg, The Weary Titan: Britain and the Experience of Relative Decline, 1895–1905 (Princeton, 1988). On the Royal Navy, see Andrew Baines, A History of the Royal Navy: The Victorian Age (London, 2014) and Peter Padfield, The Great Naval Race: Anglo-German Naval Rivalry, 1900–1914 (London, 1974). The army is covered in W. H. G. Kingston, Blow the Bugle, Draw the Sword: The Wars, Campaigns, Regiments, and Soldiers of the British and Indian Armies During the Victorian Era, 1839–1898 (London, 2007). The run-up to the outbreak of war in 1914 has been discussed in many books, such as Zara S. Steiner and Keith Nelson, Britain and the Origins of the First World War (Basingstoke, 2003); James Hawes, Englanders and Huns: How Five Decades of Enmity Led to the First World War (London, 2014); James Joll and Gordon Martel, The Origins of the First World War (Abingdon, 2007); and Christopher Clark, The Sleepwalkers: How Europe Went to War in 1914 (London, 2013).

The growth and worldwide spread of the English language has been surveyed in such works as Melvyn Bragg, The Adventure of English: The Biography of a Language (London, 2008); Philip Gooden, The Story of English: How the English Language Conquered the World (London, 2011); David Crystal, The English Language: A Guided Tour of the Language (London, 2002); and Richard Hogg and David Denison, eds., A History of the English Language (Cambridge, 2007).

Index